TWAYNE'S
RULERS AND STATESMEN OF THE WORLD SERIES

Hans L. Trefousse, Brooklyn College
General Editor

ULYSSES S. GRANT

(TROW 14)

Ulysses S. Grant

By JOHN A. CARPENTER
Fordham University

Twayne Publishers, Inc.　：：　New York

To Mimi

Preface

WHILE ULYSSES S. GRANT HAS HAD HIS SHARE OF PRAISE AS A
military man, this has not been the case with his presidency. It
has, for a good many years, been customary to relegate Grant to
the lowest rank as a chief executive. Any attempt to revise that
assessment runs into all sorts of difficulty and in writing this book
I have not tried to gloss over Grant's shortcomings, either as a
person or as an administrator. What I did strive for was a balanced view, one that gave due recognition to the positive
achievements of Grant's presidency, and especially to his Southern policy which needs a new evaluation in the light of current
Reconstruction historiography.

In the preparation of this work I visited a number of libraries
especially the Library of Congress, the National Archives, the
New York Public Library, the libraries of Princeton University,
Fordham University, and Washington and Jefferson College, the
Chicago Historical Society, and the Newberry Library. To many
persons in these libraries I am greatly indebted for able and
courteous assistance. Through the co-operation of the Scarsdale,
New York, Public Library I was able to read on microfilm the
Grant, and related papers held by the Illinois State Historical
Library. I wish to express my appreciation to the American
Philosophical Society for the financial assistance which they extended to me for this project. Professor Hans L. Trefousse, the
general editor of the series, made many valuable suggestions both
of an historical and of a literary nature. His wise counsel has
saved me from making more mistakes than I care to admit. My
wife, Frances T. Carpenter, deserves a great deal of credit for the
work which she contributed to the preparation of this biography,
and I am deeply grateful to her.

Contents

Chronology

1822	Born at Point Pleasant, Ohio
1823	Moved to Georgetown, Ohio
1839	Appointed to West Point
1843	Graduated from West Point and commissioned Bvt. 2d Lt. U.S.A.
1843–1845	Stationed at Jefferson Barracks, Missouri
1844	Engaged to Julia Dent
1845–1847	Participates in Mexican War
1848	Married to Julia Dent
1848–1849	Stationed at Sackets Harbor, N.Y.
1849–1851	Stationed at Detroit
1851–1852	Stationed at Sackets Harbor
1852	Ordered to California by way of Panama
1852–1854	Stationed at Columbia Barracks (Fort Vancouver), Oregon Territory
1853	Promoted to Captain
1854	Stationed at Fort Humboldt, California
1854	Resigns from army
1854–1858	Engages in farming in Missouri
1858–1860	Engages in real estate business and other business ventures in St. Louis
1860	Moves to Galena, Illinois
1860–1861	Employed in father's leather goods store
1861	Commissioned colonel of 21st Illinois Volunteers
1861	Promoted to brigadier general
1861	Battle of Belmont
1862	Forts Henry and Donelson, battles of Shiloh, Iuka, Corinth
1862	Promoted to major general
1863	Vicksburg campaign, battle of Chattanooga
1863	Made commander of western armies
1864	Promoted to lieutenant general and command of all Union armies

1864	Virginia campaign, siege of Petersburg
1865	Appomattox campaign, Lee's surrender
1866	Promoted to general
1867–1868	Serves as Secretary of War *ad interim* in cabinet of Andrew Johnson
1868	Elected President
1869	Black Friday episode
1869–1870	Attempt to purchase Santo Domingo
1869–1871	Last Southern states admitted to Congress
1870–1871	Negotiations with Great Britain culminate in Treaty of Washington
1870–1871	Legal Tender cases
1871	Uses Enforcement Acts to suppress disorder in South Carolina
1871–1872	Attempt to introduce civil service reforms
1872	Re-elected over Horace Greeley, Liberal Republican and Democratic candidate
1873	Salary Grab Act
1873	Panic of 1873
1873	*Virginius* Affair
1874	Sanborn Contract Investigation
1874	Vetoes inflation bill
1875	Congress passes Specie Resumption Act and Civil Rights Act
1875	Exposure of Whiskey Ring
1876	Defends Orville E. Babcock against charges of complicity in Whiskey Ring
1876	Belknap impeachment trial
1876–1877	Takes neutral position in disputed election of 1876
1877–1879	Trip around the world
1880	Loses out in bid for nomination for a third term
1884	Failure of Grant and Ward
1884	Stricken with cancer of the throat
1884–1885	Writes memoirs
1885	Dies at Mount McGregor, New York

CHAPTER I

Early Years: Success and Failure

THE STEAMER MOVED SLOWLY TOWARD THE WHARF AND made fast, and as soon as the gangplank was in place the passengers went ashore. Among them was a man surrounded by several small children and carrying some household chairs. He was short, squat, and a bit unkempt, surely no one to attract much notice. Nor did he. The same could be said of his wife, plain, squint-eyed, and anything but elegantly dressed. The four children ranged in age from ten to two, nice-looking youngsters, but obviously strangers to Galena, a northwest Illinois community on the Mississippi River. Rising high above the river loomed a bluff two hundred feet high, atop which stood houses reached by long flights of wooden steps. Galena, once a thriving community, was economically on the downgrade, but for Ulysses S. Grant, his wife, and children it represented an escape from poverty and failure.

Strange that a man whose two younger brothers had attained a degree of affluence as successful merchants in their father's leather and hardware business, should, at the age of thirty-eight, be counted a failure. Still, that was the rumor which circulated in Galena on his arrival. People knew that this older brother had one time been in the army, had even attended West Point, and had served in the Mexican War. They speculated on the reasons the former captain had resigned from the service, reasons that were not flattering. But Grant went quietly to work in the family store, remained mostly out of sight, and let the gossipers have their day.

It had not always been this way for Ulysses S. Grant. He had known success and some fame and, until a time six years before, had every reason to look forward to a secure future in the army. Such a reversal in fortune was to be the pattern for the years ahead, however, and provide the substance for an enigma never satisfactorily explained. Seldom has the combination of success and failure, the contradiction of affluence and poverty, and the contrast of tremendous mental powers set against dullness and indolence been so strongly represented in the life and person of a single individual. A character that baffled even so close a friend and associate as William T. Sherman must surely present the greatest of problems for the biographer. Some clues, however, can be found in the youth and early career of the future general and President to help decipher the mysteries of his sphinx-like character.[1]

At Point Pleasant, Ohio, a bustling river town upstream a short distance from Cincinnati, Jesse Grant, father of Ulysses, had, in 1820, obtained part interest in a tannery and was immediately successful. Leather was much in demand, and Jesse, an enterprising son of a Connecticut Yankee and Revolutionary War captain, soon established himself as one of the town's leading citizens. His mother possessed qualities and characteristics just the opposite of her garrulous husband. Daughter of a well-to-do farmer who had recently arrived from eastern Pennsylvania, Hannah Simpson kept her silence, minded her business, and did as she believed right. She had married Jesse in July 1821 and came to live at the little frame house near the tannery.

Their first child, a son, was born on April 27, 1822, although it was some weeks before he acquired a name. At the country home of his maternal grandparents a family conclave decided to commit the matter of naming the child to a vote. The fact that Hannah's step-mother favored Ulysses and her father, Hiram, might have been the explanation for the winning combination being Hiram Ulysses. So it remained for seventeen years, although all called him Ulysses or Ulys, and never Hiram. When Ulysses was a year old, the family moved to Georgetown, Ohio, ten miles inland from the river, where his father built his own tannery.[2]

Grant received rudimentary schooling both in local subscription schools and, later, at boarding schools in Maysville, Kentucky and nearby Ripley, Ohio. He did exceedingly well in mathematics, especially mental arithmetic, and performed acceptably in other subjects. While at home he was expected to work for his father, but Ulysses hated the tannery. He would find other chores to do, be they plowing, hauling wood, or going out of town on various errands—anything to get away from the smelly tanyard. This could possibly explain Ulysses' willingness to consider a West Point education as an escape from an unappealing future in his father's business.[3]

Jesse looked favorably on a West Point education for Ulysses.

For one thing it was free; but, in addition, it trained a boy to be an engineer, and engineers were in that day in great demand in civilian life. Jesse wrote his Congressman and fellow townsman, Thomas L. Hamer, asking the appointment for his son. Hamer readily complied but submitted the name of Ulysses S. Grant, believing that Grant's middle name was Simpson, his mother's maiden name. Ulysses had no real desire for a military career, but his father insisted that, if appointed, he must go. There was no escaping it; the appointment came through, and in the summer of 1839 he made ready to set out for the East. Before his departure, someone had the bright idea of putting Ulysses' initials on his trunk, but when Grant saw the result, H.U.G., he reversed the first two letters, and thus went off bearing the name Ulysses Hiram Grant.[4] The name which the Academy had received from Washington was the one submitted by Hamer, Ulysses S. Grant. Unable to convince the adjutant that this was not his name, Grant resigned himself to the inevitable.

At first West Point had no appeal for the new cadet. Shy to start with, the ridicule heaped on the newcomers by the merciless upperclassmen made him even more withdrawn. For a time, he was decidedly unhappy. In September, the cadets moved into barracks and began the regular routine of classes and other Academy activities. He did not excel in any subject although he did his best work in mathematics. The fact that he did not find it necessary to study hard indicated not only that Grant had a generous share of native ability, but is also a reflection on the academic standards of the Academy and on Grant's lack of ambition to achieve high rank in his class. At graduation he stood twenty-one in a class of thirty-nine. Grant's four years at West Point were not especially noteworthy. Of course, they had a lasting impact on him. He learned a profession which fitted him for a career and which opened the way for his receiving a command and subsequent promotion during the Civil War.

While the proof is lacking, Grant's West Point experience might very well have caused him to become sensitive over his lack of social standing as compared to young men from the East and especially from the South. Hamlin Garland, a perceptive and discerning biographer of Grant, wrote that "he belonged decidedly to the plebeian side of the class, which was sharply divided on the line of elegance and savoir-faire. ... " Grant's social position was reasonably secure in Georgetown, Ohio, but it could hardly count for much away from there. A naturally bashful and yet proud youth could without much difficulty build up a feeling of hostility and resentment towards those who by their words, their bearing, and their attitudes made it obvious that they condidered themselves socially superior. Had he not done so, it would have been remarkable, and in later life Grant's behavior on a number of occasions can best be explained by this feeling of inferiority coupled with an instinctive dislike of people who belonged to a different social group. Such a feeling would have had its origins in those terribly difficult years between youth and adulthood spent in the hothouse atmosphere of West Point.

Grant, who so disliked army life and West Point during his first year there, gradually changed his attitude. The friendships he formed, and the feeling of comradeship which comes to a group living in close, confined association over a lengthy period of time, had an erosive effect on his initial antagonism. As was true of so many West Pointers before and since, Grant came to have a strong affection for the Academy.[5]

The army did not want the new graduates until September, so Grant passed the summer of 1843 in and around Bethel, Ohio, where his family had recently moved; going out for rides, visiting old friends in Georgetown, and on one occasion taking an excursion into nearby Cincinnati. This occurred soon after he had received his new blue uniform and proudly the new brevet second lieutenant, thinking he would make a big splash in the city, wore the uniform for the occasion. But a small ragamuffin of a boy brought him down to earth by calling out, "Soldier! will you work? No, sir—ee; I'll sell my shirt first!" From that time on, Grant made no attempt to dress up but rather was inclined to go in the opposite direction.

Grant, as a brevet second lieutenant assigned to the 4th Infantry, was ordered to report to Jefferson Barracks, near St. Louis, Missouri on September 20, 1843. The post was situated south of the city near the Mississippi River and served as headquarters for most of the 3d and 4th Infantry regiments.

Grant soon developed a friendly relationship with the family of Fred Dent, his West Point roommate who lived on a farm, White Haven, only five miles from Jefferson Barracks. Frederick Dent, the father, had come originally from Maryland by way of Pittsburgh, where he had married Ellen Wrenshall and then established himself as a Southern gentleman and slaveowner in Missouri. There were several children besides Fred, including eighteen year old Julia, who happened to be visiting in St. Louis when Grant first called. In fact it was February before she returned, and by that time the young West Pointer was a frequent visitor at White Haven. Julia's bright personality, vivaciousness, and trim figure had a decided appeal to the bashful lieutenant, who scarcely noticed a slight crossing of the eyes. He accompanied her on rides into the country, their times together becoming more and more frequent. Yet neither one, apparently, suspected the deep attachment that was mutually taking hold.[6]

That spring of 1844, while Ulysses and Julia enjoyed a blossoming romance, the country moved closer to war with Mexico. The Tyler administration was bending every effort to secure the annexation of Texas though Mexico had made it clear that war would follow annexation. Since Tyler had assured the Texans that they would have the protection of the United States following the signing of a treaty of annexation on April 12, 1844, it was not surprising that the 3d and 4th Infantry regiments were sent to take up a position near the Texas border in Louisiana.

The 3d had already left, and the 4th was expecting orders at any time, when Grant took a leave of absence to visit his parents in Ohio. Away from Julia, he quickly became aware that he was in love with her, and decided he should hurry back to White Haven to tell her so. First arranging for an extension of his leave, he rushed out to White Haven, and, as he himself confessed, awkwardly made known to her his love. Julia responded warmly, and from that moment on they were unofficially engaged.[7]

Forced to move on, Grant reluctantly took leave of Julia, hoping and believing that the separation would be brief and their marriage could soon take place. He found his regiment encamped in northwest Louisiana, and for more than a year he served in the army of observation while the country passed through the election of 1844. Just before Tyler left office, Congress approved the annexation of Texas by joint resolution. Following this, the Mexican government broke off diplomatic relations, and the new President, James K. Polk, ordered troops first to the Nueces River at the edge of the disputed territory and eventually to the north bank of the Rio Grande.

Early in September, the 4th Infantry went by water to Corpus Christi, near the mouth of the Nueces. Farther than ever from Julia, Ulysses continued to hope for an end to the trouble with Mexico so that his regiment would be ordered back to St. Louis. For six months, General Zachary Taylor gathered an army of from two to three thousand men, all regulars, awaiting orders to return home or to proceed on to the Rio Grande. An excursion to San Antonio, some amateur theatricals, and other forms of diversion, filled up the time in addition to the regular military preparations.

In his memoirs, Grant stated clearly his disapproval of the policy of the Polk administration in forcing the issue with Mexico, a weak neighbor. But if these were his opinions at the time, it is not evident in the letters he wrote. In these he wrote mostly of his eagerness to return, of mutual army friends, and of the scenes and people he was encountering in Mexico. A skirmish late in April north of the Rio Grande was followed by a declaration of war by Congress on May 13, 1846. The conflict which Grant, for personal reasons, hoped could be avoided had come to pass.[8]

Grant participated in most of the major engagements of the Mexican War, that is, in the battles fought near the Rio Grande and at Monterey, as well as those battles leading up to the capture of Mexico City. Whether as company commander or later as regimental quartermaster, he obtained valuable experience in combat and in the field. He also came to know many of the officers who would later be friends and foes in the Civil War.

His first battle, and the first major engagement of the war, was at Palo Alto just north of the Rio Grande on May 8, 1846. Grant, who had by this time grown whiskers, saw action with his company. When the fighting was over, he related to Julia his impressions of combat.

Although the balls were whizing thick and fast about me [he told Julia] I did not feel a sensation of fear until nearly the close of the firing a ball struck close by me killing one man instantly. . . . There is no great sport in having bullets flying about one in every direction but I find they have less horror when among them than when in anticipation. . . . [9]

The battle of Resaca de la Palma resulted in another American victory and the occupation of Matamoras, on the south bank of the Rio Grande, on May 18. After considerable delay, Taylor next launched the campaign which eventually resulted in the taking of Monterey, an important city more than two hundred miles from Matamoras, in the interior of Mexico. To handle the difficult logistics problems entailed in this venture, the position of regimental quartermaster was created. Much against his wishes, Grant got the assignment in the 4th Infantry.[10]

Try as he would, he could not escape the duty, but he got around this by going to the front whenever his regiment was engaged. In the three-day battle for Monterey, Grant took part in one infantry charge and in another instance volunteered to pass through a section of the city occupied by the Mexicans on a mission to secure more ammunition for his regiment. As the defeated enemy forces marched out of Monterey, Grant stood watching them, sensing that the Mexican soldiers had little idea of what the war was all about, and feeling pity for them. For several months the 4th Infantry did garrison duty in Monterey, a period of loneliness and impatience for Grant. To help pass the time and to put money in the regimental fund he organized a bakery and sold bread to his own and other regiments.[11]

Eventually, the 4th Infantry joined Winfield Scott's march against Mexico City, which got under way from near the mouth of the Rio Grande in March 1847. Grant was on hand for the landing south of Vera Cruz and the subsequent investment of that important sea coast city which fell to Scott's forces on March 27. While the siege was in progress Grant performed his quartermaster duties, which to Julia he described as merely "having the Pork and Beans rolled about."

Scott needed to get out of the coastal region onto higher ground to escape the sickness which prevailed in the summer months and so put his men in motion toward Mexico City as quickly as possible. Grant was not with the advance units and so had no part in the battle of Cerro Gordo, April 8, 1847, fought in the mountains against the Mexican army led by the ubiquitous Antonio Lopez de Santa Anna. The Americans flanked the Mexicans so that Santa Anna had to flee precipitately. Grant commented to Julia that the Mexican general was "pursued so closely that his carriage, a splendid affair, was taken and in it was his cork leg and some Thirty thousand dollars in gold." He regretted not being able to share "in that brave and brilliant assault" which had brought victory to Scott's men.

All the while Grant was seeing new sights and broadening his experience. He called Jalapa, on the way to Puebla, "the most beautiful place that I ever saw," and while marking time in Puebla, which Scott occupied on May 15, had occasion to be housed in a convent and to note the extraordinary grip which Catholic Christianity had on the people of Mexico. He did not like what he saw.[12]

Scott moved on toward Mexico City and in one day, August 20, engaged in two hard-fought contests with the Mexicans at Contreras and Churubusco. Grant saw action in the latter and was also involved, on September 8, in the sharp encounter at Molino del Rey. On September 13, he took part in the show-down struggle for the heights of Chapultepec, key to the city of Mexico. The battle which began early in the morning raged all through the day and swirled around the castle of Chapulte-pec and later the gates to the city and finally in the streets of the city itself. At one point, Grant, another officer, a few men, and a disassembled howitzer moved forward to a church Grant had spotted. Its belfry overlooked a position of the Mexican defenses near the San Cosme gate. Moving up to the edifice, they talked their way past a priest, assembled the howitzer in the belfry, and began lobbing shells into the enemy defenses. This caused considerable confusion for the enemy and materi-ally assisted Scott's attack. Late in the day a delegation of offi-cials came out to surrender the city to Scott. His campaign had been brilliantly conceived and executed from the very begin-ning. It was now crowned with complete success.

That Grant's services were finally recognized by his superiors is indicated by the rapid promotions that came to him in the last days of the campaign. For his conduct at Molino del Rey he was given a brevet first lieutenancy, and because of the death of one of the first lieutenants in his regiment, Grant was raised to that rank. Then for his "gallant conduct" at Chapultepec he was awarded a brevet captaincy. He also received mention in the reports of his superiors.[13]

The fighting had ended but the American troops stayed on in Mexico City during the lengthy peace negotiations. Fortunately it was a large, cosmopolitan city with a variety of diversions, so there was no excuse for boredom. Grant tried attending a bull fight, but, repulsed by the cruelty to both horses and bulls, left before the performance had ended. On another occasion, he began the ascent of Popocatapetl but turned back when the weather turned bad. He also visited the great cavern near Cuer-navaca. Grant once more got into the bakery business for the regiment and did extremely well. He wrote in his memoirs that "in two months I made more money for the [regimental] fund than my pay amounted to during the entire war."

The treaty of peace was signed February 2, 1848, but it took until May 30 for formal exchange of ratifications by both countries. Troop departure came rapidly after that, although the 4th Infantry did not sail from Vera Cruz until July 16, 1848.[14]

Leaving his regiment in temporary quarters in Mississippi, Grant obtained a two-months' leave and hurried on to St. Louis and Julia. It took only a short time to make arrangements for the wedding, which took place in the Dent town house in St. Louis on August 22, 1848. Ulysses and Julia took their wedding trip to his parents' home in Bethel, Ohio, prior to Grant's reporting to the new headquarters of the regiment in Detroit.

Grant and his bride arrived at Detroit only to discover their assignment was to be Madison Barracks, Sackets Harbor, New York, on the eastern end of Lake Ontario. Grant later protested the irregularity of his assignment and formally requested that he be ordered to Detroit. He won his case, and in the spring they made the desired move. The most noteworthy event of the Grants' two-years' stay in Detroit was the birth of a son, Frederick Dent Grant, on May 30, 1850.[15]

Grant's duties as regimental quartermaster did not overburden him, and he spent most of his spare time with a crowd of army officers and civilians who staged informal trotting races, traded horses, and sat around the sutler's store, drinking whiskey. Presumably Grant had his share of whiskey, since this was normal, indeed expected in the army circles he travelled in. At the social affairs, and especially the dances, Grant invariably stood on the fringe, never dancing, seldom speaking. The same sense of social inferiority which seemed to have bothered him at West Point now apparently reasserted itself. At a party he felt ill at ease, clammed up, and appeared awkward.

With Julia away in St. Louis in the spring of 1851, Grant received orders to return to Sackets Harbor, a change which looked better to him now than it had two years before. But the pleasant living at Sackets Harbor came abruptly to an end in June of 1852, when the 4th Infantry received orders to proceed to the West Coast. Since Julia was again pregnant and due in a matter of weeks it was out of the question for her and little Fred to accompany the regiment on the lengthy journey by way of the isthmus. Instead, she took her son to Bethel, Ohio, gave birth to a second son, Ulysses S. Grant, Junior, on July 22, and later went to live with her parents in Missouri. It was understood that she would join her husband as soon as possible.[16]

Crossing the isthmus in mid-summer was fraught with danger to persons not accustomed to the climate. The only hope lay in a quick transit, but this was not to be. Grant, in charge of the operation, discovered that the mules contracted for were not available at the price originally agreed on. As more and more of the party contracted cholera, the affair turned into a nightmare. Grant, confronted with increasingly complicated problems, exposed to the dread disease, and worn out from constant exertion, rose to the occasion with intelligent improvisation and did a remarkable job of getting the party through to the Pacific Ocean side of the isthmus even though the casualty figures were tragically high.[17]

At length, the survivors of the ordeal arrived at Benicia Barracks on San Francisco Bay on August 17, 1852. Grant's ultimate destination was Columbia Barracks, Fort Vancouver, Oregon Territory, but they lingered almost a month in the San Francisco area. Already the pangs of homesickness were eating away at the young lieutenant. "No person," Grant wrote Julia from Benicia, "can know the attachment that exists between parent and child until they have been separated for some time. I am almost crazy sometimes to see Fred." Grant still had not learned of the birth of his second son, in fact he would not know until December, when Julia's first letter arrived.[18]

As at Detroit and Sackets Harbor, Grant's quartermaster duties at Fort Vancouver were relatively light, leaving him much time. With living costs extremely high, Grant knew that if Julia and the children were ever to join him he would need far more income than his meagre army pay provided. It seemed as if making money on the side would be easy. Grant had some success in his speculative projects, but he also ran into more than his share of bad luck. He and a couple of fellow officers tried farming, knowing the high prices potatoes and onions brought. Unfortunately, the Columbia River flooded and all they could salvage from the project were a few bushels of potatoes. An attempt to sell ice in the San Francisco market failed. Several bad debts added to his financial woes and seemed to make even more remote the possibility of Julia and the children joining him.[19]

As the lonely months passed, with few letters from home to cheer him, Grant seriously considered resigning from the army. Then early in January 1854 came the transfer to Fort Humboldt, California, an isolated post some 200 miles north of San Francisco. The long-awaited promotion to captain meant that he would command one of the companies of the regiment. Under other circumstances, this would have been a desirable step forward, but Grant, knowing that Fort Humboldt was an even more unlikely place for an officer's family to reside than Fort Vancouver, did not see it that way. The commanding officer, Brevet Lieutenant Colonel Robert C. Buchanan, had the reputation of being a martinet and difficult to get along with. Grant became increasingly morose. "You do not know how forsaken I feel here," he wrote soon after his arrival. A few days later he told Julia, "the state of suspense I am in is scarsely bearable. I think I have been from my family quite long enough and sometimes I feel as though I could almost go home 'nolens volens.' "

Duties were light, mail irregular, and there was little to do. Grant had only one letter from Julia during his stay at Humboldt and this rankled to the point where he feared that his wife was growing away from him. Shortly before he submitted his resignation he wrote: " ... how do I know that you are thinking as much of me as I of you? I do not get letters to tell me so."[20] Under these conditions Grant did more drinking than was wise. Just exactly what happened at Fort Humboldt is unclear and probably will remain so. Grant's physical makeup was such that a little liquor went a long way, and in those months at Humboldt he seems to have attracted the unfavorable notice of his commanding officer.[21]

Grant's resignation from the army because of loneliness, desire to be with wife and children, the hopelessness of his situation as it then was, the gloomy prospect of assignment to an even more isolated post, the tedium of his duties, and his unfavorable financial condition is so clearly understandable that it is not at all necessary to seek out another explanation. Buchanan may have forced Grant to resign, but the story of an undated letter of resignation to be made effective should Buchanan deem it desirable is discounted by the document which Grant did submit.[22]

What the record shows is simply a brief tender of resignation and a request that it take effect July 31. A request for a sixty-day leave was granted, Grant was relieved of his duties at Fort Humboldt as of May 1, and a few days later he departed for home by way of San Francisco. It was best for him that he was going home to be with wife and children. The career was sacrificed to be sure, but more important, he would have around him the love and affection which he needed so desperately.[23]

The first year out of the army, Grant joined Julia and the two boys at her father's home, White Haven. Colonel Dent had given Julia sixty acres of the farm but they were undeveloped and Grant would have to build his own house, as well as clear the timbered land.

In the summer of 1855, the family now increased by the birth of a daughter, Ellen, on July 4, moved into the house built by Julia's brother Lewis, still on the Dent estate. Since Grant could be considered poor so far as material wealth was concerned, it was ironic that they had the luxury of three house servants, slaves Julia had been given by her father. If Grant felt qualms about having slaves about the house he did not voice them.

That year he cut and shaped the timbers needed to build his own house, planted and harvested crops, and hauled wood. The next year he erected the house, a good sized two-story structure. With straight-faced, but grim irony, Grant named the place Hardscrabble. The results of his farming efforts in 1855 were disappointing; instead of harvesting four or five hundred bushels of wheat, he netted only seventy-five. And when Christmas came around he was out of money, so much so that he pawned his gold watch for twenty-two dollars to buy presents for the family.[24]

The next spring brought renewed hopes for a successful farming season. To his sister, Grant told not only of his third son, Jesse Root, born on February 6, 1858, but of his having rented his farm and having taken over Colonel Dent's farm with its 200 acres of ploughed land, and 250 more of woods and pasture. Grant also received from his father-in-law a slave, William Jones, and thus became what Julia already was, a slave owner. But he freed Jones shortly after the family moved to St. Louis. Since he could have sold the Negro for badly needed cash, but did not, the manumission must have been done out of principle.

The favorable prospects of 1858 faded as Grant, at the crucial time in the growing season, fell ill with chills and fever and could not keep up with the work. At about that time he came to the conclusion that he would have to abandon farming. Helped once more by Julia's father, at the beginning of 1859 Grant became a partner with the colonel's nephew, Harry Boggs, in a St. Louis real estate and rental collection agency.[25]

Misfortune continued to dog Grant. The real estate business proved not to be the answer to his career problem. The job was a made one to begin with and, besides, Grant did not have the hard-driving determination to succeed as a collector of rents.

That summer of 1859 he abandoned the effort and struck out on his own trying to land a patronage job as county engineer. Failing in this, he did in the fall of 1859 obtain a position in the St. Louis Custom House, but, with the death of the collector and the installation of a new regime, he lost even that job. With no other recourse remaining open to him, Grant turned to his father. Traveling to his father's new home in Covington, Kentucky, in March, he made arrangements to take a position in the family leather business in Galena, Illinois where his brothers Simpson and Orvil had already gone. With his brother Simpson seriously ill and thus no longer able to give his attention to the Galena store, it was only natural that Ulysses should be wanted for that spot even had he not been in need of a livelihood just at that time.[26]

To Ulysses the Galena job represented a solution to the immediate problem of how to support his family. It could hardly have been anything other than an acknowledgement of failure, however, and he could scarcely have thought otherwise as he took his wife and their four young children aboard the steamer at St. Louis for the trip up the Mississippi to Galena. He was now thirty-eight, an ex-army officer fit for nothing better than a clerkship in a leather store.

CHAPTER II

The First Campaigns: The Road Back

GALENA WAS THE END OF THE ROAD FOR GRANT. HERE HE could remain out of sight, do his job, and be with his family. The worst was over; behind were the lean years after leaving the army. But ahead was nothing better than a meagre living along with a certain amount of humiliation for having to accept help from his father. Grant had few friends in Galena. Most of the people there in later years could not remember much about the undistinguished clerk in the leather store who more often than not did not know the prices of the merchandise. He spent his off hours at home with Julia and the children. He would climb the long steps up the steep slopes to the unpretentious house above the river to be greeted by his little boys.

Occasionally he would travel to Iowa, Wisconsin, and Minnesota visiting the accounts of the family leather business. These trips were the only things to break the monotony of Grant's life. But the steady routine and humdrum existence were unexpectedly interrupted by national events moving to a climax simultaneously with Grant's brief stay at Galena.

South Carolina declared herself independent in December 1860, and six other states of the lower South followed suit by the beginning of February 1861. When Fort Sumter was attacked in April, about a month following Lincoln's inauguration, Grant had to face the question of whether or not he should join the volunteer army. He concluded that his country would now need trained men and that, since he had received his education at the expense of the government, it was his duty to offer his services.

Somewhat reluctantly, Grant was drawn into the military preparations in progress in Galena. In one instance he found himself elected chairman of a meeting for the purpose of recruiting volunteers, but he himself did not sign up. Quite properly he believed he had the qualifications for something higher than lieutenant or captain in a volunteer company. Still, he would help out whenever he could, and he did so, giving advice on making up uniforms for the men, obtaining arms, and drilling the recruits.

During these confusing weeks Grant established friendly relations with two men who would have a great effect on his military career: Congressman Elihu B. Washburne and John A. Rawlins, a young Galena lawyer. Washburne spotted Grant as a potential high-ranking officer, made him his protégé, and gave him the political influence which he would not seek for himself. Rawlins, a Democrat, attracted Grant's notice by an appealing patriotic speech to one of the mass meetings held soon after the attack on Fort Sumter.[1]

Urged by Washburne to seek a commission from Illinois' Governor Richard Yates, Grant decided against that course of action, but he did agree to travel to Springfield with the Galena company. Departing on April 25, the men arrived at the capital the next day. There followed a strange interlude during which Grant performed the duties of volunteer adjutant or clerk in the governor's office. Grant was not happy to be thus employed; he really wanted a commission as colonel of one of the regiments, but was too proud to approach Yates.

To keep himself occupied Grant accepted the assignment of mustering thirty-day volunteers in various parts of the state. He completed these duties for the governor on May 22. A letter to Lorenzo Thomas, the Adjutant General in Washington, in which he offered his services and suggested that he might be appointed to the rank of colonel should the President see fit, was lost in the bureaucratic confusion which prevailed in the War Department. Early in June, Grant visited his parents in Covington, Kentucky, across the Ohio River from Cincinnati, where the leader of the forces in Ohio, General George B. McClellan, had his headquarters. Two lengthy waits on successive days in the anteroom to McClellan's office netted him nothing. Governor Yates finally saw the light and appointed Grant colonel of the Seventh District Regiment of Illinois volunteers. On returning to Springfield, he learned of his appointment and went to his new command the next day, June 16, still in his civilian clothes.

The most pressing and immediate problem was to have the men re-enlist for the three-year period. On June 28, the day when they would make their choice, Grant was visited by two leading Democrats from southern Illinois, John A. Logan, and John A. McClernand. These politicians were to address the men, even though Grant was worried lest Logan, many of whose constituents were not only Democrats but had pro-Southern leanings, might make the wrong kind of remarks. But both men gave stirring patriotic speeches, and when Logan had concluded, he introduced the new colonel. Grant, who had a strong aversion to making any kind of speech in public, simply said, "Men, go to your quarters!"[2]

Grant spent the next few days instructing the officers and trying to instill a little discipline into the unruly boys and young men from southern Illinois. He was partially successful, and when orders came to take the regiment, now the Twenty-first Illinois, to Quincy and from there into Missouri, he could feel a little more confident about going into action against the enemy. By the middle of July the troops were across the Mississippi into northern Missouri, a region infested by Confederate partisans and guerillas.

The important but uninteresting activity of defending the countryside and drilling the troops was interrupted early in August when Colonel Grant got word that he had been promoted to brigadier general. The new rank meant a new assignment, first to Ironton, in southeastern Missouri, again to combat guerilla forces, and shortly after to command of the district of southeast Missouri which included the southern part of Illinois as well.

On September 5, a few days after Grant arrived at Cairo, Illinois, an uninspiring, overcrowded, and dirty river town, he learned of the Confederate seizure of Columbus, Kentucky which was the first time either side had touched foot on Kentucky soil. Without wasting any time, he notified General John C. Frémont, his superior, that, unless he had orders to the contrary, he was going to occupy Paducah, Kentucky, in a countermove. Receiving no reply, he moved off that night with two regiments of infantry and a battery of field artillery. Early on the morning of the sixth this small force landed at Paducah without opposition. The importance of this move cannot be overestimated because Paducah was at the mouth of the Tennessee River and near that of the Cumberland. The control of these rivers would be essential to any combined amphibious operation into the interior of Kentucky and Tennessee. If Grant had delayed for even a few hours, there is every likelihood that the Confederates would have occupied Paducah first and upset all Federal schemes for conducting a campaign using the two rivers.

In the weeks following, Confederate strength at Columbus increased, and Grant's men grew restive for want of action. This, according to Grant, explains his attack on Belmont, some-

thing smaller than a hamlet, across the Mississippi from Colum-
bus. The ostensible reason was an order to demonstrate against
Columbus to assist a Federal force operating against the
Confederates in southeastern Missouri.

On November 6 he set out down river, accompanied by
gunboats of the navy, with a force of around 3000 men. On
the morning of the seventh they went ashore a little above
Belmont. Grant took his men for more than a mile through
the woodland and fields and eventually struck an equal force
of Confederates. Fighting erupted and continued for approximately four hours. About midday or soon after, the Union
soldiers swept the Confederates back almost to the river and
occupied their camp. Victory appeared complete, but the triumph was too much for these green troops who lost any
semblance of order or discipline for the moment.

When Grant saw Confederate reinforcements crossing the
river and about to land between him and his transports he
knew that he had best get his men out in a hurry. They
managed to fight their way out of the partial encirclement
and reached the boats. The gunboats' fire kept the Confederate pursuers at bay, and the Union troops returned to
Cairo. The positive results of the raid were confined to in-
fliction of casualties on the enemy, and battle experience for
his own men.[3]

Grant was gaining experience all the time. He knew how
to command a regiment; he had faced the problems of drilling and disciplining inexperienced volunteers; he had been
given the responsibilities that go with independent command
and had proved that he could seize what opportunities came
along. He was rapidly acquiring the equipment for successful
command.

Soon after the engagement at Belmont, Mrs. Grant with
the children came to live with the general at Cairo.
Throughout the war, whenever possible, the Grant family
was together. Some time before the battle, John A. Rawlins,
the young lawyer from Galena, joined Grant's staff and practically speaking became another member of the family. Rawlins was to have a significant part in Grant's Civil War
career, becoming to a degree his *alter ego*. Perhaps as important as anything, he kept a close watch on Grant's drinking.
Rawlins, son of an alcoholic father and a strict teetotaler
himself, was good insurance against Grant's resuming his
west coast habits. In a remarkably candid letter to Wash-

burne, replying to rumors that Grant was getting drunk in Cairo, he stated quite flatly that while on occasion the general took a drink with visitors, the report that he was drinking hard was "utterly untrue."

Grant's command at Cairo and vicinity could only wait for developments during the late fall and early winter of 1861. The troops could drill, supply problems could be worked out, but that was not Grant's way of winning the war. He wanted to be moving against the enemy even if it meant doing it in cold, wet weather over bad roads.

A demonstration against Mayfield, Kentucky which Grant conducted in January 1862 was moderately successful and also opened the way to the capture of Forts Henry and Donelson. Flag Officer Andrew Foote, as eager for action as Grant, had moved his gunboats up the Tennessee River as far as Fort Henry and saw how vulnerable to attack this Confederate position was. Grant needed little encouragement, though a visit to General Henry W. Halleck, Frémont's successor, in St. Louis near the end of January to promote an attack on the Southern fort proved, for the moment, futile. But Halleck changed his mind, and on January 30 issued orders to Grant "to take and hold Fort Henry."

Delighted to be up and doing, Grant and Foote wasted little time in getting the operation started. The expedition set out from Cairo and Paducah on February 2, 1862 and proceeded up the Tennessee River to within about nine miles of Fort Henry, on the east side of the river. Grant prepared a joint military-naval attack on Fort Henry, but bad roads delayed the army's advance, and the job was done by the navy. The weakness of the position, and the loss of most of his guns led the Confederate commander to evacuate the fort. The fall of Fort Henry forced Confederate General Albert Sidney Johnston to fall back from Bowling Green, Kentucky, at least as far as Nashville. With the Tennessee River now open, Foote could send his gunboats far upstream to Muscle Shoals and Florence in northern Alabama.[4]

Thinking in terms of the capture of Fort Henry, Grant asked the navy to go round by way of the Cumberland River to attack Fort Donelson. Meanwhile, he would take his army across the fifteen-mile-wide strip of land between the two rivers. Moving as rapidly as the weather and poor roads permitted, Grant with about 15,000 men set forth on the morning of February 12 and arrived in the vicinity of Donelson about noon. By this time there were approximately 20,000 Confederates in and around the fort on the west bank of the Cumberland River. Grant set about fixing his lines for a siege of the fort. He placed General John A. McClernand's division on the right and that of C. F. Smith on the left. Two days later, sizable reinforcements arrived, and Grant placed these, along with some other units, in a new division commanded by General Lew Wallace. Wallace's division occupied a position between McClernand and Smith, which put it directly to the west of Fort Donelson.

Grant's hope for a quick end to the affair by Foote's gunboats, as at Henry, was dashed, when, on the fourteenth, Foote moving up close to the shore batteries, had to retire when his vessels suffered numerous hits. Just at this time there was a sudden change from mild, warm weather to bitter cold accompanied by sleet and snow. The men, many of whom had discarded overcoats in the sunny weather of the march, now suffered from the intense cold.

It so happened that Foote had received a disabling wound during his affair with the shore batteries, and instead of going to headquarters for consultation asked Grant to come to his flagship anchored in the Cumberland River. The meeting took place on the morning of February 15. During his absence, the Confederates, seeking to break the siege, attacked the right of Grant's line. They were at first successful but failed to exploit their advantage.

The general's reactions to these events were mixed. Believing correctly that this part of the line would have been weakened in order to add weight to the Confederate attack, he first ordered an assault by Smith on the Confederate right. He also took steps to restore the situation on his own right. Whether or not this was the crisis of his whole career as some historians have asserted, it was nonetheless a moment of testing his ability to face up to adversity. There was a note of panic in his message to Foote: "If all the gunboats that can will immediately make their appearance to the enemy it may secure us a victory. Otherwise all may be defeated. A terrible conflict ensued in my absence, which has demoralized a portion of my command, and I think the enemy is much more so." Grant was absolutely right. Generals John G. Floyd and Gideon Pillow were convinced the night of February 15 that all was lost and that their best bet was to clear out, which is what they did, turning over to Simon Bolivar Buckner the unpleasant job of surrendering the fort the next day. When Buckner asked for terms, Grant replied that he had no terms to offer but would insist on "unconditional and immediate surrender. ... "[5]

Because of these words and because of the capture of Donelson, Grant's fame spread over the land. He had gained the first truly important Union victory, and the North went wild with joy. Secretary of War Edwin M. Stanton and Lincoln agreed to Grant's promotion which gained speedy confirmation from the Senate, so that Grant was now a major general dating appropriately enough from February 16, 1862. This made him number ten on the list of general officers with only Halleck outranking him in the West. But when in July Halleck went east to be general-in-chief of all the Union armies, neither Grant nor anyone else was appointed in his place.

The capture of Donelson opened up all sorts of possibilities for the Union forces that late winter of 1862. Albert Sidney Johnston, Confederate commander in the West, abandoned Nashville as well as all of central Tennessee shortly after the disaster at Donelson. But the possibilities for further advance were even greater and Grant was well aware of this. To his wife, on February 24, he wrote that " 'Secesh' is now about on its last legs in Tennessee," and "I want to push on as rapidly as possible to save harsh fighting. ... The way to avoid it is to push forward as vigorously as possible." That there was not complete exploitation of the Donelson victory was the result of the want of aggressive leadership in the Union high command. General-in-Chief George B. McClellan, even if he had been a fighter, was too far away to have much influence over events outside Virginia; while Halleck and Don Carlos Buell in the West were both so overcome with fears of what the enemy might do that it is a wonder anything was accomplished in that theatre. Grant alone of the men in command positions in the West saw the desperate need to keep hammering away at the defeated and demoralized foe, yet he was powerless to go beyond the restrictive orders Halleck issued from St. Louis.

Nor was Halleck's ingrained timidity the only reason for the inaction following the fall of Nashville. A breakdown in communications resulting from the disloyalty of a telegraph operator made it appear to Halleck that Grant was deliberately refraining from submitting reports to his superior. To compound Grant's seeming insubordination, the victor of Fort Donelson took it on himself to proceed to Nashville to confer with Buell, on the assumption that Nashville lay within the area of his ill-defined district. Halleck did not see it that way. Halleck, no easy man to get along with anyway, reported these actions and inactions to McClellan, and for a time Grant's status was somewhat in doubt. There was even mention of his being placed under arrest. But Halleck had gone too far, and he knew it, when the White House told him to come through with specific charges, or, in effect, drop the matter. Halleck seemed glad to forget the whole business. He was canny enough, however, to lead Grant to believe that only his intercession with McClellan had saved him from serious trouble with the Washington authorities.[6]

Thus as spring approached, the opportunity for delivering a knockout blow in the West was fast disappearing. The Confederates were given a reprieve and used it to gather forces at the important railroad junction of Corinth, Mississippi, in hopes of recouping after the disasters of the previous months. Albert Sidney Johnston commanded a sizable Confederate army at Corinth and decided that he must strike a blow before Buell's army, coming southwest from Nashville, should unite with Grant's. In March, Grant advanced upriver to Savannah on the east bank of the Tennessee River, about twenty-five miles from Corinth. Farther up the river from Savannah about nine miles was Pittsburg Landing on the road that linked the Tennessee River with Corinth. The road rose quickly from the landing to a plateau some hundred feet above the level of the river. About three miles from the river, on the road to Corinth, stood the little log meeting house known as Shiloh Church. Nearby, in this early spring of 1862, when the fruit trees were beginning to blossom, were encamped the men of Grant's divisions.

By the end of March, Grant had six divisions in his army, five of which were in the vicinity of Pittsburg Landing and Shiloh. The sixth, commanded by Lew Wallace, was just to the west of Crump's Landing a few miles down river, that is north, from Pittsburg. Grant had no fear of a major attack on his position at Shiloh. He was, in fact, becoming impatient and wanted to move forward against the Confederates at Corinth. He hated to be idle, especially when it was obvious to him that the enemy was using every hour of delay to strengthen its position at Corinth. He also, characteristically, was thinking of the enemy morale, which he correctly estimated to be rocky after the Donelson surrender and the loss of Nashville.[7]

That Grant was mentally unprepared for the Confederate attack which struck on April 6 is indicated by the statement he made to Halleck on the fifth, "I have scarcely the faintest idea of an attack (general one) being made upon us, but will be prepared should such a thing take place." Confederate activity in front of the Union forces was seen as simply reconnaissance and not as movements preparatory to a general assault. This does not mean that no preparations for an attack had been made. The position was selected in part because it was defensible: creeks protected either flank, there was frequent reconnaissance, and orders were issued to cover the contingency of an enemy assault. Johnston's attack, originally set for Saturday, April 5, could not be delivered until Sunday the sixth, a matter of major importance to Grant, because during the delay Buell's advance division arrived at the Tennessee in time to reinforce Grant at a critical moment.

Grant stayed at Savannah on the fifth of April, depending on division commander William T. Sherman to keep him informed about any movements of the enemy. He reported to Halleck the arrival of Buell's other two divisions the next day. His messages were still not couched in words which would betray any anxiety or apprehension of imminent attack.

There was some fog early on that Sunday morning in April, when advance units of the Confederate army clashed with a reconnaissance force from General Benjamin M. Prentiss' division. In a short while the whole Confederate attack was uncovered, and soon the Southern forces were moving in overwhelming strength against the Yankees.

As more units of both sides became engaged, the sound of battle could be heard down river at Savannah where Grant and his staff were just beginning breakfast. Although there had been ample warning, Grant, without question, had been caught off guard by the Confederate attack. Pausing only for a moment to try to determine whether the sound was coming from Pittsburg or Crump's Landing, Grant quickly made ready to go to the scene of the action. He sent an order to General William Nelson directing him to move his command to the point on the river opposite Pittsburg, and another to Lew Wallace to hold his command in readiness to move as soon as orders were sent him.[8]

When Grant and his staff arrived at Pittsburg Landing, the battle was in full progress and he went forward immediately to the battle lines. Overwhelming Confederate strength had been hurled against the inadequately prepared divisions of Sherman and Prentiss. Soon McClernand's and W. H. L. Wallace's divisions were engaged and the fighting became intense as the Confederates tried to force the Yankees back to the river.

This was not a tactician's battle, neither for Johnston nor for Grant. It was a soldiers' slugfest which went on for the better part of two days with incredible slaughter on both sides. Noise, confusion, smoke, and shouts dominated the scene which afforded a commanding general little opportunity to display tactical skill. Still, there was much that could be done. Grant was present on the field, conspicuously so throughout the day, and this alone helped to restore confidence and reinforce the will to fight, in those troops who stayed. One of his first acts was to arrange for supplies of ammunition to be sent forward to the troops. Equally important, he sent orders to Lew Wallace to bring his division in on the Union right. But Wallace's men arrived only when the fighting was over for the day. They had set out on the wrong road, had to retrace their steps, and wasted precious hours in aimless marching.

The commanding general on several occasions visited each of his division commanders (except Lew Wallace), advising them on troop dispositions, and, when he was hard-pressed, urged Prentiss to hold his position at all cost. This Prentiss did and possibly saved the rest of the army in doing so, even though the remnant of the division, some 2500 men, surrendered late in the afternoon after having been totally surrounded.

By the end of the day Grant's men held a line fully a mile to the rear of the one they had taken up early in the morning. It was perilously close to the river; yet that very closeness held some advantage. Buell's men could more easily reinforce, the narrower line was easier to defend, and the gunboats could now come into action, hurling shells at the advancing Confederates. The stubborn Yankee defense had taken a terrible toll of the attackers, including Johnston himself, and the Confederate formations were early thrown into confusion. By the late afternoon the force of the attack was spent, and Pierre G. T. Beauregard, who had succeeded to the command after Johnston's death, found it impossible to mount another assault.

It was evident that the Union army was going to be able to keep its position. About this time, Buell crossed the river to confer with Grant and asked him what provision he was making for a retreat. In typical fashion, Grant replied that he was not contemplating retreat, but rather was going to launch a counterattack the next day.

As darkness settled down on the dismal scene of death and suffering, rain began to fall. Grant, having done all he could towards preparing for the morrow, leaned against a tree, seek-

ing sleep. Finding this uncomfortable, at about midnight, he
went to a log hut which served as a hospital. While much of the
army rested, the surgeons kept busy throughout the night attending the wounded. Their groans and cries were too much
for Grant and he returned to the comparative tranquility of the
tree.[9]

Grant ordered a general attack for the next morning. The
Confederates at first put up stubborn resistance, but the fresh
troops of Buell's and Lew Wallace's commands eventually carried the day, and early in the afternoon the whole Confederate
line drew back. The retreat to Corinth from then on was con-
tinuous.

That Grant did not relentlessly pursue his broken foe during
the remainder of Monday, April 7, and the following day has
been the subject of considerable controversy. Certainly, a
superficial glance at the situation at the time Beaureguard's
forces were staging a retreat, which Southern commanders admitted was something of a general rout, would seem to reveal
a heaven-sent opportunity to strike the crushing blow which
would obliterate the principal Southern army of the West.

The obvious reason why there was no pursuit was the extreme weariness of the troops, their broken organization, and
the muddy condition of the roads. But Grant was not one to
quit just because the troops were tired. Besides, he was capable
of assuming the exhaustion and demoralization of the enemy
forces. Why, then, was there not a more relentless pursuit? The
answer seems to lie in a statement Grant made to Buell. He
wrote, "Under the instructions which I have previously received, and a dispatch also of to-day from Major-General Halleck, it will not then do to advance beyond Pea Ridge [a point
between Shiloh and Corinth], or some point which we can
reach and return in a day." On the morning of the ninth Halleck told Grant, "Avoid another battle, if you can, till all arrive.
We then shall be able to beat them without fail." This would
seem to be the most logical explanation for Grant's failure to
follow up the retreating Confederates and to deliver the knockout blow.

Just as the war in the West reached a turning point at Shiloh,
so too did Grant's conception of the war. Believing that the
Confederacy was a hollow shell, vulnerable to one decisive
blow, Grant had expected the Southern cause to collapse after
the loss of Kentucky and much of Tennessee. In keeping with
his belief that most of the Southern people were really loyal to

the Union, he had tried to wage war in such a way that the
civilian population suffered as little as possible. But his eyes
were opened by the Confederate performance at Shiloh. An
enemy who was supposedly demoralized, broken, and on the
point of collapse had rallied and launched an impressive attack
with a superior force. Obviously, the war was by no means over;
nor would it end until the will of the Southern people to wage
it had been broken.[10]

Grant had now won two important victories in the West.
Though it was easier for the public to see the immediate results
of Donelson, the discerning observer could see that his success
at Shiloh was no less important in that it not only frustrated
Confederate hopes and plans, but opened limitless possibilities
for exploitation: seizure of Corinth, Mississippi, opening the
Mississippi River for its entire length by the capture of Vicksburg, securing east Tennessee by the prompt occupation of
Chattanooga, or a rapid advance into Alabama.

That Lincoln should have refrained from giving Grant a more
important command after Donelson is easily understood. That
he should have passed up the opportunity to reward him with
greater responsibilities after Shiloh is also understandable. The
reports that Lincoln received from Halleck and especially from
the press cast doubt on Grant's performance at Shiloh. Halleck,
soon after his arrival at Pittsburg Landing, wrote to Stanton that
it was the unanimous opinion there that Sherman saved the day
on April 6 and "contributed largely to the glorious victory on
the 7th." And while Halleck implicitly defended Grant from
charges of incompetence and misconduct, he did not clearly
convey to the President or to the Secretary of War the idea that
Grant was a great general who deserved high praise and reward for what he had accomplished.

As for the press, the attacks on Grant were such as to undermine public confidence in his ability and moral fitness to command. Though the criticism came largely from the western
papers, some of the stories were reprinted in the East. Inevitably, the charge was made that Grant had been drunk at the
time of the battle, and the story gained wide currency. Lincoln
would naturally be aware of this and be reluctant to reward so
seemingly an undeserving man. When Alexander K. McClure, a
Pennsylvania politician, sensitive to the public's criticism of
Grant, suggested to Lincoln that Grant had better be relieved,
Lincoln replied, "I can't spare this man; he fights."[11]

Now it so happened that on April 7, 1862, the date of the

second day's battle of Shiloh, General John Pope had captured Island No. 10 in the Mississippi River between Cairo and Memphis, thus opening a long stretch of the river and leading quickly to the fall of Memphis to Union forces. Pope had handled his operation with skill, and besides there were no charges of drunkenness leveled against him. The upshot was that in time Lincoln gave Pope an important command in the East, a decision which can best be described as unfortunate.

Soon after Pope went East to command the Army of Virginia, Halleck followed him there with the more exalted assignment of general-in-chief of the Union armies. Halleck had proved his organizing and administrative abilities during the time he had command in the West, and Lincoln, seeking an overall coordinator of military operations, cannot be criticized for choosing "Old Brains." But Halleck had not shone as a field commander, and he was obviously not the aggressive fighter needed for a successful prosecution of the war. Lincoln at the same time was sticking with McClellan as commander of the Army of the Potomac, despite numerous signs of unaggressiveness, and an almost paranoid mentality. Clearly, Lincoln was not displaying acute perception in singling out successful commanders and this was especially true in the case of Grant.

Not only was Grant denied increased responsibility as a result of his success at Shiloh, but he was subjected to a degrading humiliation by Halleck, so much so that this period in Grant's career is a cipher. Halleck took over active command just a few days after the battle of Shiloh and treated Grant almost as if he were in disgrace; at times, as if he hardly existed. During this time he did not directly command the Army of the Tennessee, but rather held the empty position of second-in-command to Halleck.

Grant bore the humiliation until after the fall of Corinth, May 30, 1862, and then asked for a leave. Sherman urged him not to absent himself from the army, fearing that if he did he would jeopardize his career. Halleck, even, asked Grant to stay. Grant did, and before long, he got back his old command, the Army of the Tennessee. By removing his headquarters to Memphis, he avoided having to deal directly with Halleck.[12]

By mid 1862 Grant had come a long way from the relative obscurity of the previous year and from the lowly clerkship of two years earlier. While his West Point training and previous army experience account for his first commission as a volunteer, something more must explain his sudden rise to national prominence. His success stemmed from a complicated set of circumstances which worked in his favor, but also from specific traits within his own character which only needed the right conditions to reveal themselves, conditions which had been present during the Mexican War, and on the isthmus, but which were singularly lacking on the West Coast, in Missouri, and at the leather store in Galena. These traits were determination, mental acuteness, excellent memory, ability to look into the minds of others, and a willingness to subordinate self to a cause. When these are added to the experience gained in the old army, especially in the Mexican War, and as a regimental commander during the early months of the Civil War, Grant's sudden rise from oblivion becomes more comprehensible. Even so, the transformation borders on the miraculous.

CHAPTER III

Victory at Vicksburg

FROM JUNE UNTIL EARLY NOVEMBER 1862 CONDITIONS IN Grant's department were such that he could not add to his reputation as a fighting general. With the exceptions of the battles of Iuka and Corinth, in which he did not directly participate, the important engagements took place in other theatres. His activities were mostly confined to the performance of administrative duties which devolved on the commander of an occupied territory in time of war. His experiences in this role are of significance in revealing Grant's attitudes and feelings toward slavery, the Negro, Jews, and dealers in cotton.

The general did not share the sentiments of the abolitionists, nor did he believe in racial equality. But he had no desire to see the institution of slavery perpetuated, nor could he remain insensitive to the wants and feelings of an enslaved people. Yet, far more significant in evaluating Grant's actions regarding the Negro during the war period was the fact that Grant would simply follow the orders of his superiors. However, practical problems involving Negroes kept intruding themselves, and they had to be met, not by mere obedience to orders from above, but by on-the-spot solutions formulated by the district or department commander. As the war proceeded, refugee Negroes crowded near the camps of the Union army and in cities, such as Memphis, in control of Northern forces. In seeking a solution to the problem of these numerous unemployed persons Grant, in November 1862, turned to Chaplain John Eaton of the 27th Ohio regiment. Eaton had had a varied army experience and only needed solid backing from Grant to get started a plan of putting Negroes to work primarily in cotton fields. It was a practical and humane solution to a difficult problem.

Grant also faced a touchy problem in the trade in cotton and other articles which inevitably went on in his department. Now the law did allow, under certain restrictions, cotton to be shipped from the conquered areas of the South. The result was much pressure on Grant to issue permits to Northern merchants who would go to almost any lengths to garner the enormous profits to be had from sending cotton north. The greatest embarrassment for Grant came when his own father, working with partners out of Cincinnati, tried to get in on the good thing. The partners happened to be Jews; in fact, a good many of the cotton merchants and speculators who plagued Grant were Jews. Annoyed by this vexing problem Grant issued an unfortunate order on December 17, 1862, which required the expulsion of all Jews from the department within twenty-four hours. The order was quickly repudiated in Washington and Grant obediently withdrew it. In issuing it he revealed a degree of racial prejudice not becoming a high-ranking military man who must have known (as was pointed out to him by Lincoln, by way of Halleck) that there were Jews in the Union armies and that it would be neither wise nor fair to single out any special group for condemnation.[1]

Grant could not solve the problem of cotton speculators and traders with the enemy by any number of orders; the best he could do was to keep it under reasonable control. But in so doing he picked up enemies and critics along the way. Indeed, Grant's reputation both as an administrator and as a military commander fell under a cloud toward the end of 1862 and in the early months of 1863. His campaign in Mississippi in the fall of 1862 all but collapsed by the end of the year. This campaign was preceded by two disappointing and indecisive engagements which took place in his department and were fought by troops who were under his overall command.

During the summer of 1862, General Don Carlos Buell, in command of what would soon be known as the Army of the Cumberland, set out eastward toward Chattanooga along the line of the Memphis and Charleston Railroad. He crept along at such a slow pace that Braxton Bragg, who replaced Beauregard in command of the Confederate army at Tupelo, Mississippi, saw a chance to take the initiative and make a thrust into Kentucky. Setting out near the end of August, Bragg got the jump on Buell, by-passed Nashville, and by early September was in Kentucky, heading for Louisville.

It fell to Grant to prevent Confederate forces in the vicinity of Corinth from reaching Bragg. With depleted forces, Grant found it impossible to hold the railroad east of Corinth, and when Confederate General Sterling Price moved against Iuka on September 13, General William S. Rosecrans, who was under Grant's command, withdrew westward toward Corinth and the support of another portion of Grant's forces commanded by

General Edward O. C. Ord. Grant now saw a chance to crush
Price and ordered Rosecrans and Ord to attack his force at Iuka
in such a way as to catch the enemy in a pincers movement.

Ord was in position on the eighteenth of September, but
Rosecrans was not ready until late the following day. Grant,
travelling with Ord's command, found it impossible to coordi-
nate the movements of the two forces. Meanwhile Price turned
on Rosecrans late on the afternoon of the nineteenth. The wind
was blowing away from Ord's position, and no sound of Rosecrans' battle reached Ord's men poised for the attack which
was never ordered. Rosecrans fought Price to a draw and very
early on the morning of September 20, Price abandoned Iuka.

Not long after, a Confederate force commanded by Earl Van
Dorn attacked Corinth. Again, Rosecrans had immediate command of the Federal forces, with Grant remaining behind at his
headquarters in Jackson, Tennessee. Van Dorn, now joined by
Price, moved north and west of Corinth and then came in on
that fortified town from the northwest. On October 3, the
Confederates were partially successful in driving in the defending forces. The next day Van Dorn renewed the attack, but the
impetus had been lost, and the Confederate commander decided to withdraw.[2]

Near the end of October, Grant wrote to Halleck protesting
that he had not been given any plan of operations, and that he
knew of no plans for the commanders of adjacent territory. But,
he said, with reinforcements it would be possible to move south
along the Mississippi Central Railroad and thus cause the
evacuation of the fortified and strategic river town of Vicksburg, Mississippi.

Disaster to Grant's Vicksburg campaign in December 1862
struck in the form of two raids by Confederate cavalry. One
was by Nathan Bedford Forrest in west Tennessee against the
Mobile and Ohio Railroad connecting Grant's force in Mississippi with his rear base at Columbus, Kentucky. The other by
Earl Van Dorn destroyed Grant's forward supply base at Holly
Springs, Mississippi, on December 20, 1862. Because of this
setback Grant was obliged to abandon his forward thrust toward Vicksburg made in conjunction with a river expedition
commanded by Sherman. The upshot was that, lacking the expected cooperation from Grant, Sherman, on December 29,
was badly mauled by the Confederates at Chickasaw Bluffs, on
the Yazoo River, a short distance north of Vicksburg.[3]

Grant then abandoned the project to attack Vicksburg by

way of Oxford, Grenada, and the Mississippi Central Railroad, largely because of John A. McClernand. This major general with beaked nose, full, bushy beard, and receding hairline had left the halls of Congress as representative from Illinois to become an active participant in the cause he believed in whole-heartedly. He had been a major factor in rallying midwestern Democrats to support the war effort. But regular army officers were none too happy with this difficult, and often arrogant man. For months, Grant put up with McClernand's insubordina-tion, interference, and chronic complaining, only occasionally showing his displeasure.[4]

McClernand chafed under the restraints imposed on him as a subordinate to Grant. Taking advantage of his political con-nections, he took a leave in September 1862, journeyed to Washington, and talked with the President about a plan for an offensive which he himself would lead. The plan involved rais-ing a new, independent army in the Midwest, which would operate along the Mississippi River and wrest it from the Confederates. This meant especially a campaign against Vicks-burg.

To Lincoln, who had known McClernand back in Illinois, all this sounded reasonable, but he made a mistake in giving the amateur general authority to command an independent expedi-tion against Vicksburg. Hints as to what was going on reached Grant during the last two weeks of the year, but he never was given a clear picture of what McClernand's role was by either the President or the Secretary of War.[5] One can only feel sym-pathy for McClernand who had returned to Illinois to raise the troops with the understanding that he would lead his own ex-pedition. No wonder he believed himself betrayed by the President when these troops were swallowed up in Grant's command. The blame for a badly bungled mess lies clearly with Lincoln who showed lack of consideration for both Grant and McClernand.

McClernand had waited impatiently in Springfield, Illinois, and finally appealed directly to Stanton for orders to take per-sonal command of his troops. On December 23, Stanton gave him the desired permission. But before this, on December 18, an order had gone out from Washington to Grant directing him to organize his forces into four army corps, one of which would be commanded by McClernand. This was hardly what McCler-nand had been promised, and he still believed, with reason, that he would independently command the expedition against

Vicksburg, even though nominally he would be operating within Grant's department. When McClernand reached Memphis, Sherman had already left for Vicksburg, and on December 29, as already related, suffered defeat at Chickasaw Bluffs. McClernand, senior to Sherman, hurried to the scene so that he could take command, Grant being still far down in the interior of Mississippi.[6]

At Sherman's suggestion, the troops which had unsuccessfully moved against Vicksburg now turned their attention to a Confederate position up the Arkansas River on the theory that something was better than nothing. On January 11, 1863, their overwhelming force brought about the surrender of Arkansas Post and 5000 Confederate troops. Grant was in something of a dilemma. At first he disapproved of the expedition but later softened his criticism, perhaps because Sherman, and not McClernand, had originated the plan, and because it was a success.[7]

With McClernand and Grant both on the Mississippi, the time had come for a showdown. On January 30, McClernand in a letter to Grant asked that the dispute be referred to Washington. The day that McClernand wrote that letter was the one on which Grant issued General Orders No. 13, from Young's Point, Louisiana, assuming immediate command of the expedition against Vicksburg. The result of this unpleasant controversy was that McClernand sullenly continued as commander of the Thirteenth Corps, and Grant accepted him as a necessary evil because of his political importance. The episode, however, was by no means closed.[8]

So, mostly because of McClernand, Grant found himself in command of an expedition against Vicksburg, not in central Mississippi on firm ground, but on the river with no easy way to reach his objective. One thing to do would be return to Memphis and start the overland campaign again. Grant says in his memoirs that because of the deep discouragement in the North at the time, he could not add to the gloom and defeatism by a retrograde movement. He would have to "go forward to a decisive victory."[9]

The trouble was that in that season of the year the ground along the west bank of the Mississippi and on the east bank north of Vicksburg was badly flooded, so much so that no usable roads existed along the west bank for the transfer of the army to the relatively dry ground south of Vicksburg. One possibility was to use some of the waterways both on the west and the east sides of the river, either to get south of Vicksburg or to reach dry ground east and north of the city. Between the latter part of January and the end of March, Grant had his men at work trying four different routes. To enter into the details of these efforts would hardly be profitable inasmuch as they all failed.[10]

The men, however, were kept busy and the Confederates could never be sure what Grant might try next. Yet, it is difficult to believe that these engineering projects involving canal construction, levee breaking, and the like were primarily meant to keep the troops busy and lead the country into thinking that something important was being done. Rather, Grant's correspondence reveals that he really did have confidence these projects could amount to something.[11]

Be that as it may, the failure of these attempts forced Grant into adopting the plan which eventually worked. Hindsight shows that the plan of moving the army south of Vicksburg on the west side and then crossing to the east side with the aid of the navy was simple and obvious. Yet, at the time, the obstacles and dangers appeared insuperable.

The first phase of the campaign involved moving the army from north of Vicksburg to some point south of there, where the enemy was without fixed defenses. McClernand's corps was first to move. An advanced detachment set out from Milliken's Bend March 29, and on April 6 arrived at New Carthage on the river, having found the roads difficult but passable. Grant, meanwhile, had asked Admiral David Porter to cooperate by sending his gunboats and a few cargo vessels past the Vicksburg batteries. Without the aid of the navy, the expedition could hardly succeed. Porter, skeptical but loyal, agreed to do it, and successfully carried it off the night of April 16.[12]

Grand Gulf just south of Vicksburg proved to be too strong to be taken, so Grant moved further south from New Carthage to another spot called Hard Times. A Negro, captured on the east bank, revealed the existence of a good road inland from Bruinsburg, Mississippi, ten miles south of Grand Gulf. This was just what Grant needed, and immediately he adjusted his plans to the new conditions. The landing took place on April 30, while Colonel Benjamin H. Grierson, with a cavalry detachment, was marauding through central Mississippi heading for Baton Rouge, creating confusion as he went. And up to the north of Vicksburg, Sherman's corps was staging a convincing demonstration along the Yazoo. These diversionary tactics kept the

Confederate commander at Vicksburg, General John C. Pemberton, guessing so much that he could not concentrate against Grant at Bruinsburg.

The landing on the east bank opened the second phase of the campaign, the most dangerous part, because Grant now faced an enemy force which, if concentrated, would equal his own; he was in hostile country with an attenuated, vulnerable supply line. Should he suffer a reverse it could well lead to total annihilation or capture. But Grant only felt relief to be on the same side of the river with the enemy, on dry ground.

What happened in the next three weeks forms part of the basis of whatever claim to military genius can be made for Grant. In that short time span Grant fought five battles against a scattered foe, captured the capital of Mississippi, placed his forces between the two principal opposing armies, and completed this phase of the campaign by penning Pemberton's Confederates in the fortress of Vicksburg. In the midst of all this he opened a supply line on the Mississippi north of the city, but before that Grant subsisted his army off the country, which was wholly unorthodox military behavior for that day.

Working in Grant's favor were the problems of his adversaries in divining his plan, in having to guard more than one place against possible attack, and in having a divided command. Yet it was Grant's boldness and skill, not his adversaries' problems and mistakes, which explain his brilliant success. His rapid marches (when such were needed), unexpected thrusts, and unerring decisions kept his opponents continually off balance.[13]

When McClernand's men landed at Bruinsburg on April 30, all but one division of General James B. McPherson's corps was still on the west bank, and Sherman's divisions were far to the rear. It would be necessary, therefore, to bring up the rest of the army, get all the supplies possible across the river, especially ammunition, and to start moving. So McClernand, with Logan's division of McPherson's corps, struck out for Port Gibson, an inland town on Bayou Pierre and the first stop on the way to either Vicksburg or Jackson, the capital of Mississippi. Facing them was a force of some 6000 Confederates. On May 1, McClernand, in an encounter which lasted most of the day, drove the enemy out of Port Gibson and back across the two branches of Bayou Pierre.

This victory uncovered Grand Gulf, which Union forces occupied on May 3. Grant made it a base and ordered Sherman's corps to proceed there. He also went aboard Porter's flagship to get a bath, a change of underwear, and a decent meal.[14]

After the Port Gibson engagement, Grant threw forward McClernand's and McPherson's corps an action leading Pemberton to think the Union forces would be heading straight for Vicksburg; but the confused Confederate commander also had to worry about Jackson, which lay due east of Vicksburg and which was a valuable military possession in its own right. With Pemberton hesitating and thinking in terms of defense rather than attack, there was time to bring up Sherman's corps (except for Frank Blair's division) and to distribute rations to the troops. On May 7, McPherson's and McClernand's corps set out once again toward the north over dry country roads with McPherson keeping to the right so as to be in a position to make a dash for Jackson should that prove desirable.

From May 7 to 12 the advance was more deliberate than rapid. Grant kept the Big Black River on his left; this provided a useful screen and prevented Pemberton from easily falling on his flank. During this week of slow advance, Grant's plan was fluid and consisted primarily of cautiously moving northward so as to interpose between Vicksburg and Jackson, thus separating Pemberton from the reinforcements General Joseph E. Johnston was supposed to be assembling at the capital.

On May 12, Grant had his three corps in supporting distance of each other and in a position to move east on Jackson, north to separate Pemberton from Johnston, or west toward Vicksburg. In the early afternoon on May 12, a short distance from the town of Raymond, which lay fourteen miles west of Jackson but five miles south of the railroad to Vicksburg, McPherson ran into a brigade of Confederate infantry. It took him some time to dislodge this force, but by 5:00 P.M. the Union soldiers were entering Raymond and pursuing the defeated enemy beyond.[15]

Now it was that Grant decided to strike at Jackson before turning west toward Vicksburg. The Confederates were said to have a sizable force at the capital which could prove a danger to Grant's rear during the attack on Vicksburg. It was best to dispose of this first. Now, also, Grant cut his communications and supply lines to Grand Gulf, gave orders to McPherson to move on Jackson by way of Clinton, and to Sherman to go through Raymond directly to Jackson. McClernand would stay in supporting distance and keep an eye on Pemberton, who by now was in the vicinity of Edward's Station, about half way between Vicksburg and Jackson.

Grant's third victory came with the capture of Jackson on May 14. Crafty Joe Johnston commanded an inferior force

there, and the best he could do was to delay the advance of
McPherson and Sherman (advancing on Jackson by different
roads) for a few hours only. By the middle of the afternoon it
was all over, and the Union soldiers went cavorting into Jackson. Johnston withdrew his beaten troops to the north, still
hoping that somehow he could unite with Pemberton, even if
that meant evacuating Vicksburg. Johnston ordered Pemberton
to join him north of the railroad in the vicinity of Clinton. It
was while attempting to carry out this order that Pemberton
ran into Grant's troops marching west from Jackson.[16]

This encounter at Champion's Hill on May 16 precipitated
the campaign's most decisive engagement and victory for
Grant. It was a hard-fought contest for several hours, but the
Union numbers finally overwhelmed Pemberton's Confederates
who retreated to and beyond the Big Black River on the way
to Vicksburg. The Confederates made one more stand, at the
Big Black River, where the final battle of this phase of the
Vicksburg campaign was fought on May 17. It was a short fight,
taking place on the east side of the river. But the Confederates
were routed by a determined charge and the road was now
open all the way to Vicksburg.

Two days later, on May 19, not only did Grant invest the city
but he made contact with the fleet and opened up a new supply line along the Yazoo River, above Vicksburg. Standing on
the bluffs above the river, Sherman now confessed that up until
that moment he had had no confidence in Grant's campaign,
but that now, regardless of the result of the siege of Vicksburg,
the campaign was a success.[17]

Grant tried twice, on May 19 and 22, to storm Vicksburg's
defenses. Each time his men were thrown back with heavy loss.
Grant was, however, in a safe and strong position. An abundance of supplies now poured in for his army, and heavy reinforcements reached him from Missouri, Kentucky, and other
points. There was still some concern about Johnston off to the
east, but Grant organized a force under Sherman's command to
fend off any attack from that direction. On May 24, when the
Union troops had settled down to siege operations, Grant told
Halleck, "The enemy are now undoubtedly in our grasp. The
fall of Vicksburg and the capture of most of the garrison can
only be a question of time."

The business of a siege in the middle of a hot Mississippi
summer was tedious and unpleasant. There never was an abundance of drinking water and Confederate sharpshooters were a

continuing menace. Grant conducted an old-fashioned operation of digging trenches, parallels, and the like, pressing into
service for engineering duty every West Pointer in the army.
Inexorably the lines pressed closer, and the only hope the
down-cast Confederates in Vicksburg had was that Johnston
would somehow raise the siege. It was a vain hope. Johnston
had neither the men nor the inclination, despite repeated urgings from Richmond, to do anything.[18]

It was the possibility of Johnston's trying some desperate
measure to relieve Pemberton that caused Grant to journey up
the Yazoo, early in June, to see that all was well in that sector
where some Confederate activity had been reported. This
would seem to be a routine move on Grant's part and would call
for no comment, except that the story was later related by a
newspaper correspondent, Sylvanus Cadwallader, that Grant
got horribly drunk on this expedition, and that only through the
correspondent's strenuous exertions was Grant saved from disgrace and possible capture by the Confederates. While Bruce
Catton is inclined to dismiss the story as fiction, it is entirely
possible that something of the kind did occur, making allow-
ance for the probability of a good deal of embellishment and
exaggeration by Cadwallader. Grant did drink during the war;
Rawlins is the best authority for that assertion. It was spasmodic
and on rare occasion intense. While most commentators were
discreet, reports of an occasional escapade appear now and
then, stories leaving the dispassionate observer uncertain, but
inclined to the conclusion that Grant was anything but a total
abstainer during the course of the war.[19]

Shortly after Grant's excursion up the Yazoo, he had it out
once and for all with McClernand, who issued an unauthorized
and provocative congratulatory order to his corps after the assault of May 22. When Sherman and McPherson saw copies in
a Memphis newspaper, they complained bitterly to Grant. This
was what Grant had been waiting for—a breach of orders
forbidding publication of such congratulatory proclamations
without first clearing them with department headquarters.
Grant immediately relieved McClernand and ordered him to
Illinois, and gave Edward O. C. Ord the command of the Thirteenth Corps.

As June turned to July, Pemberton concluded that it would be
fruitless to hold out longer. While his supplies were not totally
exhausted, they soon would be, and, besides, his men were
showing signs of defeatism and inability to stand the strain. On

the morning of July 3 (the last day of the battle of Gettysburg), General John S. Bowen, one of Pemberton's principal lieutenants, initiated the surrender negotiations which culminated the next day in the surrender and paroling of some 30,000 Confederate officers and men. Paroling the surrendered men relieved Grant of having to ship them north to prison camps and was probably the most practical solution, though Halleck found fault with the move.[20]

The capture of Vicksburg must be counted as one of the major turning points of the war. It cleared the entire length of the Mississippi River, thus severing the Confederacy, and opened up prospects for new military campaigns. The victory at Gettysburg, on July 3, 1863, together with the capture of Vicksburg materially aided Union diplomatic efforts abroad, severely damaged enemy morale, and at the same time revived sagging spirits in the North.

Not long after the surrender, Grant sent his adjutant, Colonel Rawlins, off to Washington with reports of the campaign and lists of prisoners. The reason for this might well have been Grant's concern about possible political repercussions following McClernand's dismissal. Rawlins did discuss the McClernand affair with Lincoln and his cabinet and successfully conveyed to them Grant's views. Grant need not have worried; Lincoln ignored McClernand's pleas for an investigation and little was heard from him for the remainder of the war.[21]

Julia came to Vicksburg to see not only Ulysses but her oldest son, Fred, who had been with the army from the beginning of the campaign. Now the whole family was together, occupying the house formerly used by Pemberton. Julia started calling her husband "Victor." The implications of that simple word are enormous, revealing as they do so much of the trials and heartaches of the troubled past. Grant had by the capture of Vicksburg assured for all time his reputation as one of the world's great military leaders.

CHAPTER IV

Chattanooga and the Supreme Command

THE CIVIL WAR OPENED UP PROMISING OPPORTUNITIES FOR many an American; yet few could point to as dramatic a reversal in the direction of a life's career as could Ulysses S. Grant. One concrete result of the capture of Vicksburg was a commission as major general in the regular army. The rank of major general in the United States Army was the highest that an officer could aspire to at that time and was reserved for the select few. Grant's future was assured.

Lincoln sent a letter of congratulations,[1] but should not something more have been done for this general who had accomplished so much for the Union? Grant had proved himself in every conceivable way, but after Vicksburg there was no change in the command structure of the Union armies. Yet the war was far from over and would not be until aggressive commanders relentlessly applied pressure to the faltering Confederacy. The situation that prevailed that summer, however, did not reflect a sense of urgency on the part of those in charge. That the Washington authorities had no immediate plans for Grant becomes obvious when one looks at what happened to Grant's army after Vicksburg. Weeks passed and there was little or no discussion of future plans, except that General Nathaniel Banks, commanding in Louisiana, and Grant both suggested to Halleck a move against Mobile. Lincoln replied that this would have to give way to an expedition into Texas. The French had just recently occupied Mexico City and Lincoln and Secretary of State William H. Seward, were intent upon re-establishing some sort of Federal control over Texas.[2]

At the very end of August, Grant went to confer with Banks in Louisiana. While there his horse became frightened by a locomotive, careened into a carriage, and threw Grant who was pinned under the horse. He sustained a serious and painful injury to his leg which laid him up for about two weeks and made walking difficult for even a much longer period. While the evidence is not conclusive, it does appear that Grant, in New Orleans, had another bout with liquor which was fortunately covered up by the accident.[3]

Back in Vicksburg by the middle of September, and still suffering considerable pain, Grant received orders from Halleck to send some of his force to aid Rosecrans, who just then was operating in the vicinity of Chattanooga. Rosecrans, facing Bragg in south-central Tennessee during much of the summer, had finally maneuvered his opponent out of Chattanooga, which the Army of the Cumberland occupied on September 9. Rosecrans then proceeded to follow Bragg into northern Georgia, only to have Bragg, reinforced by two divisions of Longstreet's corps from Lee's army, turn on him at Chickamauga Creek. The battle of Chickamauga, fought on September 19 and 20, ended in the disastrous rout of Rosecrans' army which was saved from virtual destruction only by the stubborn defense of General George H. Thomas who commanded the Union left. Rosecrans retreated to Chattanooga which Bragg promptly invested. Here was a serious crisis which called for drastic action. Two corps, commanded by Joseph Hooker, from Meade's Army of the Potomac were sent by rail to assist in the relief of Chattanooga, and Grant was called to take charge of the rescue operation. He was placed in command of all Federal forces in the West, except those under the command of Banks, and was ordered to Louisville.

Stanton, meeting Grant in Louisville, informed him he was now to command the Military Division of the Mississippi and offered him the option of keeping Rosecrans in command of the Army of the Cumberland or replacing him with George Thomas. Grant without hesitation chose Thomas, who was told to hold on at Chattanooga until help arrived, and in a short time Grant had the situation well under control.[4]

The supply problem demanded immediate attention. The Union army in the beleaguered town had connection with its supply bases by means of a tortuous wagon road some sixty miles long. The railroad and the Tennessee River, both regular supply arteries, were under the control of the Confederate guns on and near Lookout Mountain, a commanding height of unbelievable grandeur on the south side of the river. Bragg stood a good chance of regaining Chattanooga and destroying the Federal army simply by waiting for the opposing forces to starve. Putting to use a plan already worked out before he took command, Grant in a matter of a few days reopened the supply route and saved the army. The railroad between Decatur, Alabama and Nashville was quickly repaired and made an auxiliary to the one connecting Nashville and Stevenson, Alabama. Grant also ordered Sherman forward with the rest of the Army of the Tennessee.

Even though the immediate danger had passed, there was still need for urgent action because not far off, at Knoxville, General Ambrose Burnside was in trouble and calling for help. He, too, had a supply problem, and, in addition, was partially besieged by a force of Confederates, from Bragg's army, under General James Longstreet. Grant refused to allow himself to be diverted from the principal task and concentrated on preparations for driving Bragg from around Chattanooga.[5]

Once he had all his forces assembled Grant could proceed with his plan for attacking Bragg. The plan was to have Sherman attempt to turn the right of Bragg's position along Missionary Ridge just east of Chattanooga. Hooker would operate against the Confederate left on Lookout Mountain and attempt to reach the enemy rear by forcing a passage through Rossville Gap near the southern end of Bragg's position on Missionary Ridge. Thomas, occupying the Union center, would attack when the two flanking operations had been well developed.[6]

The battle was fought, thus, in three separate sectors, with Joseph Hooker starting off on November 24 by driving the Confederates from Lookout Mountain in what has fancifully been called the Battle above the Clouds. On the same day Sherman crossed the Tennessee River north and east of Chattanooga and made some progress in reaching the Confederate right. He continued his efforts on the twenty-fifth, but he never did accomplish what he was supposed to do mainly because of the unexpectedly difficult terrain and stiff Confederate resistance. Hooker, on the twenty-fifth, succeeded in crossing Chattanooga Creek after a four hour delay, and was able to threaten Bragg's left. Grant had hoped for more positive results on the flanks, but the morning had passed, the afternoon was waning, and he could not afford to wait any longer. He would have to attack with his center if he were to gain a victory that day. So he gave Thomas the order to advance against the rifle pits at the base of Missionary Ridge. He expected them to reform after this initial task had been accomplished before attempting to carry out his order to assault the main Confederate position on the summit of the ridge. Thomas' four divisions, numbering 20,000 men, easily overran the first Confederate line at the base of the ridge, and then, as ordered by their officers, kept on going up the slope. The attack against a seemingly impregnable position so befuddled the unbelieving Confederates that they hastily retreated, leaving the crest of the ridge in the possession of the Federals.[7]

While victory at Chattanooga owed much to the soldiers, a major share of the credit rightfully belongs to Grant who had withheld the frontal assault until the right moment. Even if this had not succeeded, Hooker's threat to the Confederate left would have forced Bragg to retreat anyway. As it was, Grant won a stunning victory, redeemed Chickamauga, secured Chattanooga, freed southeastern Tennessee of Confederate control, and opened the way for next season's invasion of Georgia.

The principal reason why Grant did not press the pursuit more persistently then he did was the need to rescue Burnside whose plight, so far as Grant knew, was desperate. Grant wasted no time and sent Sherman off to extricate Burnside from his predicament. At the approach of Sherman's force, Longstreet withdrew from Knoxville.

Lincoln was naturally pleased by Grant's success, and complimented him on his "skill, courage, and perseverance." Lincoln still had no plan of making Grant head of all the Union armies which reveals an inexplicable inconsistency in the President's reactions. He wanted more than just victories of the Gettysburg variety. He wanted aggressive action. Both he had had in greater abundance from Grant than from any other of the army commanders, and Grant had succeeded in fulfilling Lincoln's great ambition of freeing east Tennessee of Confederate troops. But when Grant did finally receive promotion to the command of all the Union armies it was at the direction of Congress and not the President.[8]

Congress passed a bill late in February which revived the rank of lieutenant general held previously only by Washington and Winfield Scott. Washburne was more responsible than any other individual for the bill, but the demand was widespread among Republican Congressmen. Why Lincoln failed to take the initiative cannot be easily determined. One explanation is that he suspected that Grant had political ambitions and would be a rival for the nomination in 1864. It is true that Grant had been approached by a representative of a group of War Democrats from Ohio in December but he had emphatically turned them down. While Lincoln conceivably might have hesitated making the appointment because of worry over Grant as a political rival, this does not ring true, for Lincoln in every other situation was willing to do what was necessary for victory, regardless of what might be the consequences for him personally.[9]

Lincoln may have hesitated in making the obvious appointment because he questioned Grant's ability as a strategist. In late November, Grant had proposed a dual thrust from Chattanooga toward Atlanta and another from the lower Mississippi against Mobile. The Mobile operation was one which Grant had had in mind ever since Vicksburg but Lincoln would not buy it, first because of his concern over Texas, and now because he feared that the force at Chattanooga would be weakened to provide manpower for the Mobile campaign and this would afford the Confederates the opportunity once again to take over east Tennessee.[10] More to the point was his objection to a plan which Grant, at Halleck's request, submitted in January 1864. This called for an army of 60,000 men to land on the coast of North Carolina to break Richmond's rail links to the south. This scheme ran the risk of seeing the Army of the Potomac's numbers depleted, a loss which would pose a threat to the safety of Washington, and it contemplated a move against Richmond rather than against Lee's army. On both counts Lincoln disapproved.[11]

Whatever the reason, Lincoln did not take it on himself to push Grant's promotion. As things turned out, he had only to let matters take their course, and well before it was time for the spring campaigns to begin, Congress had forced his hand. Until he received official notification, however, Grant could only act as if he were to retain his command in the West. On March 3, 1864, Grant was ordered to Washington to receive his commission as lieutenant general, the Senate having confirmed Lincoln's nomination on the second.[12]

Grant arrived in Washington on March 8 and that evening attended a reception, already in progress, at the White House. There he met Lincoln for the first time. The meeting was, as one would expect, simple and with a minimum of conversation. Grant did not excel in this kind of situation. The next day, Lincoln presented him with his new commission, Grant reading a reply of a few sentences containing platitudinous statements about "the noble armies," and "that Providence which leads both nations and men."[13]

Grant soon returned west to confer with Sherman who would now replace Grant in that theatre. Grant realized that he must be near Washington although he did not want to establish headquarters there. So he finally did what had to be done. He would not emulate Halleck and become a desk general. Rather he would take to the field and make his headquarters with the principal Federal force, the Army of the Potomac.[14] It was now March and soon the spring winds and the warm air would dry the Virginia mud and a new campaign would begin. There was little time left to make the necessary plans, but Lincoln and Grant had good reason to hope that this time the Confederacy would collapse beneath the relentless blows of the Union armies and that winter would see the country reunited.

CHAPTER V

The Last Battles

GRANT WAS NOW THE SHAPER OF GRAND STRATEGY. BETTER than any military man thus far in the war, he had a conception of what was needed for victory. For Grant, there was simply the need to apply relentless pressure on the Confederate armies, to keep pounding away until the Confederacy and the people of the South had had enough. Included in these plans was the intention of occupying enemy territory and capturing key positions such as Richmond and Atlanta. Coordination of effort, then, would be the key to success, that plus the application of superior Northern economic and manpower resources against the armies and military installations of the South.[1]

None of this would work, however, unless the Northern people could sustain the war effort through the coming months when the price of human lives was sure to be high. And there was an abundance of war weariness in the North after three years of seemingly inconclusive fighting. To add to the difficulties, 1864 was an election year and the administration, to gain re-election, could not afford military defeat or even lack of positive success. Thus an even heavier burden than normally would have been the case was placed on Grant's shoulders. But this was exactly the kind of responsibility and burden Grant, more than anyone else, was capable of assuming. Seeing what had to be done, he had the singleness of purpose and fortitude to pursue a goal until it was attained. In the spring and summer of 1864 his staying powers were to be tried to the limit.

Once he had determined on making his headquarters with the Army of the Potomac, Grant had to decide what to do about General George G. Meade. He did not want command of that army himself, yet he needed to have close supervision over its movements. Fortunately Meade was willing to assume the awkward role of an army commander who frequently did little more than transmit the orders of the lieutenant general. The arrangement was useful to Grant but to some extent humiliating for Meade.

As general-in-chief Grant had to arrange, with Lincoln, for the direction of the other Union armies. Grant had no hesitation about leaving Sherman in charge of the Military Division of the Mississippi, while McPherson would move up to head the Army of the Tennessee. This arrangement could hardly have been improved upon. The same cannot be said of the other principal armies and departments. Ben Butler, commanding the Army of the James, was sufficiently important politically for Grant to leave him where he was. This was also true of Franz Sigel in the Shenandoah Valley, and Nathaniel Banks in Louisiana. Had he insisted on tried professionals the military success which might well have resulted could have easily compensated for whatever political setback Lincoln might have suffered by dismissal of these three inept men.[2]

On April 4, 1864 Grant wrote Sherman a lengthy letter outlining his plan of campaign. The Army of the Potomac was to "operate directly against Lee's army wherever it may be found," and Sherman, with the combined armies of the Tennessee, Cumberland, and Ohio, would "move against Johnston's army [The Army of Tennessee], to break it up and to get into the interior of the enemy's country as far as you [Sherman] can, inflicting all the damage you can against their war resources." Butler would operate against Richmond along the line of the James River; Sigel's task was to move in two columns up the Shenandoah Valley and through western Virginia to strike at the Virginia and Tennessee Railroad; while Banks, if he could finish up his campaign in northwestern Louisiana, was to fulfill Grant's long-standing ambition of capturing Mobile.[3]

Grant directed that there should be an advance of all the armies beginning on May 4. In conformity to this order, the Army of the Potomac began to move across the Rapidan in the early hours of that day. It was spring in Virginia, the air was mellow, the dogwood and other spring flowers were in bloom. For the first day there was no opposition, not because Lee was caught unprepared, but rather because he saw a chance to deliver a knockout blow against the Union army. Thus, the battle of the Wilderness began on May 5, with Lee taking the initiative and striking Gouverneur K. Warren's Fifth Corps as it moved through that tangled mass of woods and underbrush known as the Wilderness. Grant allowed the battle to be fought in this hampering, congested region, even though he originally had planned to get through to the more open country beyond.

The two-day battle on May 5 and 6 defies accurate description. No two persons saw it the same way. This was a battle fought in bits and pieces. Grant did not really control it, and even Meade and his corps commanders could only have a vague idea of what the individual units were doing. It was a soldier's battle and a gruesome one.[4]

On the morning of May 7, when the fighting had subsided, Grant ordered Meade to prepare for a night march to Spotsylvania Court House. In other words, Grant would not renew the fight in the Wilderness (having failed to crush Lee's army there), but far more important, he would not withdraw to the north side of the Rapidan. While it might seem the natural decision, it was so different from what had happened previously that Grant's resolute course of action stands out as something unique. So the armies moved on to a little country cross-roads village, Spotsylvania Court House, and continued the fight in more open country. It was warm and dry and the men had been through the most brutal kind of fighting in the Wilderness, but even worse was to come. Lee's army came astride Grant's road, and by the time Warren had brought up his Fifth Corps, it was too late to achieve Grant's purpose of interposing his army between Richmond and the Army of Northern Virginia. Still, here was another chance to engage Lee and Grant did not flinch.

On May 9 and 10 heavy fighting went on with the Union forces gaining some slight advantage. On the twelfth Winfield Hancock's Second Corps launched a determined attack against a Confederate salient which came to be known as the Bloody Angle. The initial assault made under cover of woods and fog brought sensational, but very brief, success. Lee plugged up the gap which Hancock's men had opened in the Confederate line; then ensued some of the most bitter hand-to-hand fighting of the entire war. The terrible carnage, however, brought no decisive results.[5]

The day before Hancock's major attack on the Bloody Angle, Grant in reporting to Halleck, made the now famous remark, "I ... propose to fight it out on this line if it takes all summer." It might not have been necessary to fight all summer (and into the next year) had Butler and Sigel done what was expected of them, but Butler, by May 16, was effectively bottled up on a neck of land on the James River, Bermuda Hundred. He had abandoned a promising offensive operation which, had it been pressed aggressively, almost certainly would have resulted in the capture of Petersburg, rail key to Richmond, and could have materially aided Grant's operations north of the Confederate capital. And Sigel suffered humiliating defeat in the battle of Newmarket in the Shenandoah Valley on May 15.[6]

Unable to dislodge Lee from his entrenched position around Spotsylvania Court House, Grant continued his flanking maneuver and sent Hancock's Second Corps on a wide sweep to the south and east. The other corps, of course, followed closely on the heels of Hancock's men who would be used as bait to force Lee out into the open. Unfortunately for Grant, Lee refused to seize the bait and instead of going after Hancock, he rushed Ewell's Corps toward Hanover Junction. By doing this, Lee positioned himself between Grant and Richmond. That was not the only bad news for Grant, however. He found that helping to block the way were reinforcements, amounting to perhaps 9000 men, who had been sent to Lee from Petersburg and also from the Valley. Here was a disheartening reminder of the failure of Butler and Sigel to carry out their parts of the plan.

On May 23, Hancock moved across the North Anna near the Richmond and Fredericksburg Railroad crossing, and Warren made a lodgment on the bank a few miles upstream; but neither could advance far because of the strong position Lee had assumed, so strong, in fact, that Grant decided not to try to force his way through. So his forces continued their move south by the left flank. Phil Sheridan's cavalry led the way to Hanover Town on the Pamunkey. The Federal troops crossed the river and were on the roads to Richmond early on the afternoon of May 28, but the ubiquitous Confederates again were on the scene to block the way. W. F. Smith's Eighteenth Corps from Butler's army now joined the Army of the Potomac. With these reinforcements on hand, Grant now determined to try once more to break through Lee's defenses and reach a showdown.[7]

There is no need to dwell on the catastrophe that ensued on that third of June at Cold Harbor. Had Grant been successful in delivering a frontal assault, his critics would never have been able to find fault with his decision to attack; failure, however, brought severe censure. Actually, the losses at Cold Harbor were not as excessive as at Spotsylvania, for instance, but coming as they did after the terrific casualties of the previous month, the sacrifice of lives seemed all the greater. In his memoirs, Grant confessed that "at Cold Harbor no advantage whatever was gained to compensate for the heavy loss we sustained."

Stoically, Grant went on about his business while the opposition press began to criticize him for his inability to defeat Lee. Without meaning to do so, Grant was creating serious political problems for Lincoln in this critical election year. Lee's army was still intact, Grant had not taken Richmond (neither had Sherman captured Atlanta, nor had he defeated Johnston), and Grant, the one-time hero, was now labelled "butcher."[8]

As soon as the failure at Cold Harbor had become apparent, Grant turned his attention to the next move in the plan which he had worked out before the start of the campaign. This was to cross to the south side of the James River and unite with Butler. At the same time, he would destroy Lee's principal supply line to the west, the Virginia Central Railroad.[9] The Army of the Potomac began to pull away from its entrenchments at Cold Harbor on the night of June 12. With Wade Hampton's cavalry off to contend with Sheridan, who was raiding northwest of Richmond against the railroad, Lee was in trouble trying to find out what Grant's next move would be. Federal troops had arrived at the Petersburg entrenchments before Lee knew for certain that Grant's army had crossed the James and was not going to attack Richmond directly. But Grant's plan to seize Petersburg was badly bungled.

The man who seems most to blame for the failure to capture Petersburg is General William F. "Baldy" Smith, commander of the Eighteenth Corps. The Eighteenth Corps arrived at Butler's position at Bermuda Hundred, on the James, on June 14. Smith had several fine chances to seize the practically undefended city of Petersburg, but he threw them away. Not reaching the fortifications guarding the city until late on the afternoon of June 14, he had some initial success but soon called off the attack. Hancock's Second Corps had by this time arrived; yet it merely occupied some of the evacuated Confederate entrenchments. Even on the sixteenth, with most of the Army of the Potomac up, the odds were still heavily in favor of the Yankees, but the attacks came too late. When renewed attempts late on the seventeenth had some success, Beauregard, Confederate commander at Petersburg, simply withdrew to a new line closer in to the city. And on the eighteenth Lee's whole army was in the trenches, where it easily beat off the attacks that Meade launched.[10]

Failure on June 18 led Grant to the decision to rest the army for a time before attempting to move to the west to gain control of both the Weldon and Southside Railroads. The next months showed that his strategy was to hold Lee in Petersburg. Making a move to the left from time to time, Grant planned to do everything possible to prevent Lee from sending reinforcements to the Confederate army in Georgia. With Lee thus held, the work of reducing the rest of the Confederacy could go forward.[11]

For perfect success, Grant needed the utmost in cooperation from his subordinate commanders. Smith and Butler had let him down, and at about the same time, Sheridan and David Hunter, Sigel's replacement, failed to carry out Grant's intentions. These two commanders had been ordered to move against rail and canal communications linking Richmond with the west, but Hunter turned back after approaching his objective, Lynchburg, and Sheridan, hearing of Hunter's decision and having been checked in a cavalry engagement at Trevilian Station on the Virginia Central Railroad, decided to return to Grant before having completed his assignment. To make matters worse, Hunter, instead of withdrawing down the Valley toward Winchester, thought it more prudent to move westward to the Kanawha Valley and thence to the Ohio River. This left the Shenandoah Valley virtually unprotected against a Confederate advance northward. It so happened that one of the reasons Hunter did not dare risk a battle was his discovery that the Confederate force opposing him had been reinforced by the Second Corps of Lee's army, commanded by Jubal Early.[12]

Lee saw the chance for a diversionary strike against the North and willingly sanctioned a raid on Washington by the testy, hard-swearing Early. For a time, his strategy worked. Not only did Grant have to detach troops from his army around Petersburg (the Sixth Corps), and divert reinforcements on the way from Louisiana, but he, himself, was obliged to leave Petersburg to see to the defense of the capital and the conduct of operations against Early. Thus, while the Confederates did not capture Washington, the summer's campaign against Lee was decidedly upset and delayed.[13] Eventually, at Lincoln's prodding, Grant appointed Sheridan to command in the Valley and in September and October the aggressive cavalryman won three smashing victories over Early. The lieutenant general's plan to render the Valley useless as a granary for Lee's army was at last fulfilled.

As these dramatic events were taking place around Washington and in the Valley, Grant proceeded to press the siege of Petersburg, convinced that relentless application of pressure would cause Confederate resistance to crack. To make progress against Lee, however, was far from easy and on several occasions, Grant found that there was still plenty of fight in the Army of Northern Virginia.

The attrition that sapped the strength of Lee's army had taken its toll of the Army of the Potomac as well. Many of the field officers had been killed or wounded since May 4, and the quality of the troops deteriorated as green conscripts and bounty men replaced the veteran volunteers, casualties in the hard fighting of the previous months.[14] Not only had the quality deteriorated but the number of troops in the Army of the Potomac declined appreciably during the spring and summer of 1864. Some reinforcements did arrive, but nowhere near enough to make up for the losses. It has been often asserted that while Lee's army could not make good its losses, Grant was receiving a steady flow of reinforcements and thus could afford to adopt the attrition tactics he allegedly used in his Virginia campaign of 1864. Since just the opposite happened, that is, Lee did obtain sizable reinforcements and Grant lost more men than he gained, a reassessment of Grant's performance in the campaign is in order. Rather than fighting a war of attrition, Grant employed tactics which, while costly, had other goals in view than simply the killing off of the enemy army.

One source of reinforcements Grant refused to tap was the Southern prison camps. For the first two years of the war a regular exchange occurred, but, by the summer of 1864, this had broken down, largely because of the complication created by the fact of Negro soldiers serving in the Union army. Confederate authorities refused to treat these, when captured, as prisoners of war; rather they were seen as escaped slaves. Stanton would not allow any regular exchange as long as the other side adhered to this policy and he had the strong backing of General Grant. Besides, both Stanton and Grant saw the exchange system as merely a means by which the South's armies could be replenished. Hard as this was on Northern prisoners confined to such hell-holes as Andersonville, it was, they believed, one way of shortening the war.[15] But their stand was unpopular with many in the North who, with reason, believed it was costly in human lives and not worth the price.

Grant's problems with subordinates continued to plague him during that long, hot, and discouraging summer. Something had to be done about Baldy Smith and Butler. They could not work together, and aside from the obvious fact that Butler was not capable of handling an army in the field, despite his recognized

administrative abilities, Grant was now coming to the conclusion that Smith was deficient in leadership qualities. When
Grant at first moved to strip Butler of active command of the
Army of the James Butler fought back vigorously, so much so
that Grant quickly abandoned that scheme and dismissed Smith
instead. It was evident that Butler's political influence was too
great for him to be shoved aside in an election year. But Smith
later charged that Butler threatened to expose Grant's drinking
unless he was retained in command, and that therefore, he,
Smith, had to be sacrificed. This is not a very likely story, since
Grant could easily grasp the importance of Butler as a political
asset to the administration, and, after the election, did dismiss
him.[16]

Another thorn-in-the-side for Grant was Ambrose Burnside,
commander of the Ninth Corps, who was the general most responsible for the mismanagement of the Petersburg mine. At
one point in the extensive works surrounding Petersburg the
opposing trenches were less than two hundred yards apart and
the commanding officer of a regiment of Pennsylvania volunteer infantry, made up mostly of miners, had the idea of digging
a shaft under the enemy position, exploding gun powder, and
following that up with a charge through the gap thus created.
This regiment was in the Ninth Corps, and when Burnside
heard of the scheme he took to it immediately. Meade, however, was anything but enthusiastic, and Grant had no confidence at all in the project. Still, he allowed it to proceed and
did what he could to assure its success. But once again subordinates failed to live up to their trust. The explosion went off all
right, on the morning of July 30, but the follow-up was poorly
handled, and the result was, in Grant's words, "a stupendous
failure." Burnside was largely responsible for the inept handling of the assault which, with proper leadership had a good
chance of succeeding. But Grant cannot escape ultimate responsibility for what happened. A short time later, he relieved
Burnside from command of the Ninth Corps, replacing him
with John A. Parke.[17]

Since Grant had charge of the operations of all the Union
armies his attention was frequently directed to what his subordinates were doing. Thus the events around Richmond and
Petersburg were a part of a much larger whole and Grant never
ceased to concern himself with these other far-flung operations.
Mention has already been made of events in the Shenandoah
Valley which had a direct impact on what went on at Peters-

burg. But especially, Grant watched Sherman's progress from the northwest corner of Georgia towards Atlanta. Always did he worry lest troops from Lee's army be detached to aid Joseph E. Johnston's Confederate forces, and often his moves against Lee were made to prevent this. He rejoiced with the country in Sherman's capture of Atlanta, on September 2, 1864, but would not rest content with that. Rather, his active mind immediately began thinking of the next move. He held out a suggestion for a campaign against Savannah and Augusta, but, characteristically, asked Sherman's opinion in the matter. In the end he let Sherman do what he wanted, which was to leave Thomas in Tennessee with a sufficient force to guard against an invasion of that state, and to take his army on a march of destruction through Georgia.[18]

General E. R. S. Canby also figured in Grant's thinking. Canby, who had replaced Banks early in May, Grant believed, should direct his attention to Mobile and from there cooperate in a combined move with Sherman against Savannah and Augusta. But interest in Mobile as an object of attack lessened following Admiral David G. Farragut's successful entry into Mobile Bay on August 5, which rendered the port useless to blockade runners.

Sherman's march began on November 15. He made contact with the fleet on December 13, and Savannah fell on December 21. Thomas' crushing victory over John B. Hood (Johnston's replacement) on December 15 and 16 at Nashville finally vindicated Grant's faith in the ponderous but dependable Virginian. Grant put in some really bad days in December waiting for Thomas to launch his attack against Hood who had brought his army up from Georgia to besiege Nashville. It even came to the point where Grant actually sent General John A. Logan out to Nashville to relieve Thomas. And finally Grant himself set out for the west, but he had traveled no further than Washington (and Logan had only reached Louisville) when word of Thomas' great victory arrived.[19]

At the time these events occurred, the Army of the Potomac was relatively inactive. Grant had gone into winter quarters at City Point, his headquarters ever since the start of the Petersburg campaign. The camp site was on a bluff overlooking the James River, giving it easy access by water to Washington and points north. Grant lived simply in a tent large enough merely to provide an outer office and an inner room for sleeping. When winter approached he moved into a rude cabin. During the summer evenings, Grant liked to sit outside and converse with members of his staff or with what visitors happened to be around. Grant in such company was not his usual reserved self but could become quite talkative. Visitors to headquarters came and went almost uninterruptedly. Lincoln came down from Washington on several occasions, so did Stanton and other cabinet officers and Congressmen.

Mrs. Grant and the four children who had been staying in St. Louis came east that summer, staying for a time at City Point, and then repaired to Burlington, New Jersey, where the children were placed in school for the fall term. Mrs. Grant returned for a more lengthy stay after Grant had gone into winter quarters. Occasionally Grant left the Petersburg region for a quick visit to Washington, or to Sheridan in the Valley, and once he went as far as Philadelphia and New York.[20]

Abandoning a proposal to have Sherman's men shipped to Virginia by water, Grant gave his approval to Sherman's suggestion of a winter campaign through South and North Carolina, a part of the Confederacy which had scarcely been touched by the war. Grant also concerned himself with the reduction of Fort Fisher, guarding the entrance to Cape Fear River and the city of Wilmington, North Carolina, the last major port open to blockade runners. Butler had made an abortive attempt to capture the fort late in December doing his usual inept job. Now it was that Grant moved swiftly to have Butler removed. The election was over, and Butler was no longer necessary to the administration. Lincoln quickly responded to Grant's broad hint that he wanted to be rid of Butler. Grant wasted no time in appointing General Alfred H. Terry to replace him. Terry, with the close cooperation of Admiral David D. Porter, moved decisively against Fort Fisher reducing it with relative ease on January 15, 1865.[21]

Grant's strategy that winter was to hold Lee fast to his Richmond-Petersburg defenses, knowing that active operations in the winter months were impractical, and to permit his subordinates farther south to take the initiative. Sherman began to move his forces out of Savannah late in January and had set his two columns in motion toward Columbia, South Carolina by the early part of February. Knowing that Sherman would probably encounter increasingly stiff opposition as he moved northward, Grant ordered John M. Schofield's Twenty-third Corps to come east from Thomas' army to land on the North Carolina coast and move inland to seize the key rail junction of Goldsboro, North Carolina, in time to link up with Sherman.

He also ordered Thomas to set General George Stoneman in motion from eastern Tennessee into South Carolina, and to launch an offensive under his own direction from Tennessee toward Selma, Alabama. He directed Canby, in southern Louisiana, to move against Mobile and then to turn north toward Montgomery and Selma. Finally, on February 8, Grant ordered Sheridan, who had wintered in the vicinity of Winchester in the lower Valley, to strike at the Virginia Central Railroad and the James River canal. As in 1864, Grant wanted all forces to move simultaneously to keep the Confederates as tied up as possible in all theatres.[22]

As usual, not all of Grant's plans worked out as he had anticipated. By the time Stoneman set out, Sherman had marched out of South Carolina. Stoneman's orders were changed so as to have him threaten Lynchburg and to invade western North Carolina. Canby made Grant impatient because of his inability to act promptly. Eventually he did capture Mobile, but not until April 12, 1865. General James H. Wilson, in command of Thomas' cavalry, led the raid into Alabama from the north, capturing Selma on April 2. Yet, as Grant pointed out later, these expeditions were not of much use to him or to Sherman.

Sheridan, Schofield, and Sherman, however, did their work promptly and efficiently. Sheridan, as soon as the roads permitted, advanced up the Valley and easily routed Early at Waynesboro on March 2, 1865. He then proceeded to destroy enough of the canal so that it was no longer of any use to Lee. He did the same with the Virginia Central Railroad west of Richmond and then rejoined Grant at Petersburg.[23]

Schofield's corps arrived in the Washington area on the last day of January and from there proceeded by ship to the North Carolina coast. They captured Wilmington on February 22, and then, in cooperation with Terry, moved inland toward Goldsboro, arriving there on March 21.

Sherman's march had been largely unopposed until he was well into North Carolina. Gathered to impede his progress was a conglomerate force of Confederates led by Joseph E. Johnston who fought a drawn battle with Sherman at Bentonville on March 19 and 21. But Johnston's force was too small to do more than annoy Sherman, who was on the point of joining with Schofield, so Johnston broke off the engagement and Sherman, needing supplies and wanting to give his men a rest, was content to let Johnston go and he continued on to Goldsboro which he reached on March 23.

Lincoln paid Grant a short visit, following his abortive conference with a group of Confederate peace commissioners at Hampton Roads, and returned later in March, at Grant's invitation, for a more extended stay. The President liked to sit around in the evening at Grant's headquarters, getting the latest military information, telling stories in his inimitable way, and thoroughly enjoying the brief respite from the burdens of his office.[24]

The day after Lincoln arrived at City Point, that is on March 25, Lee did what Grant had been expecting him to do for several weeks. He launched an attack against the Union right with the hope of forcing Grant to reinforce from his left which in turn would give the Confederate army a short time in which to make a withdrawal from Petersburg and to join forces with Johnston in North Carolina. The Confederates struck quickly and successfully at Fort Stedman. But the success was only momentary, and in a relatively short time the break had been mended.

Two days later Sherman came up by water from Goldsboro for a person-to-person discussion of immediate plans. Lincoln was there for this meeting too. Sherman said he would not be ready until April 10 at the earliest and wanted Grant to wait until then, but Grant was determined to move at the earliest possible moment hoping to deal finally with Lee's army without waiting for help from Sherman. Grant's plan, contained in his orders of March 28, was to hold his intrenchments in front of Petersburg with reduced force and to use his cavalry and two corps of infantry for a turning movement around Lee's right. It would take just twelve days from the start of the spring campaign of 1865 to bring about the surrender of the Army of Northern Virginia.[25]

Spring comes early in southern Virginia and by the end of March peach trees were in blossom, grass was green, and days were becoming mellow and warm. Not all the mud had dried yet, and spring rains could make roads impassable, especially for wagon trains and artillery. But Grant could not afford to wait as long as he had the year before.

All eagerness to be up and doing, Sheridan, to whom Grant had given the principal role in his offensive plans, set out at the appointed time, and, despite heavy rain on March 30, arrived at Dinwiddie Court House, fifteen miles southwest of Petersburg, and moved north to a strategic road junction known as Five Forks. Possession of this point would assure control over the Southside Railroad and would force the evacuation of Petersburg, and thus of Richmond too. Well aware of the importance of Five Forks, Lee detached a force of some ten thousand infantry and cavalry under George Pickett to defend the place.

Anticipating this move, Grant made provision for infantry support for Sheridan. The Second and Fifth Corps drew out of the Petersburg trenches, moved west in the direction of Five Forks, and on March 31 engaged the Confederates occupying the extreme right of Lee's line. On that same day, Pickett drove Sheridan away from Five Forks toward Dinwiddie, and while this placed the cavalry leader in something of a dangerous position, it also opened up possibilities of striking a decisive blow against Pickett's isolated force.[26] Grant now sent Warren's Fifth Corps to Sheridan. Having greater confidence in Sheridan than in Warren, he gave Sheridan complete charge of the whole operation, even the authority to relieve Warren from command, should this be necessary. Late on the afternoon of April 1, Sheridan, now joined finally by the Fifth Corps, fought the battle of Five Forks, completely smashing Pickett's force and taking upwards of 5000 prisoners. Angered by Warren's slowness in arriving, by his deliberate manner of preparing for the attack, and finally by his alleged faulty tactics and lack of inspirational leadership, Sheridan relieved Warren of command of the Fifth Corps, even though the battle had already been won.

News of the victory of Five Forks was brought to Grant that evening as he sat around a campfire with members of his staff. The imperturbable Grant simply asked, "How many prisoners have been taken?" And when he had extracted all the details from the messenger, Grant walked inside his tent to write out the next set of orders which were for Meade to make a general assault against what Grant knew must be severely weakened enemy lines. He had estimated the situation precisely. Early on the morning of April 2, Horatio Wright's Sixth Corps easily broke through the fortifications in front of Petersburg and fanned out to either side, bagging prisoners, capturing guns, and in general so jeopardizing Lee's position that evacuation of both Petersburg and Richmond became mandatory if Lee's army were not to be cut off.[27]

Anticipating Lee's abandonment of Petersburg, Grant immediately laid plans for breaking up and capturing Lee's al-

ready shattered forces. When Sheridan told him that
Confederate troops were retreating westward to Burkeville,
the junction of the Southside and Danville Railroads, he
sanctioned Sheridan's request for a move westward.

The next days saw Sheridan out on the flank with Meade
following Lee in hot pursuit. The Twenty-fourth Corps of the
Army of the James, John Gibbon commanding, kept to the line
of the Southside Railroad fairly constantly throughout the campaign, and it was this corps, along with the Fifth, that finally
stood athwart Lee's path and forced his surrender. But no
amount of strategic planning would have done much good had
the men not been pushed to the extreme.

The end was brought visibly nearer on April 6, a day of
disaster for Lee's dwindling army. On that day, at Sayler's
Creek a few miles east of Farmville, both Sheridan with his
cavalry and Wright with the Sixth Corps inflicted virtually total
defeat on the Confederate rear guard. At the close of the day's
action, Sheridan reported to Grant that, "If the thing is pressed
I think that Lee will surrender." When Lincoln got Sheridan's
dispatch from Grant, he telegraphed in reply, "Let the *thing*
be pressed."[28]

Some of what was left of Lee's army found provisions at
Farmville, but before all could be fed, units of the Army of the
Potomac interrupted their hurried repast and forced the
Confederates to vacate the town. They went west, instead of
south toward Danville as originally planned, because the road
south was blocked.

Grant established headquarters at a small brick hotel in Farmville and passed the evening of April 7 sitting on the porch, as
units of the Sixth Corps paraded past him in an impromptu
review. Here it was that he learned of Stoneman's presence at
Lynchburg. Actually, only a small part of Stoneman's force
came anywhere near the town, but Grant, unaware of this fact,
believed it was possible that Lee's retreat west would be
blocked. Additional favorable news came that evening from
Sheridan, who reported that he had a cavalry column moving
on Appomattox Station. Should Sheridan's men arrive there first
the Union cavalry would be west of the Confederate army and
in a position to bring about its surrender.

Grant learned indirectly from Confederate General Richard
Ewell, captured at Saylor's Creek, that the surrender of the
Confederate army was a distinct possibility, and, being con-
vinced himself that the end was near, sent a note through the

lines to Lee urging on him the desirability of giving up. Lee in his reply cautiously requested to know what terms Grant would offer. To this inquiry Grant wrote that he would simply require that men and officers of the Army of Northern Virginia cease taking up arms against the United States until properly exchanged. Lee believed it still possible that he might effect his escape, and, trying to stall (which was accepted military practice) inserted in his reply to Grant a mention of the restoration of peace, or in other words, a political matter which he knew Grant had no authority to act upon.[29]

By the time Grant had a chance to answer this message, the military situation had developed to the point where he could do pretty much as he pleased, so far as the Confederate army was concerned. For on the evening of April 8, General George A. Custer, commanding a division of Sheridan's cavalry, rode up to Appomattox Station and seized three of four provision trains. Much depended on whether or not the infantry could come in time. The chances were good, according to Gibbon, who reported his position to Grant that evening as five miles from Appomattox. With only three hours rest, after an all-day's march, these men once more took to the road and went the four or five additional miles to where Sheridan was astride Lee's line of retreat. The forced marches of these infantrymen brought the campaign to a close. Once Lee realized that infantry as well as cavalry blocked his way he knew that there was no choice but to surrender. It is also significant that Lee's plan of retreat for that day (April 9) involved a change of route. Because of Federal forces believed to be at or near Lynchburg, Lee ordered his army to move southwest to Campbell Court House and in the general direction of Danville. Lynchburg was a last source of supplies, so even if Lee had manged to break through Sheridan's line at Appomattox Court House, it is hard to see how the end could have been long postponed.

For a time, during these last days, Grant was with Meade's forces north of the Appomattox River, ahead of his headquarters wagons and thus dependent on others for his meals. He slept in whatever farm house happened to be handy. Probably because of the pressures on him, he developed, on April 8, one of the sick headaches to which he was occasionally prone. The next morning the headache quickly disappeared when, in the saddle and on the way to join Sheridan's column, he received word from Lee that he was prepared to surrender.[30]

In due time, Grant, with some of his staff, met Lee and one

aide in the parlor of the McLean House at Appomattox Court House, a sleepy village which was the center of a rural region untouched by the war. There on a warm April afternoon an exchange of letters resulted in the surrender of the Army of Northern Virginia. Dressed in a private's uniform, displaying shoulder straps of a lieutenant general, slightly disheveled, and hardly up to Lee in his style of dress, Grant tried hard to soften the blow for his adversary. Himself terribly sensitive about individual feelings, he could appreciate the mortification which he knew Lee must be experiencing. So he kept the negotiations as simple and informal as possible. Lee's army would be paroled, and all arms, artillery, and other equipment would be surrendered, except that Confederate officers would be allowed to retain their side arms and horses. When Lee hinted to Grant that some of the Confederate soldiers owned their own horses, Grant made it clear that when arms and other property of the Confederate army were surrendered, those enlisted men possessing horses would be allowed to take them away, "to work their little farms." A few more details were attended to including arrangements for rations to be sent to the Confederate troops, and Lee left the house to ride back to his men, while the Union soldiers, on hearing of the surrender set up shouts and cheers. Grant quickly put a stop to that for he had no desire to exult and add to the discomfiture of the defeated foe.[31]

Grant met Lee once more the following day, between the lines, and then set out for City Point. Within a few days he was in Washington to confer with the President and Secretary of War. On Friday, April 14, he talked with Lincoln at the White House and turned down the President's invitation to him and Mrs. Grant to attend the theatre that evening. He had already arranged to go to Burlington, New Jersey, where the Grant children were in school. He had only reached Philadelphia when he recieved word of Lincoln's assassination, and after depositing Mrs. Grant at Burlington, immediately returned to Washington.

Grant regretted Lincoln's death as much as anyone, for he sympathized fully with Lincoln's ideas about reconstruction, and he had come to appreciate Lincoln's qualities of greatness better than most Americans at that time. No doubt President Andrew Johnson's (and Stanton's) reaction to the terms of surrender negotiated by Sherman and Joseph E. Johnston accounted in part for the general's lack of confidence in the new

President. Sherman's terms went beyond strictly military matters and embraced political matters. He had acted in good faith
and yet had exceeded his authority. Grant, ordered to Raleigh
to straighten out the confusion, did it with a minimum of of-
fense to the sensitive Sherman. He stayed out of the way while
Sherman renewed negotiations with Johnston to arrange for the
Confederate's surrender on the same terms that Grant had
given Lee. Then, as quietly as he had arrived, Grant returned
to Washington.[32]

It was only a matter of a few weeks before the rest of the
Confederate troops laid down their arms. The final collapse of
Confederate resistance resulted from a combination of causes,
but one of the principal reasons for Confederate military defeat
was the relentless pressure that Grant, as general-in-chief, applied in all areas where the South still maintained the fight. As
soon as he obtained top command, Grant did what the situation
demanded, but which few others had had the vision to comprehend: he made effective use of the North's superior material
and human resources to reduce to immobility the South's
capacity to wage war.

As a strategist, Grant was unequalled among Civil War generals. He grasped easily the requirements of an operation starting with the capture of Forts Henry and Donelson and
proceeding through the Vicksburg, Chattanooga, Virginia, and
Appomattox campaigns. His most brilliant feat was Vicksburg,
but the pursuit and capture of Lee's army must also rank high
in strategic conception and execution.

Grant does not show up as well as a tactician. For one thing,
he did not have enough of the small command experience
which would have developed a superior tactical ability. Even
so, he reacted correctly at Fort Donelson, and, at Shiloh Grant's
persistence and willingness to assume the offensive on the second day, showed an understanding of the requirements of the
situation. Little tactical skill was demanded in the Vicksburg
campaign, and at Chattanooga the holding out of Thomas' command until near the close of the day was the decision of a
commander who had an instinct for correct timing. In the east,
Grant left the tactical decisions relating to the Army of the
Potomac to Meade.

Where Grant excelled many of his colleagues was in his un-
canny ability to assess the situation in the enemy army, and
especially to read the mind of his opponent. He seldom
overestimated the size of the opposing force and always bore in

mind that if his men were worn out from marching, lack of sleep, or extended fighting the enemy must be equally affected. Finally, he believed in the axiom that in every battle there comes a moment when, with both sides equally exhausted, victory will come to the army that exerts the final last effort. This conviction would help to explain his willingness to order frontal assaults on entrenched positions at Spotsylvania, Cold Harbor, and Petersburg.

The overall estimate must be that Grant merited the praise accorded him by the people of the North, by the Congress, and by most of his military colleagues. Especially after Vicksburg was there a deep-seated confidence in Grant, an assurance that where he was, things would go right. Grant spread confidence partly because he himself never doubted the ultimate outcome.

The Civil War came at an opportune time for Grant. Trained as a soldier, he was out of his element in civilian life, as he would be again when he resigned a second time from the regular army in 1869. With qualities that could be cultivated and nurtured only in time of war, Grant proved his greatness when tried in the fires of civil conflict. A down-and-out failure in 1861, he had emerged the nation's foremost hero with a reputation that would endure through the many trials of the post-war years especially those of his presidency. For the lovers of the Union, all who had in some way sacrificed something during the war, Grant would always be the man who first brought victory and the one man who had the secret of continuing success against the rebel forces. He was the personification of victory; he had saved the Union.

CHAPTER VI

Reconstruction under Johnson

THE FOUR YEARS BETWEEN THE END OF THE WAR AND
Grant's inauguration as President served as Grant's apprentice-
ship to his later career in national politics. Still in the army as its
top uniformed commander, Grant, because of his residence in
Washington, and his close association with the President and
Secretary of War, found himself, more or less by sheer force of
circumstance (as well as by the fact of his enormous popularity)
immersed in the bitterest factional political dispute the country
had witnessed since the days of Andrew Jackson. Neither by
temperament nor by training was Grant prepared for this type
of combat. He was swept along by the tide of events until, in
1869, he found himself President of the United States. It was
almost inevitable, no doubt, but Grant, while he saw it coming,
made no conscious effort to gain the prize, nor did he have to.
It was only a question of which party would capture him as its
own, and in April 1865 it was by no means certain that the
Republicans would emerge victorious. Four years of witness to
and participation in the most vicious political infighting conceivable must have made Grant better equipped in 1869 than he was
in 1865 for his presidential experience; yet he was still a novice
when he entered the White House. Undoubtedly this was because most politicians tried to befriend him, and, except for the
unhappy experience with President Johnson over the office of
Secretary of War, Grant could deceive himself into thinking that
he was above politics. After all he was a military man and a hero
to all the people, and he was told this often enough so that he can
be excused for some of this self-deception.

It all started out in a non-political manner during the summer
of 1865, when Grant's responsibilities were altogether military.
There were difficult problems of demobilization, but Secretary of
War Stanton was really more involved in this matter than Grant,
who even found it possible to take an extended vacation trip into
New England, Canada, and the Midwest. In city after city the
general was received with tumultuous welcome, although he re-

turned the honors with scarcely any words that might be termed a speech. For the first time in over four years, he visited his old home at Galena, where the local citizenry had erected a sign which read, "General, the sidewalk is built." During the war, Grant had insisted that the only public office he might be interested in was that of mayor of Galena just "long enough," he said, "to fix the sidewalks, especially the one reaching to my house." Along with the sidewalk, there was the gift of the house which the Grants had lived in prior to the war. The usually imperturbable man of iron nerve was reduced to tears when his fellow townsmen made the presentation. After a brief stay with his parents at Covington, Kentucky, Grant finally returned to Washington. It had been a triumphal tour and proved beyond a doubt that, of all living Americans, Ulysses S. Grant had the strongest grip on the affections of the people of the North. This conclusion was reinforced by a magnificent reception, lasting several days, in New York. There were gifts from admiring countrymen including a house in Philadelphia and another in Washington.[1] Grant accepted all these presents with thanks but without contemplating their implications.

Back in Washington, the general had to address himself to the daily routine of army business, and concern over the continued presence of French troops in Mexico. At the war's close, he had Sheridan placed in command in the southwest and indicated in his letters a strong sympathy for the Liberal government of Benito Juarez. But he was forced to yield to the more cautious policy of Secretary of State Seward, who, by regular diplomatic means, impressed upon Napoleon III the desirability of withdrawing his forces from Mexico.[2]

Closer to home was the problem of reconstruction in the South. Johnson, through the summer and fall, had instituted a simple plan of restoration which was well on the way to completion by the time Grant returned in November from his brief stay in New York. Conventions had been held, ordinances of secession repealed, Confederate state war debts repudiated, and the Thirteenth Amendment ending slavery had been ratified. No state had provided for even nominal Negro voting, but all had elected prominent ex-Confederates, and several had adopted so-called Black Codes of varying degrees of severity to establish regulations for the conduct of the freedmen. Republicans saw in the plan the return to power of the Democratic party; the old abolitionist group were concerned over the implications of the plan for the freedmen; and staunch Unionists disliked seeing rebels treated so leniently. But other Northerners who hoped for a speedy restoration of the Union and who did not particularly concern themselves over such matters as Negro voting applauded Johnson's mild, conciliatory program.

In an effort to determine more accurately the state of affairs, President Johnson commissioned several persons to visit the South and to report on their findings. One of those asked was Grant who returned after a two-week trip to only four states with a report generally satisfactory to the President. A closer examination of the report, however, reveals that Grant did not advise the immediate removal of troops. He went further to point out that both whites and blacks required the protection of the national government, and indicated his belief that the Freedmen's Bureau should be continued for "a few years." The report contained indications of some of the causes for disagreement with the President in the months to come.[3]

While Johnson moved swiftly toward a full restoration of the Southern states by the time Congress met, Grant was in no such hurry. Conservative by nature, and no extremist on the race question, he nonetheless was convinced that the Union cause in the war was just, that the national authority ought not to be questioned, and that the sacrifice of 360,000 Union soldiers ought not to be casually ignored. Anything resembling reenslavement of the freedmen, the assumption of political power by the Copperheads of the North in alliance with ex-rebels, or attack on the officers and men of the United States Army was a reflection on the cause he had fought for and an indirect slur upon him and his colleagues. Thus Grant's behavior in the four years after the close of the war was perfectly consistent; he did not start out a conservative and end up a Radical. Rather, he entered this period as a moderate in his attitude toward the South and toward the Negro. Rejecting the policies of the President when these policies appeared to be resulting in the sacrifice of the results of the war, he embraced those of the Radicals as the only feasible alternatives, or as the expressed will of the people speaking through Congress. In June 1868 Sherman wrote to Grant that "the war, no matter what its cause or conduct, was an epoch in our national history, that must be sanctified, and made to stand justified to future ages."[4] Grant could have written those words; they help to explain his behavior through all this confusing period of Reconstruction.

Grant's actions from the time Congress met in December 1865, reveal a man who was not at all ready to consider reconstruction completed. First of all, on December 25 he issued an order to his subordinates in the South to report to him on "all known outrages" of whites against blacks and vice versa. These reports indicated a considerable amount of lawlessness and unrest in the former rebel states, a conclusion which the Joint Committee on Reconstruction, created by Congress in December 1865, was arriving at independently. To provide protection for army officers from hostile law suits against them in the courts of the Southern states, Grant issued on January 3, 1866 General Order No. 3, permitting army personnel as well as certain other categories, including freedmen, to avail themselves of federal or Freedmen's Bureau courts when impartial treatment could not be had in the civil courts.[5]

Johnson was committed, however, to a different policy, and shortly after vetoed the Freedmen's Bureau and Civil Rights bills. Also on April 2, 1866, he issued a proclamation that the rebellion was over, an announcement which implied that normal government was fully restored in the South. This appeared to nullify General Order No. 3, but, with Stanton, Grant on April 9 issued secret orders to army commanders in the South giving them authority to continue to use the courts of the Freedmen's Bureau and other military tribunals.

Grant moved still further from the President by War Department Order No. 44, dated July 6, 1866, conferring upon army officers of certain rank power to enforce the Civil Rights Act, which Congress had passed over Johnson's veto, when civilian officials refused to do so. Johnson countered with a proclamation on August 20 that civilian authority prevailed everywhere in the country. Again, Grant and Stanton had seemingly been bested by the President, and Grant, admitting as much to Sheridan, stated that he construed General Orders No. 3 and No. 44 nullified by the proclamation. But on November 22, Grant wrote to Stanton that Sheridan was the only one to be told this, that his orders had never been revoked, and that the Civil Rights Act could not be enforced without General Order No. 44 or something comparable. Clearly Grant (with Stanton) and the President were pursuing different courses throughout 1866.[6] Grant was not obvious or blatant about it, but he was determined to protect the army and to carry out the will of Congress as expressed in the Civil Rights Act, the Fourteenth Amendment (passed by Congress and submitted to the states on June 16), and other legislation.

Johnson was having his troubles with the Radical Republican

element in Congress, but he continued to pretend that he and Grant were essentially in harmony.[7] It was for this reason that he was so insistent upon Grant's accompanying him and a party of other dignitaries to Chicago, ostensibly to dedicate a monument to Stephen A. Douglas, but actually to present the President's case against the Radical Republicans in connection with the forthcoming Congressional elections. The tour, soon labeled "The Swing Around the Circle," turned out to be an embarrassment to Grant who was, in a sense, being used by the President. At one point the general left the party, because, the Radical press maintained, he was disgusted with Johnson's behavior. The opposition contended, with probable accuracy, that Grant was drinking too much and was put aboard a lake steamer to sober up. The report that Grant left the party at Cleveland to rejoin it at Chicago because he had been drinking heavily is categorically denied by Benjamin C. Truman, secretary to the President. Gideon Welles, on the other hand, asserts that Grant was drinking so much by the time they reached Cleveland that he had to drop out of the party.[8]

Grant returned from the trip convinced by the behavior of the hostile crowds that Johnson did not have popular support. Riots involving the death of many Negroes in Memphis and New Orleans, the Southern states' rejection of the Fourteenth Amendment (except Tennessee), in part because of Johnson's advice, and a dispute with the President over whether or not to send troops to Baltimore (in behalf of the Copperhead element) in October at the time of the state elections in Maryland all contributed to a growing conviction on Grant's part that Southerners could not yet be entrusted with control over their internal affairs, and that President Johnson was too willing to befriend former rebels.

Johnson, aware of Grant's unwillingness to give him full support, now sought a way to ease Grant out of the picture by attempting to bring in Sherman whose views on Reconstruction were in line with his own. The scheme proposed by Seward was to send Grant on a trumped-up mission to Mexico in company with the minister to that country so as to have the general out of the way in the event of a civil disturbance, believed to be extremely likely in that period of tension before the Congressional elections. Johnson was foiled, however, by Grant's absolute refusal to go (the general said that he could not be ordered on a purely civilian mission), and by Sherman's equally adamant unwillingness to become embroiled in any plan that

would work to Grant's discomfiture. The upshot of the whole
business was that Sherman offered to go in Grant's place, and
Johnson, realizing it was futile to contend against both men,
accepted this way out.

The result of the 1866 Congressional elections, on top of the
response of the crowds in the Swing around the Circle, confirmed Grant in his opposition to the President's policies. The
people had spoken, and they let it be known in no uncertain
way that they wanted a Republican Congress. Grant, believing
in the supremacy of Congress as representing the will of the
people, now began to persuade himself that he was needed to
preserve the results of the war and to thwart designs by the
President and his followers to overturn those results.[9]

While the general was still able to approve Johnson's veto of
a bill giving the freedmen the vote in the District of Columbia,
he was nonetheless adhering to a position which was becoming
increasingly differentiated from the one maintained by the
President. In January, he wrote General O. O. Howard, Commissioner of the Freedmen's Bureau, requesting a list of murders and other outrages committed against freedmen and
Unionists in the Southern states for the last six months or year.
"My object," he wrote " . . . is to make a report showing [that]
the courts in the states excluded from Congress afford no
security to life or property of [the freedmen and Unionists] and
to recommend that Martial Law be declared over such districts
as do not afford the proper protection."

When the report was sent in from Howard and Grant, Stanton presented it to the cabinet, much to the disgust of Gideon
Welles who called it "an omnium-gatherum of newspaper gossip, rumors of negro murders, neighborhood strifes and troubles. . . . " More and more was Grant convinced that Johnson,
and conservative members of his cabinet like Welles and Orville Browning, were blind to the true conditions in the South.
They seemed too willing not only to defy Congress but to listen
to former rebels and to disregard the appeals of the Union men
and Negroes.[10]

The growing hostility of virtually all the Republican members
of Congress to the President, an antipathy arising out of Johnson's Reconstruction policies, conditions in the South, and the
results of the recent elections, led to the adoption on March 2,
1867 of three momentous pieces of legislation, all three extremely significant in the life of Ulysses Grant.

Most far-reaching in its importance was the Reconstruction

Act. It inaugurated Congressional Reconstruction in ten Southern states by placing them under military government in five
districts each to be headed by a general officer of the army. It
laid down for each state specific stages of reconstruction: a
constitutional convention selected by universal manhood suffrage (which of course meant Negro voting), new state governments whose legislatures would be required to ratify the
Fourteenth Amendment, and finally, if Congress so decided,
admission of the state's senators and representatives to the national legislature. Grant would have a great responsibility in the
execution of the new law, because, in another action, approved
the same day, Congress stipulated that all orders to the army
from the President had to go through the general-in-chief and
that he could not be removed nor his headquarters relocated
without approval of the Senate. The third measure was the
Tenure of Office Act designed to protect officers of the executive departments from removal by the President without the
Senate's consent. Johnson vetoed all three measures, but Congress quickly overrode the vetoes.

The Reconstruction Act was needed, Grant believed, to give
the nation security for the future, and from the day of its passage, in all the disputes between President and Congress over
its implementation, Grant unswervingly aligned himself with
the Congress. But the country was not really aware of this.
Grant still maintained, outwardly, a formal correctness in his
relations with the President, efforts made more convincing by
the overt attempts by Johnson to make it appear that the general still sympathized with the administration. Johnson's motive
is clear enough, he needed Grant's support; he dared not risk
his open opposition in view of Grant' enormous popularity in
the country. So when it came to appointing the five district
commanders specified in the Reconstruction Act, Johnson
freely consulted with Grant. The names of Sheridan, Daniel
Sickles, and John Pope in the list of five is proof of the fact that
Johnson was not the sole determiner of the final selections.[11]

While all of the district commanders from time to time ran
into difficulties in administering their satrapies to the satisfaction of the local citizenry, none had the explosive experiences
which beset Sheridan. In charge of the Fifth District compris-
ing Texas and Louisiana, Sheridan moved swiftly to exercise
full authority by wholesale removals from office of those whom
Sheridan considered obstructionists. These controversial actions
annoyed Johnson and those who disapproved of military gov-

ernment, but Grant gave his unalloyed confidence and support to Sheridan.[12]

Even this controversy did not destroy the outward appearance of harmony between Grant and Johnson. While the Attorney General ruled that the powers of the district commanders were limited, Grant told his commanders in the field that they could interpret the acts as they saw fit, because this was what Congress intended. Grant, so far as the country knew, was carrying out his duties to the satisfaction of the President in his accustomed unobtrusive way. Few were aware of the deep gulf which existed between them on the subject of Reconstruction policy.

In July, Grant, with members of his family, paid a visit to ex-governor Hamilton Fish at the latter's summer home in Garrison, New York, opposite West Point. Then he spent a week at Long Branch, New Jersey. He was back in Washington by the end of the month to participate in the events surrounding Johnson's attempt to replace Secretary of War Stanton, who for many months had been working actively against the President and his policies. When Stanton would not resign, Johnson suspended him and named Grant Secretary of War *ad interim.* The general's acceptance of the position puzzled a good many at the time and led some to believe that a close understanding existed between Grant and Johnson. Thomas Ewing, Jr., General Sherman's brother-in-law, later remarked that Grant was staying on as Secretary of War because he had full control of the army, ruled "the whole army his own way—all which suits him exactly. . . . " Ewing put his finger on the reason, but failed to note that Grant's satisfaction at having the army under his control was, as he admitted to Johnson at the height of their personal dispute, to keep it out of the hands of a secretary who was not in sympathy with the Reconstruction policy of Congress.[13]

Johnson's motive is more difficult to ascertain. Welles said he was "at a loss as to the policy of the President. . . . " But the most logical explanation is that he wanted to have on his side (or as close to him as possible) the most popular man in the country, who was being talked of as a presidential candidate for 1868.

Grant, as Secretary of War, soon was crossing swords with Johnson. Earlier he had pleaded with the President not to remove Sheridan from command of the Fifth District, but no sooner had Grant taken over his new position (an additional job for him since he remained as general-in-chief of the army) than Johnson told him to replace Sheridan with Hancock. Grant, remonstrating strongly in a letter to Johnson urging the President to rescind the order, showed once again that he would go to any lengths for his favorite. It did no good, but Johnson was doing the one sure thing that would further alienate Grant from the administration.[14]

On October 12, Johnson called on Grant at the War Department to have a confidential talk on the subject of the Senate's possible attempt to reinstate Stanton when Congress convened in December, and the course Grant would adopt should there be an attempt to arrest the President. Johnson came away from the interview reassured that Grant was reliable. He had obtained from the general a promise to inform the President should there by any shift in his position regarding the office of Secretary of War.

Grant's sphinx-like behavior can be readily understood if we see him as a man being pushed by events into a position he did not particularly desire. It is impossible to know whether or not, at this time, he wanted to be president. He always said he did not. Senator John Sherman, brother of the general, believed that he did. Never one to promote his own candidacy—he had a pronounced aversion for anything smacking of self-advancement—he could nonetheless see that his duty might lie in taking the presidency, to do what was needed, as General Sherman expressed it, "to protect the negroes and Union men against legal oppression, or the acts of badly disposed ex-Rebels." Events and men were pushing him into the contest. Prominent New Yorkers, led by the merchant A. T. Stewart, organized a rally endorsing Grant for the office. The general, however, was behaving as if he were still on good terms with Johnson, hardly the way for a presidential hopeful to act.[15]

This outwardly harmonious relationship broke up completely following the rejection by the Senate of Johnson's explanation for his suspension of Stanton. The Senate committee reported on January 10, 1868 that the explanation was not satisfactory, so that it was only a question of time before the full body would declare that the suspension was invalid and that Stanton was still rightfully the Secretary of War. These developments would place Grant in an uncomfortable position. Should Johnson decide not to obey the terms of the Tenure of Office Act, Grant would have to choose between his obedience to the commander-in-chief and his loyalty to the authority of Congress. The day after the committee made its report, a Saturday, Grant went to the White House to inform Johnson that he had examined carefully the Tenure of Office Act. Having noted that there was a fine of $10,000 and a five-year prison sentence for attempt to retain office illegally, he would not run the risk by keeping the office after the Senate had formally acted on the committee's report. Johnson offered to assume the responsibility for the fine and prison sentence, but Grant would have none of it. Further argument proved of no profit to either man and something was apparently said about a renewal of the discussion on Monday. In view of the certainty that the Senate was due to act at any time (after Sunday), Johnson was risking a good deal in any delay. He might have asked for Grant's resignation on the spot and sent to the Senate the name of some other person acceptable to him and to the Republican majority. As it turned out, the name of Governor Jacob D. Cox of Ohio was suggested to Johnson on Sunday through the efforts of General Sherman and Senator Reverdy Johnson, but the President chose to ignore the advice. Whether or not Grant promised Johnson that he would see him on Monday (before surrendering the office of secretary) became the subject of an acrimonious dispute between the two. The general's prediliction for silence, his reputation for being thoroughly honest, and Johnson's insistence on his own interpretation of events make it extremely likely that there was a misunderstanding. In any event, Grant did not visit the President on Monday, apparently because there was no reason to do so, but he did ask Sherman to visit Johnson and inquire about Cox. But Sherman was unable to induce Johnson to commit himself. Late that day, the Senate, voting to accept the report of the committee, refused to allow Johnson to dismiss Stanton and so notified Grant. It seems odd that when Grant attended a White House reception that very evening, the President made no mention of Grant's failure to appear at the White House earlier in the day.[16]

The next morning Grant went to the War Department, locked the door to the secretary's office, turned the key over to the adjutant-general, and went directly to his office as general-in-chief. He then sent a message to the President stating that because of the Senate's action his functions as Secretary of War, *ad interim*, had "ceased from the moment of the receipt" of the Senate's notice. Another letter reached Johnson some time that day from William S. Hillyer, once of Grant's staff, still a friend of the general, but also on speaking terms with the President.

Hillyer had seen Grant that morning and received at first hand the account of recent events and especially assurance from Grant that he had "never had any conversation or collusion with Mr Stanton in regard to his (Stanton's) restoration to the war office. ... " This is convincing evidence that Johnson was wrong in believing that Grant was acting in concert with Stanton to deprive Johnson of the opportunity to test the constitutionality of the Tenure of Office Act in the courts.

Meanwhile, Stanton had appeared at the War Department, had repossessed his old office, and, as one of his first acts, sent Grant a brusque note summoning him to appear, an action which did not please the sensitive general. Never one to feel an intimacy with the frequently rude War Secretary, Grant, all through this episode, was inclined to hope for Stanton's replacement by someone with whom he could feel more at ease, and in so doing he was not be any stretch of the imagination doing Stanton's bidding.[17]

That Tuesday afternoon, Grant, learning indirectly that he was expected at the cabinet meeting, went to the White House convinced he was no longer a member of the cabinet. He was treated as such, however, and, when it came his turn to report, let it be known that under the terms of the Tenure of Office Act he could not be the Secretary of War. This led to Johnson's interrogating Grant about their previous agreement, another instance of which Grant and Johnson later gave opposing versions. Johnson, supported by the testimony of the rest of the cabinet with the exception of Seward who hedged, insisted that in answer to one of his questions Grant had admitted having promised to see the President on Monday. Later, Grant insisted that he had admitted no such thing. While the weight of the testimony appears to support Johnson, again there exists the strong possibility that there was a difference in interpretation of what Grant said. The general appears to have been flustered, and, with the President firing questions at him, he might have been led into unintended admissions. Grant could hardly have deliberately lied to the President (though this is what Johnson, Welles, and Browning believed), and when he was accused of falsehood he naturally was offended. Since there was an honest difference of opinion, it behooved Johnson to act with moderation, since he could hardly profit (nor did he) from a fruitless argument with the popular military hero. Furthermore, he was obviously trying to use Grant for his own purposes, and Grant, understanding this, did not care to be so used.[18]

It is hardly necessary to go into the later stages of this quarrel which went on by personal interview and later by letter for some days after that stormy cabinet session. Grant, believing his honor and word had been impugned, brought the matter to a head with a letter, reportedly doctored by Rawlins to make the break more decisive, stating that Johnson, not wanting to take the responsibility, had attempted to get him to violate the law and, "thus . . . destroy my character before the country." One more letter from each only made things worse and the breach was irreparable.[19]

Johnson's next move was to try once more to bring Sherman into the picture, first as commander of a new military division with headquarters in Washington and with the brevet rank of full general, and later as Secretary of War. Sherman, who hated politics, had considered resigning his commission to avoid being made a pawn in Johnson's game and being forced into a rivalry with Grant. His strong stand finally convinced the President that it was futile to try to commit Sherman to actions of which he disapproved, so Johnson gave up the idea.[20]

Meanwhile, Stanton tenaciously held on to the office of Secretary of War, despite some effort by Grant and Sherman to persuade him to resign. This unprecedented situation continued for more than a month until, throwing away all caution and moderation, Johnson dismissed Stanton once more and named Lorenzo Thomas, adjutant general, to the office of Secretary of War. Stanton conferred with Grant and decided, possibly because he now knew he could count on Grant's support (as well as that of the Radical senators), to hold the position in defiance of the President's order.

It was during this sequence of events that the House voted to bring charges of impeachment against Johnson, especially for his open violation of the Tenure of Office Act in his attempt to put Lorenzo Thomas into the war office. Grant, prior to his break with Johnson, had not been in sympathy with impeachment, but when the effort actually was made he showed a desire for conviction. The President, however, was acquitted when the vote in the Senate fell just short of the two thirds necessary for conviction.[21]

By this time it was a foregone conclusion that Grant would be the Republican nominee, and that the convention to be held in Chicago on May 20 would be a mere formality. In keeping with his practice of not seeking place or position, Grant had done nothing to gain the nomination. But he did not try to discourage those who were seeking it for him. His name had been suggested as early as 1863 as a potential candidate, and ever since the end of the war there had been a good possibility the Republican party would want the war's number one hero as its standard bearer. But Grant's actions were so noncommittal that the country was not sure whether or not he sympathized with Johnson until the break with the President in January 1868. From that time on there were no further obstacles. The convention delegates made him their unanimous choice, selected Schuyler Colfax for the vice presidency, and adopted a platform endorsing Radical Reconstruction.

In typical Grant fashion he displayed no emotion whatsoever when Stanton brought him the news, but to his friend Sherman a short time later he told of his reluctance to accept the nomination. He was, as he said to Sherman,

forced into it in spite of myself. I could not back down without, it seems to me leaving the contest for power for the next four years between mere trading politicians, the elevation of whom, no matter which party won, would lose to us, largely, the results of the costly war which we have gone through.

His acceptance letter said that he could not properly lay down a policy for an administration of four years' duration, knowing how often circumstances changed. It was his belief, as he stated in the letter, that "a purely administrative officer should always be left free to execute the will of the people." Since to Grant Congress expressed the will of the people, here was a clue to his two administrations. The conclusion of the letter was the memorable phrase, "Let us have peace."[22]

Grant considered himself above party and did not take an active part in the campaign; neither, for that matter, did his Democratic opponent, Horatio Seymour, former governor of New York. In June, Grant visited West Point where his oldest son, Fred, was a cadet, and then, with Sherman and Sheridan, went west as far as Denver. But this was really not a campaign tour in that Grant did not deliver any political speeches; he scarcely spoke at all. By the latter part of July he had returned to Galena, where the townspeople had made ready his modest home even to the point of preparing the first meal.

While the general thus remained out of sight during most of the canvass, and did not express himself on the major issues of Reconstruction and monetary policy, his supporters conducted a spirited campaign emphasizing the dangers inherent in a Democratic administration: the enthronement of rebels, repudiation of the national debt, and other dire catastrophes. They told the voters of Seymour's Copperhead leanings. The Democrats naturally regaled their listeners with stories of Grant's addiction to alcohol and insisted that Grant still went on drinking bouts.[23]

These issues had little bearing on the outcome of the election. The Republican leaders who nominated Grant did so because they were fully conscious of his great popularity with the white voters of the North and, incidentally, the colored voters of the South. That they estimated things correctly is borne out by the election results. Grant carried twenty-six out of thirty-four states and had a 300,000 popular majority. Negroes voted in great numbers in the South and delivered six states of the former Confederacy, as well as two border states. Grant was an overwhelming victor in many of the Northern states, polling 55 percent or better in thirteen of these (including Ohio and Illinois), obtaining over 78 percent of the popular vote in Vermont, and just under 70 percent in Massachusetts. It is not true, as has been frequently stated, that without the Negro vote Grant would have lost.[24] Even had Seymour carried all the states of the former Confederacy which took part in the election and had carried all the border states as well, Grant would still have won the electoral vote 157 to 137. Furthermore, to state that Grant did not receive a majority of the white vote of the country is true but misleading. When the votes of the white Democrats of the Southern states are subtracted from Seymour's total (it could hardly be expected that any significant number of Southern whites would vote for the Republican candidate no matter who he was) Grant ends up with a comfortable margin. And if one counts Grant's vote in only those states where the Negro vote would not be significant, he comes out with a plurality of over 400,000 votes in a total of 4,418,000, although he *lost* the states of New York, New Jersey, and Oregon.[25] New York was Seymour's home state and New York City could be counted on to deliver a sizable Democratic majority. New Jersey had been in the Democratic column since 1848, yet Grant polled 49 percent of the vote there, as opposed to 47.3 percent for Lincoln in 1864. That Grant carried such states as Connecticut, Indiana, and Pennsylvania was a great tribute to his vote-getting ability.[26] Everything considered, it was an impressive triumph.

Grant never had any doubt about the outcome, and while sitting with friends at Washburne's home in Galena the night of the election he showed little emotion. When the returns showed that he would be the winner, he stepped outside to speak a few words to townspeople who had gathered to cheer him. Thanking them for their help, he concluded his brief remarks with, "The responsibilities of the position I feel, but accept them without fear."[27] Well might Grant feel the responsibilities of his new office because the nation still had a long way to go along the road to reunion, and, this being a post-war era, the country's moral stamina was weakening and a heightened spirit of materialism and acquisitiveness had already gripped the American people. The new President would need a wealth of experience and political sagacity with which to confront the major problems of the day. Grant was nowhere near as well provided with these as he needed to be.

CHAPTER VII

Let Us Have Peace

As the time for Grant's inauguration approached, it began to dawn on the country—and especially on the Republican leaders—that Grant really believed himself to be above party. For one thing, he did not consult with the Congressional leaders of the party about his inaugural address, his cabinet selections, or the basic presidential policies. True, the platform had something to say about the latter, and Grant was believed to be a sound money man as well as a supporter of the Congressional plan of Reconstruction, but he remained, even so, something of an enigma. His willingness to cut loose from the professional politicians had its appeal; yet there were dangers in trying to run a politically oriented system of government without the assistance of experienced professionals. This is undoubtedly why Orville E. Babcock, a member of Grant's staff, in October of 1867 had stated to Washburne his belief that it would be "a great misfortune" to Grant himself if ever he should become President, or why Rawlins, in a conversation recorded by Browning a year earlier, was quoted as saying that Grant "is not a politician or statesman—he knows how to do nothing but fight—would fail in other positions. . . . "[1]

All this became manifest during Grant's presidency. But a man can learn in office, even though the price might be costly (as it was with Grant), and by the time his eight years were up he understood professional politics as well as anyone could.

The key to Grant's presidency lies not so much, then, with his lack of experience as a politician, or, putting it in reverse, with his military training and background, as with the personality traits which were to stay with him all his life. Surely one of these was a loyalty to those who had befriended him and remained loyal to him. How much this stemmed from his earlier troubles in the years prior to the Civil War (and the period of the war itself) one can only speculate, but Grant, a highly sensitive and appreciative person, would naturally want to stand by the men who had done the same for him.

Linked with this was a sense of inferiority in two spheres. Grant had failed in business and knew what it was like to be poor; he thus came to admire the man who was successful in business and who was rich. While it might have turned out the other way —a jealousy and dislike for the successful business man—Grant in the years after the war obviously enjoyed the company of wealthy men and believed that such men necessarily were endowed with talent and brains. The general also was conscious of his own intellectual shortcomings. That is, he lacked the classical education common to men of culture and education in that day, and while he was not unread he nonetheless would hardly feel at ease with a Charles Sumner or a John Lothrop Motley, men of the highest erudition.

Necessarily, then, Grant felt more comfortable with military men, self-made businessmen, or the politicians who did not, like some men in public life, consciously or otherwise, assume a patronizing attitude toward the simple tanner from the West with only a West Point education. That there were exceptions does not negate the essential truth of the assertion. One of the most obvious exceptions was Hamilton Fish, a true aristocrat enjoying a high social position in New York, who was able to break through Grant's self-imposed reserve and establish a genuinely close relationship with the otherwise diffident President. Much of Grant's reserve and his preference for men more like himself can be traced to his unwillingness to appear intellectually inferior in the company of men whom he believed to have a condescending attitude toward him.

None of this would interfere with Grant's determination to do his duty as he saw it, but it can help to explain some of the peculiar events that occurred during the early stages of his first administration. So, for instance, Grant consulted only a military aide, Adam Badeau, in preparing his brief inaugural address, which, while devoid of grace and depth, nonetheless stated in clear terms what Grant wanted to accomplish as President. He said, in words that no one could misunderstand, that he was going to pursue a conservative monetary policy. That meant payment of the national debt in gold (where this was called for) and a return to specie payment as soon as possible, all of which was reassuring to the business community. In stating that all laws would be enforced, Grant was only reiterating the political philosophy of a lifetime. He was also letting it be known that he accepted the policy of Reconstruction then in effect. He promised that the revenues would be faithfully collected, a mat-

ter of considerable importance just then when it was generally
understood that the Treasury was losing millions each year because of unfaithful agents. He also gave indication of a new
direction for the government in its policy toward the Indians,
and assured his listeners that we would expect all nations to
respect American rights. This was a sign to Great Britain that
the United States would expect redress of grievances inflicted
by Britain during the Civil War. He also must have had in mind
the revolution then in progress in Cuba and Spain's infringe-
ment on the rights of Americans on that strife-torn island.[2]

Another oddity of the early part of Grant's presidency was
the secrecy that surrounded his cabinet choices, a lack of can-
dor followed by considerable embarrassment when two major
appointments were given to men who failed to fill the positions,
and when in the case of some of the other appointments Grant
showed that he was wanting in political finesse. Of course, that
is exactly what might have been expected from a man who was
determined to assert his independence of the professional
politicians.

When the preliminaries were over Grant emerged with a
cabinet which in most respects would have done credit to any
administration. The first position went to Hamilton Fish (following a courtesy appointment of a few days to Elihu Washburne)
whose importance to the Grant administration cannot be
overestimated.

Grant called Fish to the position without any prior consultation with the former New York governor, a method adopted for
all but three of the choices. In two instances, those of John A.
Rawlins, Secretary of War, and Washburne, Grant found it
necessary to give out the information prior to the inauguration
to quiet the fears of those two close associates. He notified
Alexander T. Stewart, the New York merchant, that he would
be named Secretary of the Treasury in order that he might
arrange his affairs, but the public was not informed. When it
turned out that Stewart was ineligible for the office (because of
a law dating back to Washington's administration declaring that
a man engaged in trade or commerce could not hold the office),
Grant, unsuccessful in his efforts to have Congress change the
law, appointed George S. Boutwell of Massachusetts to this important post.[3] Boutwell was a Radical who had been one of the
House managers in the impeachment trial but he had served as
commissioner of the Internal Revenue Bureau during the war
period and his sound money views were acceptable to conserv-

ative businessmen. The nominations of E. Rockwood Hoar to be Attorney-General and Jacob D. Cox as Secretary of the Interior, while coming as something of a surprise to the politicians, could not be criticized on the basis of suitability, for both men had excellent qualifications. But Grant courted ridicule when he presented the name of Adolph E. Borie for the Navy Department. Borie, a wealthy but obscure Philadelphian, had no interest in the position and accepted on the understanding he would shortly resign, which he did. John A. J. Cresswell of Maryland was Postmaster-General, and he proved to be able in administration as well as adept in handling the patronage of his office.

Throughout the next eight years numerous changes occurred in Grant's cabinet, shifts which could be interpreted as a sign of instability in the administration. Yet Fish remained throughout the period and George M. Robeson, who early succeeded Borie in the Navy Department, held office nearly as long. Others remained for from four to six years, offsetting to a degree some of those who held office only briefly.[4]

The fact that the politicians were displeased with most of Grant's original appointments need not have made much difference to the success of the administration, since Grant could ride along on his popularity and fulfill the duties of the presidency, which were, in his eyes, simply to carry out the will of the people as expressed by Congress. What has branded the Grant administration a failure is, of course, the all-too-numerous instances of scandal, especially in the second term. But when one examines the eight presidential years, omitting the scandals, the record is one of accomplishment and even outstanding success. Coming to office when the nation was torn by dissension, when the Southern problem still rancored and would not down, when the price of gold in greenbacks was still dangerously high and so was the national debt, when touchy problems remained unsolved with Great Britain and when a bloody revolution was in progress in Cuba, Grant's administration found solutions for most of these problems and even made a stab at civil service reform and a more humane Indian policy. True, more deep-seated national evils began to demand attention—problems related to industrialization—but these were incipient in the early years of the Grant administration and the general, though not universal, assumption was that it was improper for the national government to concern itself with such economic questions as big business, the plight of the farmer and industrial worker, or even the exploitation of natural resources. Unfortunately, the scandals of the Grant administration did occur, did bring shame to persons close to the President, and inevitably lowered the prestige of the administration including that of the man at the top. The remarkable thing is that Grant retained as much of his popularity as he did; indeed he proved eminently successful in riding out the storm and emerging, not unscathed, but at least with the respect and admiration of the great majority of his countrymen from the North. Grant's name still stood for victory against rebels; millions of his countrymen could never forget Donelson, Vicksburg, Chattanooga, and Appomattox and the success he gained when so many others had failed. Such a reputation could withstand almost any kind of assault largely because, to the American who saw Grant as the savior of the Union, he could do no wrong.

While the first weeks of the new administration were largely taken up with patronage matters, Grant did give some attention to the major problems confronting him in March 1869. So often is the assumption made that the general had been taken in completely by the Radicals that the essentially conservative character of the administration frequently goes unnoticed. Yet the fact remains that Grant was not a Radical when he took office, nor had he ever been one. His pre-war politics were relatively simple and could be termed national. He had not been an abolitionist, not, at least, until the war was well under way. Throughout the war he had displayed moderation toward Southerners and the South; never had he favored a vindictive policy. At the time the war ended he had not been in favor of giving the franchise to the freedmen and would have supported Johnson had there been greater willingness on the part of Southerners to acknowledge the supremacy of the national government in all matters concerning Reconstruction and the Negroes. Only when it appeared to him that the President was carelessly tossing away the fruits of victory did he part company with him, and then in such a quiet way that few knew it had happened. The support he gave to Congressional reconstruction stemmed from his strong sense of duty to the people and their representatives in Congress and his equally strong belief in the supremacy of the national government in dealing with the conquered South. Thus, as President, he had no desire to punish; his sole aim was to carry out and enforce the laws.

His Secretary of State, Hamilton Fish, had a conservative Whig background, had never shown any radical tendencies, had, in fact, given his approval to Johnson's veto of the Freedmen's Bureau bill and disapproved of certain features of the Fourteenth Amendment.[5] Fish not only handled the affairs of the State Department in a restrained and conservative fashion, but exercised a moderating influence on his cabinet colleagues, especially those who might be considered Radical. Furthermore, Grant appointed to his cabinet a number of other conservative Republicans as well as some former Democrats. Examples are Benjamin H. Bristow, William W. Belknap, and Jacob D. Cox.

It was Grant, however, who set the tone of the administration, and despite some superficial Radical signs, it was essentially conservative. But there is no evading the scandals, and for these Grant was partially responsible. The trouble lay first in the fact that he lacked experience as an administrator in a civilian capacity. In many matters relating to the presidency (his relations with Congress, for example) he was out of his element. Grant was too sensitive of the feelings of others, too unready to believe evil of others. It should also be borne in mind that Grant happened to be President at a time when the level of morality both in public and private affairs dipped to a new low, or so the incidence of scandal in and out of public office would seem to show.

That the Congress had a mind of its own and would exert its authority even against such a popular figure as Grant shows that Grant was at no time master in his own house. Grant was not in the position where he merely had to ask and the obedient Congress would act as he wished. What this meant was that he constantly had to keep in mind the Republican leaders in Congress, powerful men, capable of making or breaking any piece of legislation or any nomination for office the President might happen to make. Grant, aware of this, and more convinced than some that Congress spoke for the nation, for practical reasons found it expedient to accept the fact that no matter what he might want, if the Congress saw fit to turn him down, it would do so.

He learned this lesson very early. The Tenure of Office Act was still in effect when he assumed the presidency. Naturally, Grant did not want to be bound by the restrictions the act placed on his control of the executive branch of the government. He believed the act had been intended to control Andrew Johnson but not him. When the House voted for repeal but the Senate refused to relinquish a useful weapon, the President faced the choice of fighting for what he wanted or submit-

ting to the superior power of the Senate. He decided to accept
a compromise, which was tantamount to defeat, for the Senate
had maintained the principle even while surrendering some of
the actual power.[6] Many more times in the years ahead Grant
would be made to feel the force of Congress' power. This is not
to say, however, that the Congress was not alive to the force of
Grant's popular appeal and it frequently responded with alac-
rity to the President's requests. This was especially true of what
was commonly known as the Southern problem.

One of the major accomplishments of Grant's first administration was the completion of Reconstruction. So frequently is the
year 1877 used to signify the end of Reconstruction we are
prone to forget that Reconstruction officially ended when senators from Georgia took their seats on February 24, 1871. At the
time of Grant's inauguration, the only states not represented in
Congress were Georgia, Mississippi, Virginia, and Texas.
Within a year, all but Georgia had fulfilled the requirements
laid down by the Congress and the Congressional representatives of these states were allowed to take their seats. Impetus
for this action came from Grant, who, on April 7, 1869, sent a
special message urging speedy action to bring the four states
into a proper relationship with the national government. Showing a willingness to co-operate with the President and to wind
up the process of Reconstruction, Congress speedily passed and
Grant signed the act calling for new elections to be held on the
constitutions of the states of Mississippi, Virginia, and Texas
with Grant having the authority to permit separate votes on
disfranchising clauses unacceptable to conservative whites.
That Grant favored these separate votes, with the knowledge
that the chances were good the disfranchising clauses would be
defeated, shows clearly that he wanted an end to Reconstruction as quickly as possible and that he would not favor a pros-
criptive policy toward the South. Georgia, whose white
legislators had arbitrarily excluded duly elected Negroes, was
the subject of special legislation which led to that state's being
allowed representation in 1870, although, as earlier noted, her
senators did not actually take their seats until February 1871.
While Republican regimes controlled several of the Southern
states, this was not true of all in 1871 and even in the Republican states, control was divided between carpetbaggers and
scalawags. In other words, native Southerners frequently were
in positions of prominence in the Republican regimes of several
of the states.

None of this, however, was officially the business of the national government. It was assumed that the reconstructed Southern governments could handle their internal affairs without interference from Washington. That Grant believed this and made it his policy is borne out by the fact that his annual messages, after that of 1870, make infrequent and only brief mention of Southern affairs.[7]

Grant, in his inaugural address, inserted a plea for ratification of the Fifteenth Amendment which only a few days earlier had been passed by Congress. When ratifications of the constitutional change to secure the right of the freedmen to vote lagged, Grant, in November, asked the governor of Nebraska to call a special session of the legislature to help put it across. By the end of March 1870 Grant could notify Congress that the necessary number of ratifications had been secured and that the Fifteenth Amendment was part of the Constitution. In doing this, Grant could assume that Reconstruction was that much nearer to being over.[8]

The fact that the Grant administration and Republicans in Congress pursued a vacillating and erratic policy of intervention in certain of the Southern states between 1870 and 1877 has led to the general assumption that Reconstruction continued without interruption during those years. A motive often assigned for this intervention was the reluctance to see the Southern states fall under Democratic control. But Grant, and certain members of his cabinet, especially Fish, opposed intervention and deviated from a hands-off policy only when there was a request from the governor of one of the states, or when the federal law clearly called for such action. While in some instances the federal troops were used to support regimes of questionable respectability, the need was legitimate in others, and in a few cases failure to intervene would have been gross negligence and dereliction of duty on the part of the President.

There was a time when historians could find no excuse for Grant's policy of intervention, when the carpetbag governments and their scalawag and Negro adherents had the most despicable reputations. Recent scholarship has brought about a reassessment of these regimes and the result is a more balanced version of this phase of Reconstruction. As the carpetbag governments have risen in respectability, so too has the policy of supporting them by the federal government. For, if the freedmen were going to enjoy to even the least extent their newly-won rights, under the Thirteenth, Fourteenth, and Fifteenth

Amendments and the Civil Rights laws they would need the
protecting arm of federal courts and federal military forces.
Seen in this light, the record of the Grant administration is
spotty at best, for it was in these eight years that the downward
trend in the status of the Negro in the South set in. It started
as early as 1869 in Tennessee, and 1870 in Georgia and North
Carolina. Every place where the Ku Klux Klan and similar
groups operated the Negroes were victims of outrages and violence of the most frightening kind. Not everyone in the North
could callously sit by and see the degradation of the newly-
created citizens without a feeling of revulsion and an urge to
see the results of the war upheld. The motive undoubtedly was
frequently mixed: a genuine desire to keep the faith mingled
with feeling of apprehension over the possibility that the
Democrats and former rebels would win control of the national
government and all that that entailed from a political and economic viewpoint. But surely, the need to fulfill the national
commitment to the freedmen—the promise that they would
really be free—can be counted as a genuine and legitimate
motive for federal intervention. The record of the Grant administration falls far short of what it should have been. Instead
of too much interference, there was too little. Not that there
was ever a real possibility for a full-scale program of rigid control over the lives of the Southern people during these years.
But there might have been a more vigorous effort to suppress
disorder, violence, and outrage. Grant at least made some attempt in this direction, and if he erred, it was on the side of
restraint rather than of excessive zeal.

Considering the enormity of the problem, the weapons that
Grant had at his disposal were few indeed. To be sure, Congress gave him legislative authority in the form of two acts in
1870 and 1871 to enforce the Fourteenth and Fifteenth
Amendments, especially in Congressional elections, but the
forces and funds available for implementation were not equal to
the task, and Grant, believing, as did most Americans of the
day, that the rights of the states ought to be preserved as much
as possible, was reluctant to intervene.[9]

The situation in 1871 became so bad, however, that the
President was constrained to act more decisively. Defeated in
most places at the polls, white Southerners turned to intimidation both to reduce the size of the Negro vote and to maintain
white supremacy in every area of human existence. The mid-
term elections of 1870 showed considerable activity in this di-

rection. An abortive attempt was made to overthrow the Republican administration in South Carolina, and a similar effort in Florida, while unsuccessful in the short-run, paved the way for a conservative-type government later on. The Democrats, resorting to widespread violence and intimidation, gained control over the government of North Carolina. A Congressional investigation which revealed the extent of the atrocities gave Grant and the Congress still more reason for adopting drastic measures.[10]

Evidence that widespread disorder existed in the South was readily available, and Grant and his administration had to face the decision of whether or not to intervene. Early in the year Robert K. Scott, carpetbag governor of South Carolina, urgently asked the President for troops to suppress disorders in his state. Grant, believing that this was a legitimate appeal, responded by sending twelve infantry and four cavalry companies. On March 9, 1871 he wrote to James G. Blaine, Speaker of the House, informally suggesting an act to assist in the restoration of order in certain parts of the South where "a deplorable state of affairs" existed. Grant went out of his way to assure Blaine that he had no intention of telling Congress what to do. But Northern Congressmen, sensing that their constituents did not really want coercive legislation, would not act without a request from the President. Reluctantly, Grant, accompanied by Boutwell, made the trip to the other end of Pennsylvania Avenue and summoned leading Republican senators to the President's room in the Capitol. At first he insisted he could not make a specific request for the kind of legislation he believed was needed to suppress disorder in the South, and reminded his listeners that he had already been charged with allowing the military too large an influence in his administration. What he wanted, of course, was Congressional action without the President's request. Because the Senate leaders were unwilling to comply, with misgivings, he wrote out a brief special message addressed to the Senate and the House recommending "such legislation as in the judgment of Congress shall effectually secure life, liberty, and property and the enforcement of law in all parts of the United States." The Republican majority, despite the opposition of some who doubted the constitutionality of the proposal, on April 20, 1871 enacted a measure known as the Ku Klux Act giving the President authority, for a limited time, to revoke the writ of habeas corpus and to impose martial law in places where the local authorities could not or would not protect the rights and liberties of citizens.[11]

Grant soon after issued a proclamation urging the suppression of disorders where they existed, stating his reluctance to use the authority recently granted him but asserting emphatically his obligation to use all the energies of the national government "for the restoration of peace and order throughout the entire country." Since there was no abatement during the summer of the outrages committed in the South, especially in South Carolina, Grant somewhat tardily decided to make an example of that state, singled out nine of the northern counties, and issued a warning to the armed conspiracies there to disperse in five days. When there was no response, in characteristic fashion he carried through his threat and suspended the habeas corpus to contain what he called rebellion. Troops entered these counties, a good many arrests were made, some convictions were obtained, and the net result was a temporary curtailment of disorder. Additional prosecutions under the Ku Klux Act continued into 1872 in other parts of the South as well, but, while the results may have been salutary, there was no significant reversal of the trend toward conservative control of the former Confederate states. Grant had neither the means nor the will to reimpose military rule on any extended scale and without these there was little hope for either the freedmen or the Republican regimes.

On several occasions Grant passed up opportunities to intervene or to take sides in factional disputes. Thus in February 1871, when trouble broke out in Arkansas, and when it would have been possible to take an active hand, he told the Secretary of War to order the commanding officer in the state to do what was necessary to keep order but to avoid aiding either faction. A similar opportunity arose in December to intervene in the fight for the governorship in Georgia, but Grant stated in cabinet his desire for the states to handle such problems by themselves. A short while later, when the chronic political turmoil in Louisiana threatened to boil over, Grant wrote a member of Congress that while the condition of affairs in that state was undoubtedly bad, "I have not been able to see any justification for executive interference." A year later a serious dispute erupted in Louisiana over the question of which of two factions should have political control of the state. Grant's instructions to the commanding officer, General William H. Emory, via the Secretary of War, were to avoid taking sides, maintain order, and wait for the courts to decide "which of the two bodies is the legal legislature." The following month in a special message to Congress, he put the problem up to the law makers by stating his unwillingness to interfere in the affairs of a state. His hope was that Congress would take the responsibility in the matter of a legitimate government for Louisiana, but if nothing were done he would be obliged to act.[12]

Grant's sense of duty, and occasionally his partiality to Republican regimes, prompted the interventions that did occur. There was also an awareness of the true state of affairs in the South in which Negroes and white Republicans did not enjoy the usual freedoms of American citizens. In a message to the House, explaining his actions in South Carolina, Grant let it be known that he was sensitive to the plight of the freedmen, and alive to the designs of the Ku Klux Klan whose objectives were

by force and terror to prevent all political action not in accord with the views of the members; to deprive colored citizens of the right to bear arms and of the right to a free ballot; to suppress schools in which colored children were taught, and to reduce the colored people to a condition closely akin to that of slavery; that these combinations were organized and armed, and had rendered the local laws ineffectual to protect the classes whom they desired to oppress; that they had perpetrated many murders and hundreds of crimes of minor degree, all of which were unpunished; and that witnesses could not safely testify against them unless the more active members were placed under restraint.[13]

In view of what everyone in responsible places knew of conditions in the South, then, there might well have been far more intervention by the national government than there was. The legal authority as well as the moral justification existed. But Grant faced a dilemma. His natural inclination was to enforce the law, punish the perpetrators of crime, vindicate his own work in the war by keeping inviolate the achievements of the conflict, and to carry out the mandate given him by the electorate and by the Congress to enforce the new amendments to the Constitution. Yet he disliked assuming the extraordinary powers needed to protect the freedmen; he had the advice of men like Fish who insisted that either because of constitutional or political reasons military intervention was wrong; and he also came to see that the government's support frequently went to assist one faction of Republicans in the South against another or to prop up a regime whose reputation was none too savory. In his dilemma, Grant pursued an erratic and inconsistent course, but more often than not refrained from interference. This was largely because, considering Reconstruction completed, he felt that it was best for each state to handle its own internal affairs according to the precepts of the federal system. All of which is understandable but Grant reaped a harvest of ill will for the intervention that did occur and yet failed in any conclusive way to halt the trend toward subjugation of the black race in the former rebel states.

Closely related to this question of ending Reconstruction in the South was the amnesty problem. When Grant assumed office, the Fourteenth Amendment excluded from office in state and national government all who had, before the war, taken an oath to uphold the Constitution, and who had subsequently engaged in rebellion. While the Congress, under the provision of the amendment for removal of the disability, had enacted special pardons for a great many ex-Confederates, there were still some 150,000 ineligible for public office. Grant appeared to be moving toward a more extensive general amnesty in March 1870.[14] But just at this time several states were requesting federal aid to suppress lawlessness, and the President decided against a declaration, which, he told a cabinet meeting, would make

Aleck Stephens, Jeff Davis & Robert Lee & others eligible to seats in the Senate or House of Representatives. He [Grant] had hoped for the early & full readmission of all the rebel states, & their entire pacification, had that been accomplished & quiet fully restored, he would have been glad to recommend a general amnesty.[15]

Nothing more was done until the following spring, when the House passed an amnesty bill, but the Senate did not act until January 1872, and then only to defeat the measure. Defeat came because a number of Senators refused to accept Charles Sumner's entire civil rights bill tacked on as an amendment. Just prior to this in his annual message in December, Grant had urged passage of an amnesty bill to be extended to all except possibly a few of the "great criminals, distinguished above all others for the part they took in opposition to the Government. . . . " Following the set-back on January 1872, Congress took its own time to act, but at length on May 22, 1872, Grant signed a general amnesty bill after Sumner's attempt to attach his civil rights bill had been voted down in the Senate. The act removed the prohibition against office holding from all but about five hundred men who had been in high position in the federal government before joining the Confederacy. Congress even then could still pass acts of pardon for individuals, a process that continued until 1898, when a complete amnesty was adopted.[16]

These steps taken by the Grant administration—the readmission to the Congress of the remaining unreconstructed Southern states, support of the Fifteenth Amendment, the amnesty act, as well as the enforcement acts, the Ku Klux Act, and the employment of troops in certain instances in compliance with federal law and the requests of individual governors—constitute a reasonable and practical Southern policy, one that erred, if at all, on the side of too much restraint. Shortly before the 1872 election, Hamilton Fish addressed a Southern correspondent on the subject of the accomplishments of the Grant administration. His assessment is worthy of note.

You have had [Fish wrote] four years experience of Gen Grant's Civil administration. Coming into office at a period when much of the animosity excited by the war still remained when the states which had seceded were still out of the Union, when vast numbers at the South were disfranchised, & incapacitated from holding office, we now see a general feeling of kindness, & a return to the fraternal recognition between North & South which marked the era of the past. Every State is now represented in the Senate of the U. S. Every Congressional District has its representative in the House of Representatives. No man at the South is disfranchised by any Law of the United States & with the exception of a very few (probably not to exceed a hundred) no man is disqualified from holding office. ... Although much remains to be accomplished, it cannot be denied that much has been attained, & I feel justified in saying that to Gen Grant is due in a very large degree the credit of securing what has been accomplished. ...

Grant, let it be said, faced an impossible task of bringing peace and tranquility to the country following the upheaval of civil war and of assuring fair treatment to the freedmen. That he fell short of complete success in the first, and failed in the second was not his personal responsibility. The road to reunion stretched out over many decades and the failure to solve the nation's racial problems stemmed from the deep-seated prejudice of the Northern whites who would not follow through with the policy of equality initiated during the Civil War and brought to a climax in the legislation and amendments of the Reconstruction years. The failure resulted also from the determined and often violent opposition to the uplifting of the black race on the part of virtually all the white population of the South. The first Grant administration showed evidence of the

inevitable drift to white supremacy and the triumph of the
Democratic party in the Southern states.[17]

CHAPTER VIII

Finance and Foreign Affairs

THE SOUTHERN QUESTION DID NOT RECEIVE ALL THE ATTEN-
tion of the President and his cabinet. During the first administration important financial and diplomatic problems had to be
faced. In the area of monetary policy Grant was content to turn
over the conduct of the Treasury Department to the secretary,
George S. Boutwell. This does not mean, of course, that Grant
was not concerned about fiscal affairs, nor does it mean that he
neglected to oversee the formulation of basic policy, but he took
the military commander's attitude that a subordinate should be
given authority and be allowed to carry out his own plans. Just
as this policy worked well with a Sherman, a Sheridan, or a
Thomas, and just the opposite with a Butler or a Burnside, so too
its results varied with different cabinet officers. Fortunately for
Grant, Boutwell turned out to be an acceptable Secretary of the
Treasury and conducted the affairs of his department along lines
of moderation and to the satisfaction of the conservative, hard-
money, businessmen of the day. Since Grant did not become
intimately involved in the financial affairs of the Treasury Department, it would hardly be necessary to dwell at length on the
various measures and policies entered into during the early
period of his administration. Suffice it to say that Boutwell pursued policies wholly in keeping with the lines laid down by the
President in his inaugural address. Hardly had the administration
been safely launched when Congress passed the Public Credit
Act (March 18, 1869) stating that the policy or the government
was to repay the bonded debt in coin (and at that time, that
meant gold) unless the terms specified some other form of payment. One of the issues of the previous election had been the
so-called Ohio idea which was a scheme to repay the war debt
in greenbacks, or inflated currency. The action of Congress,
which accorded neatly with the views of both Grant and Boutwell, reflected the strong desire of those business and financial
interests who feared above all else the threat of inflation and a
currency not tied to gold.

A little over a year later, in July 1870, Congress passed and
Grant signed a funding bill which lightened the task of the Treasury in paying interest on the war debt and meeting payments
on short-term bonds, and an Internal Revenue and Tariff Act
which retained the wartime policy of high protection, and ended
the unpopular income tax (to take effect in 1872). While Grant
and his administration wished in principle that there be a resumption of specie payment various factors prevented this until
the very end of the decade although the resolve to redeem the
greenbacks in gold was announced in 1875.

These policies, while hardly imaginative or liberal in their
tendencies, did serve the immediate needs (and desires) of
most of the business community, and the prosperity prevailing
in these years of the early 70s earned the Grant administration
the general approval of the nation. In addition, Boutwell not
only effected reforms in the collection methods of the Treasury
Department but also reduced the national debt by some 100
millions in his first year in office and by 364 millions during the
four years of his tenure. Grant took considerable pride in this
and the country, generally, liked the idea of whittling away at
the over two billion dollar war debt.[1]

The record of both Boutwell and Grant in the Black Friday
episode is a good example of the character of the administration. During that first summer when in most respects the affairs
of the nation seemed to be progressing in smooth fashion,[2] the
President and the treasury secretary were made to look foolish
by the machinations of the notorious New York financiers, Jay
Gould and James Fisk. That Grant could allow such a debacle
to happen to him can only be explained by his inexperience,
his willingness to believe the best about anyone, and his lack of
understanding of complicated financial dealings. Even when all
the excuses and the last extenuating circumstance are considered, the President's faulty judgment and unwise associations
cannot be gainsaid. Unfortunately, this was to be more or less
typical of the administration as a whole — mature and wise
handling of some truly difficult problems of both domestic and
foreign character, but some incredibly inept bungling in others.
This contrast, so typical of the general's life as a whole, is what
made him so enigmatic. How could a man so brilliant in war, so
sound in his judgments of men in most instances, so experienced in life, who had spent four years in Washington,
where he had a chance to see all aspects of public affairs and
had personally been in the midst of a ruthless personal dispute,

commit such follies as President? There is no satisfactory answer; the best that can be offered is that intellectually Grant did not measure up to the vigorous demands of the office. That is, he did not possess the broad background to enable him to deal in all instances intelligently with administrative, political, fiscal, and foreign policy matters.

Moreover, in the early years, at least, Grant did not feel socially secure and was so undiscriminating that he could on the same trip away from Washington accept the hospitality of Jim Fisk on the one hand and Hamilton Fish on the other and apparently not be conscious of the wide gulf separating the two. Grant's own upbringing was not such as to prepare him for social contacts with cultivated gentlemen. The superficial gloss of wealth dazzled Grant's eyes to the point where all financially successful men appeared on the same social level.

In any event, Grant, for a time, fell victim of a scheme (not a true conspiracy, although that term has been freely used to describe these happenings), not illegal but of dubious propriety, to raise the price of gold for personal profit. For the plan to succeed the cooperation of the administration was needed, since the Treasury Department, following Boutwell's policy of regularly replenishing the gold supply needed for commercial (mostly international) purposes, sold gold, taken in as customs receipts, on the open market in New York City. Should the Treasury refrain from selling gold for even a short time, the merchants engaged in international transactions, and gold speculators who contracted ahead of time for gold, could be forced into paying a high premium to Gould, who planned to buy up gold and thus drive up the price. At the time Gould conceived his plan it took approximately $135 in greenbacks to purchase $100 in gold. With gold at that price, reasoned Gould, American farm crops would not find a market in Europe, but if the price could be driven up to $145, not only would the European buyer get more American farm products for his money but the American farmers would be more interested in selling.

Naturally, the scheme would not work unless Gould and his partner, the former Yankee peddler, Jim Fisk, could somehow persuade the President or the Secretary of the Treasury, to withhold gold from the market. The best way to do this was to try to convince Grant that the farmers of America would benefit if the price of gold, in greenbacks, were made to go up. Useful to Gould was Abel Rathbone Corbin, elderly New York manipulator who just happened to be married to Grant's sister,

Jenny. Corbin was a man of dubious ethics when it came to making quick money, and he readily fell in with Gould whom he tried to convince that he had a good deal of influence with Grant. He was wrong, but the country did not know it.

Grant's biggest mistake in this whole unsavory episode was his acceptance of Fisk's hospitality and permitting himself to be seen in his and Gould's company. Had he possessed a true sense of propriety he would never have allowed his own reputation and that of the office he filled to be besmirched by association with men whose standing was such that even he himself is said to have remarked that Fisk was "destitute of moral character." But the President, as already noted, was unable to discriminate in such matters, and Gould was a friend of his sister's husband. Out of loyalty to a member of the family he would of course accept her husband's friends.[3]

Gould's initial efforts to persuade Grant to keep gold off the market were unavailing, but about September 1, the President notified Boutwell that he believed it would not be wise to sell gold in the amounts the secretary had disposed of during the summer, because he wanted to keep the price from dropping. Gould, in all likelihood, found out about this decision, and on the basis of that information, proceeded to purchase gold in considerable quantities on the exchange in New York.

Increasing the possibilities of a favorable result for the plan, Grant on September 13 left for Pennsylvania, to visit his wife's cousin. With Grant away from both Washington and New York, the chances for complete success seemed favorable. Gould also enlisted Fisk's financial support in buying up gold by assuring him that not only Corbin but also President and Mrs. Grant were in on the scheme. The two manipulators were able to drive the price up from 135½ on September 13 to 140½ on September 22.

Gould, however, was worried lest Boutwell on his own initiative sell gold to relieve the pressure. Rumors were circulating that this might be done after the secretary had visited New York. So, to reassure Gould, Corbin agreed to write Grant a letter reviewing the crop-moving theory and again stressing the necessity of having the Treasury keep gold off the market. Corbin's letter, sent by special messenger, made Grant suspicious, and he asked his wife to write to Mrs. Corbin to have her husband stop his speculations. When Gould found out about Mrs. Grant's letter he knew that he must unload quickly. But he failed to notify Fisk, who continued to buy until the price reached 163½ just before noon on September 24, Black Friday.[4]

The President arrived in Washington on the twenty-second to be greeted by frenzied stories of the chaos in New York and of the pleas of those short of gold, and indeed of disinterested parties, to have the government sell gold immediately.

Boutwell's policy was not to interfere with Wall Street affairs, as he assumed correctly that for every person who wanted the price of gold to rise there was another who wanted it to drop. But the situation was getting out of control, innocent persons were being injured, and normal business was seriously disrupted. Even then, neither Boutwell nor Grant took any action until the morning of Friday the twenty-fourth, when it was agreed that the Treasury, in New York, should sell four millions of gold. Gould's sales, those of some powerful bears, and now the treasury announcement, broke the price about midday; it tumbled to 133 in only fifteen minutes.

Black Friday was the subject of a House investigation the next year, but the Republican majority treated the whole thing quite gingerly, especially when the trend of the investigation began to get too close to the President and his wife. The Democratic minority made broad hints that Grant was more deeply involved than the testimony revealed, but there is no evidence that he was guilty of anything other than indiscretion.

The associations with Gould and Fisk could only make people wonder what kind of judgment Grant possessed. Few believed him guilty, but many had doubts about Boutwell's wisdom in delaying so long in his decision to sell gold, and about Grant's choice of an assistant treasurer in New York, General Daniel Butterfield, who, it turned out, had been involved personally in the speculation and was obliged to resign.[5]

Grant handled more adroitly the matter that came up a few months later involving the greenback question, and also appointments to the Supreme Court. The administration's monetary policy had been theoretically stated in the Public Credit Act, but in practice there was no intention of an immediate return to a metallic currency. In the previous administration Secretary of the Treasury Hugh McCulloch had followed a policy of contraction, which proved unpopular in that it led to a reduction in prices and a relative scarcity of money. Grant and Boutwell, therefore, had no intention of retiring any more greenbacks, at least in the immediate future. The greenback had willy-nilly become an essential element in the nation's monetary system. There were 356 millions in greenbacks outstanding at the time Grant assumed office, and, while of less value than gold dollars, were nonetheless used as legal tender as provided by the wartime acts of 1862 and 1863.

In a 5–3 decision in the case of *Hepburn* v. *Griswold* handed down on February 7, 1870, Chief Justice Salmon P. Chase, speaking for the majority, pronounced the Legal Tender Acts unconstitutional insofar as contracts entered into prior to enactment were concerned. The decision was a shock to Grant, Boutwell, and others of the administration who envisaged economic chaos stemming from so immediate a return to specie payment. There existed at the time of the decision, however, hope, even expectation, that the decision would be subsequently reversed.

Fortunately, at this very time, Grant had the opportunity to appoint two new members to the Supreme Court. On the day of the *Hepburn* decision, he named Joseph P. Bradley of New Jersey and William Strong of Pennsylvania, both Republicans and already on record as supporters of the constitutionality of the Legal Tender Act. In other greenback cases then before the Court, the two new justices sided with the old minority, thus giving a 5–4 decision in the cases of *Knox* v. *Lee* and *Parker* v. *Davis*, in May 1871. This reversal was undoubtedly best for the country at the time.[6]

Of course, Grant's political enemies made the charge of court packing, and to a certain extent this was true, if Grant was seeking a reversal of the decision and had a good idea ahead of time how his appointees would rule in any new case before the Court. But Grant was not adding new members to the legal constitution of the Court, nor did he in any way seek to exact pledges from Bradley or Strong. They were qualified men who served capably on the Court, and Grant had every right, constitutional and ethical, to appoint them. All things considered, the financial affairs of the nation were competently handled during the first Grant administration. The nation prospered and the business community in general was satisfied.

Foreign affairs absorbed much of the attention of the Grant administration in its first year in office. Grant ordinarily wanted the individual cabinet member to run his own department, but the State Department was a notable exception at this stage of Grant's presidential career. During these first months three major problems existed in this field, the most outstanding being the unsettled depredation claims against Great Britain, commonly known as the Alabama Claims. The second, and the one which caused Hamilton Fish the most worry, was the Cuban revolution. Finally, there was the controversy, mostly of Grant's own making, over the proposed annexation of the Dominican Republic, usually referred to as Santo Domingo. In the later years of the administration, Grant seldom interfered in Fish's department other than to have a voice in appointments, but at this time, Fish had to fight off an inordinate amount of well-meaning but largely inept interference from the inexperienced President. This is all the more strange when it is realized that Grant had every confidence in his secretary and recognized his growing dependence on him.

As for the problem with Great Britain, soon after Grant took office, the Senate overwhelmingly rejected the treaty negotiated by the Johnson administration (the Johnson-Clarendon Convention) for the settlement of the Alabama Claims, in part because Senator Charles Sumner, chairman of the foreign relations committee, delivered an excessively bellicose speech opposing the treaty. Fish thus had to start anew. As minister to England, Grant somewhat against his desires appointed the historian John Lothrop Motley, Sumner's close friend. Since the senator wished to direct foreign policy in person, he expected Motley to follow his instructions rather than those issued by Fish. And Grant could hardly appreciate Motley. He complained to Badeau that the historian parted "his hair in the middle" and carried "a single eyeglass"; he might also have admitted to a feeling of uneasiness, even of inferiority, in the presence of a man of such erudition. Beyond that, Motley disobeyed orders, and Grant could never tolerate insubordination. So when he learned, through Badeau, who was secretary of legation in London, of Motley's intention to do Sumner's bidding rather than to obey Fish in continuing the negotiations over the Alabama Claims, he wanted him dismissed forthwith. Fish, with some difficulty, persuaded Grant to leave Motley alone so as to avoid a rupture with the influential Sumner, but he did take the negotiations into his own hands, leaving Motley with only ceremonial functions to perform in London.

That summer Fish had some informal conversations with the Canadian, John Rose, initially on the subject of a reciprocity treaty, but soon about the topic of the Alabama Claims question and the possibility of discussions being held in Washington. All the while Fish worried lest Sumner and Grant unite in an aggressive policy against England which might lead to war, a

conflict which Grant, at least, would have no hesitancy in accepting. But the summer passed, and then the fall; relations
with Britain remained unfriendly, but neither side showed any
disposition to proceed farther toward an open rupture. One
reason for Grant's unwillingness to press the British government on the early recognition of the belligerent status of the
Confederacy was his obvious desire to extend recognition of
belligerency to the Cuban insurgents, at this time in the second
year of a revolt against Spanish rule.

The Cuban rebels had declared independence but had failed
to establish any sort of real government, controlled no important cities, and maintained no capital. Their small, ill-equipped
army mainly conducted guerilla operations against the Spanish
forces.

American sympathies inevitably were with the Cubans, and
considerable aid was extended by virtue of filibustering expeditions, shipments of arms, and especially monetary support to
the junta operating out of New York. Members of Congress
frequently expressed their sympathies for the insurgents and
urged recognition not only of Cuban belligerency, but even of
independence. Grant shared some of this sentiment and inclined toward a proclamation extending belligerent recognition
to the Cubans, and in this desire he was strongly influenced by
his Secretary of War, John A. Rawlins. Fish especially feared
Rawlins' influence upon Grant. What the secretary hoped to
avoid was a conflict with Spain which would be an unwanted
war, since there were so many pressing domestic problems to
solve, particularly those of a financial nature. Furthermore he
objected to interference in his department. Fish suspected, but
did not have solid proof at the time, that Rawlins held a considerable number of bonds of the incipient Cuban government,
which made him something less than a disinterested advisor to
the President. To direct Grant's attention away from a proclamation that might lead to war with Spain, Fish initiated an
attempt to induce Spain to relinquish her hold on Cuba in return for a money payment from Cuba guaranteed by the United
States. Fish's efforts were, however, unavailing.[7]

The President, urged on by Rawlins, and convinced that order could never be restored by Spain, told Fish in August that
he had drawn up a proclamation of recognition of Cuban belligerency to which he wanted Fish to apply the Great Seal. Fortunately for Fish, the negotiations for the liberation of Cuba were
moving along favorably at that time in Madrid under the direc-

tion of General Daniel Sickles, and he took advantage of an opening Grant had given him to delay issuance of the proclamation. On August 31, the President authorized him to urge on the Spanish government a settlement of the Cuban question with a veiled threat of possible American intervention should this not materialize.

Then, suddenly, but hardly unexpectedly, the situation improved with the death of Rawlins on September 6. Rawlins had suffered from tuberculosis for a number of years and in recent months had grown progressively worse. Grant, who had left Washington for Saratoga after the August 31 cabinet meeting, now rushed back to Washington to see once more his faithful lieutenant, only to arrive an hour late.

With Rawlins not present to press for recognition, the pro-Cuban faction drifted leaderless, and Fish could gain a brief respite in a contest which lasted throughout the Grant administration and which ceased only when the revolution petered out in 1878. In his first annual message to Congress, Grant, following Fish's lead, reiterated the administration's policy of no recognition in view of the Cubans' inability to make good their claim of independence.

Congress, however, would not let the matter drop. When Grant showed signs of weakening, and when the press, much of which favored Cuban recognition, claimed that the President and Fish were at odds over Cuban policy, Fish asked Grant to send a strong message to Congress stating in emphatic words that the administration was opposed to recognition. The President had a different idea: to transmit to Congress Fish's views with a covering letter. Fish, in effect, said no thanks. The letter would only reinforce the impression that he had one policy and the President another. He believed strongly that Grant should personally assume all the responsibility for administration policy and that if he could not have Grant's support he (Fish) had better resign. Unable to allow this development, the President had to yield to the secretary's terms. Grant sent the desired message to Congress just as a debate began, which, had the President not intervened, might well have resulted in a resolution calling for recognition of Cuban belligerency. The President's request had the anticipated result, for on June 16, 1870, the vote in the House was 100–70 against a resolution for recognition of belligerency. Fish naturally was elated over the outcome, and a short while later Grant conceded that Fish had saved him from a grievous error.[8]

One reason why Grant was hesitant about according belligerent recognition to the Cubans was the fear that this would jeopardize the American case against the British. Another factor in his failure to press the matter any harder than he did (in addition to his unwillingness to have Fish quit the cabinet) was his greater concern over the proposal to annex the Dominican Republic.

Grant's obsession with this endeavor is another element in the enigma of his character. Intrinsically, there was nothing bad about the idea of annexing the Caribbean republic; on the contrary there was much to commend it. The oddity of the whole affair was the manner in which the President made it so all-important, the way he bent every effort to accomplish his goal long after any seasoned politician would have seen the futility of trying further. The upshot of it was a humiliating defeat for the President and further questioning of his good judgment. The explanation for Grant's behavior in this episode must lie in his innate stubbornness and his strong desire to win once the battle was engaged. But in this instance he staked too much on a prize that was not worth the consequences of defeat.

The idea was not Grant's in the first place; rather it came from probably two sources: the then government of the Dominican Republic itself, and Grant's boyhood friend and wartime comrade, Admiral David Ammen. Ammen believed in the need for a Caribbean base to protect a future isthmian canal, and the Dominican government was seeking an easy way out of its perennial difficulties, mostly financial. Interest in a canal was nothing new, and in the previous administration, Seward, who appreciated the obvious need for a naval base, had made several moves toward acquiring territory in the Caribbean, notably a treaty with Denmark for the sale of the Danish West Indies to the United States (a treaty still pending when Grant took office), and an abortive effort to acquire a lease of Samana Bay, Santo Domingo's major harbor. The time was not right, however, for acquiring new territory, especially after Alaska had been added in 1867. Manifest Destiny languished during this post-war era and the public simply was not interested. Congressmen felt no pressure from their constituents. While all this would change before the end of the century, it was Grant's misfortune to meet up with massive apathy in trying to promote this expansionist scheme.

Yet the most immediate reason for objection to the annexation of Santo Domingo was the unsavory characters associated with the enterprise, and the possibilities for personal gain on the part of some men close to the President, notably General Orville E. Babcock. Despite the fact that Babcock was probably innocent of any wrong-doing, and despite the safeguards against corruption written into the treaty of annexation, the whole scheme smelled bad to the public and Grant could never dispel the aroma.[9]

The two principal promoters were a couple of American adventurers, Colonel Joseph W. Fabens and General William Cazneau, who were in league with the President of the republic, Bonaventura Baez. All of these stood to gain if the United States could be persuaded to purchase the country. Approaching Fish on April 5, 1869, Fabens suggested that the United States might want to buy Santo Domingo. Fish, naturally cautious, and having no real interest in such an idea, put Fabens off. The next day he brought up the matter at a cabinet meeting but expressed his opposition and suggested that the impetus should come from Congress. Grant showed considerable interest, however, and decided to find out more about the possibilities presented by Fabens. A naval vessel was dispatched to the region, yet the reports the commander brought back were inconclusive. Then, at Grant's request, Fish selected another man to investigate, but he became sick and was unable to go.

Grant then turned to Orville Babcock, his military secretary, in whom he had the utmost confidence. Thus far, Babcock had merited that trust, proving himself to be a bright, energetic, and ambitious young man. He was rapidly working himself into a position of power next to the President, and he naturally liked it. Later, the assumption was that Grant, without notifying anyone, not even Fish, sent Babcock off with authority to sign a treaty of annexation, and that when the young officer returned with such a treaty the whole cabinet was astounded and embarrassed. But Fish knew all about Babcock's mission; in fact, he wrote his orders, and it was distinctly understood that Babcock, an army officer, could have no diplomatic authority whatsoever. Babcock did, however, go beyond the harmless instructions Fish had written, and returned with a *projet*, or draft treaty of annexation which was binding on neither party. Even so, the terms of this preliminary agreement were potentially compromising in that the United States would be obligated to extend military protection to the Baez government against foreign aggression (a veiled reference to Haiti).[10]

With Grant out of town in Pennsylvania, just as the gold crisis was reaching a climax, Fish wrote to the President giving him an account of Babcock's report in a strictly factual way, neither expressing approval nor disapproval. When the matter was discussed at a cabinet meeting, Grant announced Babcock's return with a draft treaty. While Cox, who wrote about this many years later, was probably correct in asserting that the announcement was greeted by embarrassed silence, he was wrong in his statement that Grant took everyone by surprise, because Fish certainly, and others probably, were well acquainted with Babcock's mission. At a later meeting, on October 19, 1869, Fish presented the draft of a treaty of annexation which he himself had prepared, only to find that the cabinet was divided on the idea, with several members indifferent.

In November, Babcock returned to Santo Domingo, and, with the United States commercial agent, Raymond H. Perry, officially signing, concluded two documents, one a treaty of annexation, the other a convention calling for a lease of Samana Bay, to take effect only in the event that annexation failed. Although the cabinet heard of Babcock's accomplishments on December 21, Grant did not send the documents to the Senate till after the beginning of the new year.

Before doing so, he made a visit to Charles Sumner, hoping to enlist the support of the chairman of the Senate Foreign Relations Committee. Grant did not help things by two or three times referring to Sumner as chairman of the Judiciary Committee. A discussion ensued in which neither man really understood the other. Grant rose to leave, after telling Sumner that Babcock would come around the next day with more information on the treaty and the convention, and Sumner, going to the door with the President, remarked something to the effect that he was an administration man and would carefully consider the subject. The remark became the subject of much controversy in the weeks to follow, with Grant contending that Sumner had clearly stated his willingness to support annexation, but Sumner merely admitting to a promise to consider the matter carefully. Here was the occasion for an open break between the President and Sumner, a relationship which was tenuous at best, and considerably strained ever since the Motley business some months earlier, and especially after Sumner found out that he was not going to direct the nation's foreign affairs according to his own desires.[11]

Grant sent the treaty and convention to the Senate on January 10, and then had to wait while that sensitive body went through the process of making a decision. The President must have assumed immediate popular support for annexation, because there was no attempt made to educate the public. Rather the news broke amidst rumors of corrupt deals and other types of fraud connected with those private interests eager for annexation.

Fish faithfully supported Grant throughout the struggle for the treaty. It is uncertain whether this was strictly because of loyalty, because Fish sincerely believed in annexation, or because, as some historians assert, he had a greater concern for avoidance of a resolution recognizing Cuban belligerency, and hoped that by keeping Grant diverted by the annexation business, he could have a better chance of keeping in his own hands the forthcoming negotiations with England. The evidence to support the latter position is mostly circumstantial. The secretary himself never stated it; rather most of his diary entries either do not indicate any strong hostility to annexation, or show just the opposite—a willingness to see it occur.

Grant shamelessly worked on individual senators to try to win over the wavering and to convince those opposed. It was futile. The opposition to the treaty had built up to the point where a Republican-dominated Foreign Relations Committee voted 5–2 against approval of the treaty. There followed a full Senate debate, highlighted by a lengthy speech by Sumner on March 24. The debate dragged on with no appreciable change in the attitude of the senators one way or the other. Grant sent to the Senate a special message of his own composition offering some safeguards against financial deals that would benefit individuals, but keeping the essential features of the original agreement. Becoming quite eloquent (and not altogether accurate) in his predictions of the benefits that would flow from the union of the two countries, he went over again all the arguments in favor of annexation. Needless to say this did not sway any senator who had already made up his mind; there was, in fact, some objection to the President putting his reputation on the line in such a reckless way.[12]

The inevitable defeat came on June 30, after the opposition had exposed the imprisonment in Santo Domingo of an American citizen who happened to oppose annexation and who could have been released had Babcock cared to take the trouble to request it. Naturally, the assumption was that Babcock wanted to have the man out of the way while the treaty was being acted upon. That the proponents of annexation would stoop to such vile tactics ruined any slight chance the treaty might have had, and the final vote, 28-28, constituted a crushing defeat for Grant. Nineteen Republicans and nine Democrats voted in opposition to the President. One wonders why he had allowed such a state of affairs to come to pass.

No speculation is needed to explain his pursuit of the matter after what should have been the final *coup de grâce*. Grant felt the need to vindicate himself and his friends. The attacks had been especially vicious; his motives had been challenged, and his honor besmirched. Victory might have evaded him, but at least he could prove to the country that the right was on his side. Thus he turned to the idea of a commission, made up of disinterested men, who would visit Santo Domingo and give an unbiased report on the desirability of annexation. They would also be authorized to negotiate a new treaty of annexation. The annual message contained such a request, but Grant's friends, knowing full well that there was no chance of the Senate approving an annexation treaty, introduced instead a resolution authorizing only a commission of inquiry with no power to negotiate a treaty of annexation. Grant seized at this half a loaf, and, after some refusals, put together a highly respectable three-man commission: former Senator Ben Wade, Andrew D. White, president of Cornell University, and Samuel Gridley Howe, philanthropist from Massachusetts, famed for his work with the blind. In addition, the Negro leader, Frederick Douglass, went along as assistant secretary, and also included in the group were expert geologists and other scientists, as well as a large delegation of reporters. Fish was pleased with the make-up of the commission, telling Washburne that "their names disarm criticism and inspire every one with confidence, and present the most emphatic rebuke to those who attempt to question the sincerity of the President's motive, ..." A report sent to the Senate in reply to charges of Sumner will, Fish continued, lead unprejudiced minds "to find that the President's action has been more deliberate and more in the line of enlarged and wise statesmanship than those who denounce his course, in the Senate and in the press, have been willing to accord him."[13]

The commission arrived in Santo Domingo January 24, 1871, and remained until the latter part of March. While the members probably saw mostly the favorable side of things during their stay, they were men of sufficient intelligence and sense of responsibility to present something other than a whitewash to clear Grant's good name, for they were under no obligation to do that. That the report in every way vindicated the President, recommended annexation, and dismissed the charges of corruption is worthy of note. Yet all it afforded Grant was a certain sense of satisfaction. He submitted the report to the Congress on April 5, 1871, stating that the investigation had demonstrated the good faith of the President and those serving him, but that "now my task is finished, and with it ends all personal solicitude upon the subject." Nothing more was done about Santo Domingo, except that Grant mentioned it again in his last annual message in 1876, showing that he still believed he was right.

In addition to forcing the Republican party into a dangerous internal struggle, the Santo Domingo imbroglio had an indirect effect upon negotiations with England over the Alabama Claims in that it destroyed any chance that a Grant-Sumner combination would force a showdown that might lead to war. Fish, who desperately wanted a reasonable and peaceful settlement of the nation's difficulties with Great Britain, might well have welcomed not only the diversion of Santo Domingo but also the cooperation of the President which inevitably resulted from his (Grant's) bitter quarrel with Sumner. The President could more easily accept Fish's position if the despised Sumner adhered to an opposing foreign policy view.

The problem of Sumner was a chronic one, and it was only a question of what form it would overtly take. For Sumner expected to direct the foreign policy of the United States. The first sign of difficulty was over Motley's disobedience of Fish's instructions as soon as he arrived in London. But Fish persuaded Grant to allow Motley to retain his post so as to keep the peace with the senator. So Motley continued to represent the United States in England; yet he exercised no real authority. Even that arrangement did not satisfy Grant, and the day after the Senate rejected the treaty, Grant asked Fish to recall the historian. This was no sudden decision, for Grant had mentioned the matter to Fish some days earlier, but the two events did appear to be related, as they undoubtedly were. The only trouble was that two of Grant's choices for Motley's successor, Senators Frederick Frelinghuysen and Oliver Morton, refused the assignment, and, defiant to the last, Motley refused to give up the position. Grant became impatient and finally dismissed Motley, a most unusual step in the case of a first-class diplomatic position. It was something that had to be done and only Motley's stubbornness, encouraged by Sumner's hostility toward the administration, made it possible. Early in December, Grant selected for the London mission General Robert C. Schenck, Congressman from Ohio who had been defeated in the recent elections, and who could be counted on for loyal support to the administration.[14]

Motley's dismissal caused Sumner to sever all ties with the Grant administration, even with Hamilton Fish, with whom Sumner had long been on intimate terms. Sumner's open hostility caused Fish to state his belief in Sumner's insanity. With the chairman of the important Senate Foreign Relations Committee no longer on speaking terms with either the President or the Secretary of State, the time had come for another man to take his place as chairman. The administration had the right to expect the majority party to place a man in that position who had the trust and confidence, to say nothing of the cooperation, of the heads of the executive branch. This was sufficient reason for the action against Sumner, although there is no denying Grant's hostile feeling toward Sumner on personal grounds.

Grant could, at times, take a mildly amused attitude toward Sumner, as for instance, his reply to the remark that Sumner did not believe in the Bible. Grant's wry comment was, "no, I suppose not, he didn't write it." The fight over Santo Domingo, of course, influenced Grant in his desire to see a change in the chairmanship, for the general could be vindictive at times. Ordinarily he had a forgiving nature, but on occasion, and especially when he believed that he had been wrongfully abused (and Sumner had been unfairly abusive), he could be implacable in his hatred. Yet Fish was equally eager to see Sumner removed, and no reasonable man could take exception to the wish. After the Senate Republicans had voted to deprive Sumner of the chairmanship, Fish again referred to his belief that Sumner was crazy. The victory was not without its cost; Sumner, until his death in 1874, excoriated Grant with an acid tongue, and contributed considerably to his discomfort, even though Sumner's animosity seemed not to have any marked political effect. Grant disclaimed any intention of wishing to punish the senator for his opposition to Santo Domingo, rather, he insisted that all he asked was "that the Chairman of the Committee on Foreign Relations might be some one with whom the Secretary of State and myself might confer and advise. This I deemed due to the Country in view of the very important questions, which of necessity, must come before it."[15]

Sumner could do nothing to interfere with the negotiations with England which resumed early in the year. Grant, in his annual message of 1870, briefly mentioned their suspended status and expressed hope for a renewal of the efforts to bring about a settlement. He also, at Fish's suggestion, included a recommendation that Congress create a claims commission to collect evidence to support the American position, a gentle hint that American patience might not last forever. But the message also stated that the President would welcome a change in the British attitude.

Discussions between Fish and the British minister in Washington, Edward Thornton, did resume in January, the uncertainties of the international situation brought about by the Franco-Prussian War aiding the American cause. The Canadian, John Rose, now returned to Washington and the progress made was so great that early in February the two governments had agreed on a formal arrangement, under the terms of which each nation would appoint a commission of five to assemble in Washington for the purpose of negotiating a settlement of the Alabama Claims and other outstanding difficulties, such as the perennial fisheries question, and the dispute over ownership of the San Juan Islands in Puget Sound. After consultation with Fish and the rest of the cabinet, Grant appointed, in addition to Fish, General Schenck, the former Attorney General, E. R. Hoar, Senator George H. Williams of Oregon, and Justice Samuel Nelson of the Supreme Court. The British commissioners shortly after arrived in this country and met with the Secretary of State on February 24, 1871. Formal meetings began three days later.

Fish had complete charge of the negotiations. He had reached a point in his relations with Grant at which the President had perfect confidence in him. It is thus unnecessary to cover in any detail the deliberations leading up to the Treaty of Washington signed on May 8, 1871. Needless to say, Fish kept Grant informed as the talks proceeded, although they were not the subject of extended cabinet discussion.

The settlement, which left some matters for future arbitration and final disposal, was everything Americans could have justly desired: a virtual apology by the British for dereliction during the Civil War with agreement as to the proper behavior of neutrals in the future. The only matter not fully disposed of was that of the indirect claims, which would not get final burial until the Geneva meeting, when an international commission would meet to decide on the extent of the damages due the United States. Sumner, in particular, pressed these indirect claims. He believed that since Britain's actions had enabled the South to continue the war two years longer, the offending government must therefore assume the cost of the war for its last two years, a figure put at roughly two billion dollars. Fish did not favor this position and only failed to squelch it at the time of the negotiations because he worried over the possibility that Sumner might use this as an excuse for defeating the treaty in the Senate.

Approval by the Senate proved comparatively easy. Grant had called a special session for May 10, and, since Sumner proved tractable, the treaty encountered little opposition. The vote on May 24 was 50 to 12 in favor of ratification, which formally occurred June 17 in London. Grant could then proclaim the treaty in effect on July 4.[16]

It would be an injustice to Fish to give credit for this major diplomatic achievement to Grant. The President, at first, did not fully agree with his secretary on the line of approach to the Alabama Claims question, and it was Fish, who, virtually single-handedly, carried the negotiations through to a successful conclusion against the bitter hostility of Sumner. But Grant, after he had learned to trust Fish's judgment following their differences over Cuban recognition, had the good sense to leave the conduct of the negotiations to Fish, where they properly belonged. If Grant is to bear the blame for the sins of some of his other cabinet officers he should also be allowed to assume at least some of the glory for the magnificent handling of foreign affairs by his talented Secretary of State.

CHAPTER IX

The Struggle Over Reform

HAMILTON FISH PROVED TO BE MORE THAN A CAPABLE SECRE-
tary of State; he served the Grant administration in a number of
ways, particularly as a prudent adviser on domestic policy.
Within a short time, Grant came to realize how much he depended on Fish, how valuable the secretary was to the administration. Time and time again (one of these was after the treaty
had been approved by the Senate) the secretary tried to resign.
Each time Grant urged the dignified New Yorker, who had a
strong sense of duty, to remain. When Fish even went so far as
to present his resignation, a group of forty-four senators, along
with the Vice-President, did the unprecedented thing of writing
him a letter urging that he stay on as secretary. Fish yielded to
these pressures, especially the strong pleading of Grant himself,
and agreed to remain until the end of the term.

The relationship between Fish and Grant bears some examination. The fact that the secretary identified himself with the Grant
administration for all of its eight years is of considerable importance. Other men of honor, distinction, and ability held places in
Grant's cabinet, but none of these deserved the reputation of
Hamilton Fish, a patrician of the highest integrity to whom honor
and good name meant everything. The usual explanation (and it
could be the correct one) for Fish's willingness to bear the stigma
of an association with a regime whose reputation for respectability and integrity was not the best, is that his strong sense of duty
led him to make the sacrifice. Able to contribute something to his
country and to the Republican party by remaining in the cabinet,
he stayed on. Thus not only did he keep the foreign policy of the
nation on an even keel, but he also prevented the office of Secretary of State from falling into the hands of someone who might
easily adopt reckless and ill-advised policies. Grant, everyone
knew, could make some strange appointments, and there was no
telling who might be selected for this important office. The safest
thing for Fish to do was to hold on to it himself, make the sacrifice
of personal comfort, and risk a tarnished reputation for associat-

ing with the somewhat disreputable Grant administration.

This may all be true. But it ought not to be assumed that Fish merely tolerated Grant. On the contrary, a bond of affection grew between them which was freely admitted by both. In 1870, for instance, Fish wrote that he had "a very strong affection for the President, he is a very true man, and warm friend. ... " Grant frequently visited Fish in the evening, spending several hours at a stretch with the secretary. Nor did the President display toward Fish the extreme reticence he usually showed in the presence of those to whom he felt intellectually inferior. Fish had somehow penetrated Grant's armor, won his confidence, and established an intimate relationship which was of the utmost value to the President. To make this even more binding, Mrs. Fish in an unobtrusive and non-patronizing way became the social guide for Mrs. Grant, who appreciated her warm, friendly, and frank ways. Frequently Mrs. Grant would ask Mrs. Fish and other cabinet wives to assist her at receptions. What would seem, then, at first glance as almost an impossibility, that is, a genuinely intimate relationship between Grant and Fish, did exist. This is not to say that the secretary always appreciated or approved of the President's erratic behavior and sometimes thoroughly exasperating ways. The Fish diary contains any number of entries in which the secretary deplored some of Grant's inexplicable appointments or the backstairs influence of such men as Orville Babcock. No doubt Fish put up with an awful lot, but he did not always appreciate the political pressures under which Grant labored, nor the need, at times, to place political expediency ahead of an ideally desirable course. Naturally, they did not always agree, but Fish enjoyed the full confidence of the President and Fish quite clearly looked on Grant as a great man who was worthy of his full support but who needed steady guidance in the face of pressures not the healthiest.[1]

Grant was not always so fortunate in his cabinet choices, and at times, when he had a good man, he failed to keep him. In the first administration, the two obvious examples are E. Rockwood Hoar, Attorney General, and Jacob D. Cox, Secretary of the Interior. Both were of the highest integrity and ability, not the kind of selection the hard-bitten politicians would have made, but men who would do an outstanding job. Yet each ran afoul of the spoilsmen who had no genuine interest in the cause of reform.

Hoar was the first to go. Grant of course had known for a long time that many of the leading Republicans in Congress were quite unhappy over the Attorney General's scrupulous handling of patronage. Hoar was doing a fine job in most respects, but according to Boutwell, things reached the point where certain senators told Grant they would not visit the Justice Department as long as Hoar remained in charge. Furthermore, Ben Butler disliked Hoar and wanted the patronage which Grant had handed over to the Attorney General. Butler had given full support to annexation as well as to other administration policies and the Massachusetts Congressman's eagerness to see Hoar replaced could not easily be disregarded.

In addition, Grant was desperately trying to line up votes for the Santo Domingo treaty and especially wanted the whole-hearted support of the cabinet. But Hoar, while not actively opposing, had never shown any enthusiasm for annexation. Grant was well aware of this, mentioning the fact to Fish just two days before Hoar left the cabinet. Since both Hoar and Boutwell were from Massachusetts there had all along been some talk about Hoar's resigning; in fact he had told Grant repeatedly that his resignation could be had at any time. This provided a convenient excuse when Grant found it expedient to give a cabinet post to a Southern man. Southern Republican Senators had told Grant that to gain their support for the treaty, the South would have to get a cabinet position. Without any explanation whatsoever, Grant, on June 15, 1870 sent Hoar a terse note requesting his resignation. The Attorney General replied in kind, not because of any desire to show disrespect, but because he believed that his dignity precluded any other kind of reply. Then, in his note to Hoar accepting the resignation, Grant praised him for his patriotic and devoted service and expressed appreciation for the pleasant personal relations they had enjoyed.[2]

The loss of Hoar was bad enough, but Grant compounded the error by appointing in his place an obscure Georgian and ex-Confederate, Amos T. Akerman. This was the Southerner whose appointment would help win votes for the treaty of annexation. But the few votes this maneuver might have picked up were not enough and Grant lost not only the treaty but Hoar as well. Akerman served without distinction for a little better than a year then gave way to another second-rater, George H. Williams.

A second serious loss to the administration was the Secretary of the Interior, Jacob D. Cox. Cox administered his department

with ability and strict honesty, not bending to the demands of
the spoilsmen, but holding out courageously for a non-political
civil service. Also, it was under Cox that a more humane Indian
policy was initiated. In his inaugural address Grant had called
for "proper treatment of the original occupants of this land,"
and promised to "favor any course toward them which tends to
their civilization and ultimate citizenship." This was a hint of
the policy Grant would follow throughout his eight years in
office. The policy was one of peace, not war; of civilization, not
extermination, and though humanitarians and religious bodies
in the East could applaud the peace policy, Westerners, most
army men, and politicians interested in patronage and graft
were none too happy. Specifically, the plan called for all Indians not then under any governmental supervision to be placed
on reservations as quickly as possible, the Indians to be treated
in a humane, Christian manner. The hope was that the Indians
would take up agriculture and other civilizing pursuits and
would gain the benefits of education and Christian teaching.
What especially characterized the administration's policy was
the employment of denominational groups which had been active in Indian missionary work for the nomination of Indian
agents. Another feature of the policy was the Board of Indian
Commissioners, unpaid and with only advisory powers, which
would oversee, in cooperation with the Secretary of the Interior, the expenditure of funds for the various Indian reservations.

It was Cox who convinced Grant to have denominational
groups nominate the agents, and as early as May 1869 broad-
brimmed hats of members of the Society of Friends were seen
in the Interior Department offices. The experiment began with
their being given two agencies. Later other denominations sent
agents to the various Indian reservations.

The policy was not an unqualified success. The War Department never liked it and preferred the more direct approach.
Politicians resented the intrusion of amateurs into the business
of making government appointments. Nor did the denominational groups always nominate persons qualified for the job of
Indian agent, with the result that mismanagement and corruption were by no means stamped out. Frequently, the politically-
minded Secretary of the Interior, Columbus Delano, who
succeeded Cox in 1870, overrode the recommendations of the
Board of Indian Commissioners, and showed that he was not as
interested as they in rooting out inefficiency and corruption.

Even Grant did not always give firm support to the policy he himself had inaugurated. The most flagrant instance of this was the appointment of his brother Orvil to four agencies, which was not only nepotism, but morally indefensible.[3]

Secretary Cox had had an important hand in formulating and implementing the peace policy and earned the praise of humanitarians and reformers. He, however, was not popular with the Radicals, not only because of his conservative views on Reconstruction but also because of his intense interest in civil service reform. He had disappointed Grant by not supporting the annexation of Santo Domingo, but the President had reciprocated by failing, as Cox saw it, to support him in his efforts to keep the spoils system out of the Interior Department. At a cabinet meeting on October 4, 1870, with Cox absent, Grant, according to Hamilton Fish, related that, while he had been at Long Branch, Cox had written him that "he had labored to administer his Department honestly & to keep it free from fraud & corruption, & that if his efforts in that direction were not sustained by the President he would desire to be relieved from his office." Grant added that "he was fond of Cox & appreciated his thorough integrity, that his Dep't had been better administered by him than ever before, but this remark had 'cut him severely.' " So, when Cox, the next day, submitted his resignation, again referring to their difficulties on civil service reform, Grant wasted no time in accepting it. His letter was gracious, commending Cox for his fine work in administering his department, but the President was relieved to have him go. Columbus Delano, Ohio lawyer, former Congressman, and more recently head of the Internal Revenue Department, replaced Cox. He served without distinction, even with some question as to his integrity, for the odor of corruption surrounded his administration of the department.[4]

Although Grant's concern for civil service reform surely did not measure up to the expectations of Carl Schurz, Jacob Cox, or George William Curtis, the President, to his credit, did introduce the first serious reform into the government service and allowed the experiment a fair trial.

Civil service reform did not originate with Grant. The matter had been agitated for a number of years ever since the Civil War, especially by a Rhode Island Congressman, Thomas Allen Jenckes. Jenckes had several times introduced measures to establish a civil service commission and institute competitive examinations for civil service positions. In doing so he gained the support of a group of dedicated persons who were frequently from old New England families, descendants of merchants, clergymen, or civil servants, who lived on inherited wealth and deplored crass materialism. Often they had been free-soilers, rather than abolitionists, and in this post-war era were advocates of Negro suffrage with an educational qualification. In addition to being eager for civil service reform, they were promotors of low tariffs and hard money. In the years to come they would oppose unrestricted· immigration, organized labor, imperialism, and big government. What made their reforming demands somewhat suspect was the fact that in several cases they were disappointed office seekers themselves! Charles Eliot Norton, the Adams brothers—Henry, Charles Francis, and John Quincy—Charles A. Dana, and George William Curtis, either actively sought or would gladly have accepted places under Johnson and Grant, but they were not called. Then, in their disappointment and frustration, they joined the ranks of the reformers, consciously or unconsciously attacking the system because it had no place for their kind. Since these men were the most articulate group in the land, they helped to create the lasting impression that the civil service was more corrupt and evil during the Grant administration than at any other time in the nation's history. Yet the truth is that Grant made the only real effort toward civil service reform between the administrations of John Quincy Adams and Chester A. Arthur.

Grant did not embrace civil service reform naturally and with any enthusiasm. He made no mention of it in his first annual message and possibly came around to adopting a reform program more because of political reasons than any other. Both Boutwell and Cox had, on their own, done much to improve procedures in their departments. Boutwell had introduced rigid tests for prospective treasury employees and held the first competitive examinations in the history of the United States government in 1870. He did this not because of any deep concern for reform but rather because he recognized the need to fill the positions in his department with competent, skilled employees. Cox also instituted meaningful tests for his employees and made a genuine effort to rid such agencies as the Indian and Patent Offices and the Census Bureau of spoilsmen. He particularly fought the time-honored institution of assessing employees for campaign funds, and allowing them time off from work to go home to vote. Since Cox's resignation came because of a dispute with Grant over reform and the move was timed to coincide with the mid-term 1870 elections, it was inevitable that one conclusion to be drawn from Republican losses in those elections, especially in New York, was that the electorate was interested in civil service reform.[5]

Grant's annual message, coming on top of the party's election setback, contained a request for Congressional action in the field of hiring government employees. But Congress, instead of adopting procedures of its own, remanding the problem to the executive, authorized him to appoint a commission to establish rules for examining civil service applicants.

Grant then proceeded to assume the responsibility placed on him and as long as there was the least indication that Congress wanted the experiment to continue, with only a few glaring exceptions, he conscientiously and in good faith carried out the mandate. He made some excellent appointments to the nation's first Civil Service Commission. Heading it was George William Curtis, editor of *Harper's Weekly* and an avid reformer. Another prominent member was Joseph Medill, publisher of the *Chicago Tribune.* Through 1871 the members worked out a method of administering competitive examinations and other regulations governing the hiring and promotion of government employees. Grant could accept, revise, or reject the recommendations of the commission, but the regulations, as drawn up by the commission were accepted in principle by the cabinet on December 19, 1871, after the formal report had been handed to the President the day before. Grant had promised in his annual message of December 1871, to give the reform measures a fair trial and, somewhat to the surprise of his detractors, promulgated the new regulations on January 1, 1872, to go into effect immediately. Although it took a number of months to implement the system, which did not yet cover all government employees, it can be fairly stated that, in general, United States government employees were subject to a workable and fair civil service system for the next four years.

Yet it proved impossible at that time to establish anything permanent, for the system immediately produced numerous practical difficulties. Not desired even by some conscientious governmental leaders, it especially ran counter to the interests of the politicians. Even such an upright and conscientious public servant as Hamilton Fish had his doubts about the practicality of civil service reform, especially as it applied to the State Department.[6]

Grant himself was quite ready to make exceptions. For instance, when in cabinet meeting Fish complained that the regulations demanded examinations for prospective consuls, Grant replied, "Not if I suspend them, and direct the appointments." Nor could Grant pose as a friend of reform after his flagrant use of the patronage in such instances as the appointment of Thomas J. Murphy to the lucrative post of collector of the port of New York. Murphy turned over to George K. Leet, a member of Grant's war-time staff, part of what is known as the general order business, permitting Leet to collect storage charges on imported goods not picked up within two days. The charges, under Leet, became so exorbitant that merchants, including A. T. Stewart, complained to Grant. The President urged Murphy to get rid of Leet, but the collector convinced Grant that this was not necessary. A Senate investigation of the New York Custom House in 1874 revealed gross irregularities, not necessarily corruption, connected with the general order business as well as the moiety system, whereby the leading officials of the Custom House shared in fines imposed against importers who misrepresented the value of goods. The upshot of the investigation was that Leet was dismissed, the general order business was reformed, and the moiety system was eventually ended by Congressional action in 1874. Sometime before this, in November 1870, when Murphy was under attack in the press, he submitted his resignation. Grant wrote a warm testimonial stating his confidence in the collector and his belief in his entire innocence in charges brought against him.

Grant further antagonized the reformers by his failure to appoint an acceptable replacement for Alonzo Cornell, surveyor of the port of New York. Roscoe Conkling used his influence with Grant to induce him to appoint George H. Sharpe, in March 1873, without the knowledge of Curtis, and not according to the civil service regulations. On hearing of the appointment, Curtis resigned. But Grant did not give up on the new program. He showed his good faith by appointing Dorman B. Eaton, another ardent friend of reform, and Samuel Shellabarger to replace Joseph Medill, whose duties as mayor of Chicago forbade his remaining longer on the commission. In accepting Medill's resignation, Grant assured him "that the spirit of the rules adopted will be maintained."[7]

Part of Grant's trouble was the fact that he was under considerable pressure from his supporters in Congress, to whom he owed much, especially after the election of 1872. The Liberal Republicans, civil service reformers all, had attacked Grant for his nepotism and failure to go with them all the way on the road to reform. Thus the reformers were his enemies and the regular politicians, who did not care for civil service reform, were his best friends. And when these men wanted favors, Grant was not inclined to deny them. Both Butler and Conkling could obtain favors from Grant because the President found them loyal to him and his policies. They supported him down the line in the Congress; they spoke out for his administration and its policies both in Washington and on home soil. It is difficult to assess just how much influence each man had with Grant; Conkling probably had more than Butler. But the President would at least do his best to satisfy their patronage requests.

Yet it was not Grant who should bear the responsibility for the failure to establish a permanent civil service system. Rather the blame must fall on Congress, which had ample opportunity to enact the necessary legislation, but which failed in the end to do so. Congress, in May 1872, did appropriate $25,000 to continue the work of the commission, but it several times passed up opportunities to make the regulations which were set forth by the commission, and, incidentally, widely adopted throughout the federal service, extend beyond the Grant administration. It did give legal sanction to a continuation of the commission in 1874 but failed to make an appropriation. Furthermore, the Republican state conventions in 1875, with only one exception, failed to make mention of civil service reform.

Meanwhile the Panic of 1873 had diverted attention to the economic plight of the country. Civil service reform, never popular in Congress, was being forgotten. Some departments, notably Treasury and Interior, frequently ignored the regulations. So, in New York, Murphy's successor, Chester A. Arthur, with impunity followed the usual old-time patronage practices, even though he administered the custom house with a degree of efficiency.

Grant in his annual message in December 1874, reiterated his belief in the principles laid down in the civil service regulations then in effect, but reminded the Congress that it would have to give its support or else the system could not function. If the Congress failed to act, he wrote, competitive examinations would be dropped. Possibly Grant's appeal was not entirely convincing—perhaps his actions in some degree belied his words. Or, more likely, Congress was simply expressing the feelings of most politicians of that day. Whatever the reason, the legislators saw fit to ignore Grant's request and to Grant that was all that was needed. In March 1875, Grant announced to the cabinet that competitive examinations would no longer be held, and in July he as much as permitted the collection of campaign funds from federal employees.[8]

In the midst of a relatively busy public life, involving matters of state, Grant, as President, had to carry on a public social life. This, at first, was not altogether to his liking since he did not feel comfortable in a formal setting, resented having to wear evening dress, and preferred the company of his family or intimate personal friends. His inability to address a group with impromptu remarks undoubtedly contributed to his unease, as well as his sense of inferiority in the presence of men and women of culture and intellect, of whom there were many in the Washington of the Reconstruction period.

Despite his misgivings, however, Grant performed the necessary social duties and even came to temper his dislike of them. Indeed, he and Mrs. Grant set the standard for a gay and interesting Washington society which was the brightest and most active since the days before the Lincoln administration. Both the President and his wife took their social responsibility seriously, yet did not hesitate to introduce new practices and conventions whenever they saw fit. Thus, Mrs. Grant began the custom of receiving at her weekly afternoon receptions with other ladies of official Washington instead of doing it all herself, and Grant broke precedent by inviting only those Congressmen he chose to invite rather than running through the entire list, as in previous administrations.

Gradually, Grant overcame his diffidence, and, by the time of his second administration, was much more at ease with persons who were not known to him or were mere acquaintances. This is not to say he entirely overcame his tendency to remain silent, especially when he was in disagreement with the person with whom he was conversing. But the demands of his position forced him into a more natural attitude all the while retaining his geniality, humor, and conversational ability with intimates.

White House dinners were characteristically formal with a continental chef serving up multi-course repasts. While wines and liquors had their place at the White House table, there is no evidence whatsoever that Grant had any further difficulties in controlling his appetite for liquor. Earlier escapades had a psychological explanation, particularly the loneliness and insecurity Grant at times had to contend with. His last descent from grace appears to have been during the Swing around the

Circle in 1866, an exceptional aberration which was never again repeated. Before his election, Grant had informed General O. O. Howard that he was not then drinking, would not during that year take even any wine, and probably would abstain for the rest of his life. In 1872, Hamilton Fish gave emphatic assurance to a correspondent that Grant had never, to his knowledge, overindulged in drink.[9]

Aside from the public social functions he was obliged to attend, Grant and his family lived simply. His diversions were few, an interest in horses being the most absorbing. Occasionally, he would play cards with some close friends, or talk at length with wartime associates. Grant did not read for intellectual enrichment, and his literary tastes did not mark him as a man of erudition and culture. His mind was erratic. At times it would function so efficiently that those close to him would be astounded at the power of his mentality. But after these spurts of activity came stretches of indolence and seeming dullness. This contradiction, frequently noted by his contemporaries, has never been satisfactorily explained.

Though on occasion Grant paid lip service to the institutional church, he had no genuine interest in or concern with religion as such. Not that he had any doubts about an all-powerful God in Heaven, but all this was somehow not very close to him and he did not attend church regularly, nor was he an active member of any religious body. The habits he displayed in his later years simply were a continuation of those formed in childhood and as a young man. If he did accompany Mrs. Grant to services he went to the Methodist church, but more often than not, Grant remained at home on Sunday mornings.

Living virtually within the family were several young men who had served on Grant's staff during the war, and who were now detailed to the White House to perform secretarial duties. Among these was scholarly Adam Badeau, who briefly remained to complete his history of Grant's campaigns but who later went to England to serve as secretary to the legation in London. Very useful to Grant were Horace Porter, son of a former governor of Pennsylvania, and acquainted with the ways of society, and Julia's brother, Frederick Dent, who performed the duties of social secretary. But the man who most consistently and for the longest time had the ear of the President and who headed the backstairs group in the White House, was Orville E. Babcock, West Pointer, nephew of Grant's financial advisor, J. Russell Jones of Chicago, and husband of a Galena girl, Annie Campbell. Babcock, youthful, handsome, and sporting an imperial moustache and beard, had a gracious and disarming manner. No crude manipulator, Babcock had ability and above all ambition for power. Outwardly loyal to the President, he covertly pursued his own interests which may or may not have been dishonest. Most authorities believe the former. Grant trusted him thoroughly, and frequently allowed himself to be guided even in the most crucial state decisions by this young adventurer, much to the alarm and disgust of Hamilton Fish who deplored Babcock's influence over the President in the Cuban and Santo Domingo affairs.[10]

Because so many men of military affiliation were in such close proximity to the President, critics charged that the country was being run by a military clique. To the extent that Grant thought in military terms and considered the office of President equivalent to a generalship in the army, the charge had substance, but the idea of a militarily oriented administration was far from Grant's mind. He performed his duties in the only way he knew, and the loyalty displayed toward his military associates stemmed not from their being army officers, but rather from his genuine need for reassurance, a need that he had felt since the dark days before the war. Grant had a deep-seated respect for democratic government and the right of Congress to represent the will of the people. If at times he experienced frustration in dealing with Congress, he never allowed this to overcome his willingness to abide by whatever decision the lawmakers might make.

Grant had military men near him because these were the men he knew best and in whom he trusted. But he most enjoyed the company of his wife and his children. No one could be more the devoted family man than Grant. His love and affection for Julia were genuine and her influence on him was profound. While he seldom allowed her to interfere with his conduct of the office of President, Grant did listen to his wife in other matters. Thus, for example, it was she who may have induced him to accept gifts from friends, and even from strangers, since she wanted these things. And because she seems to have enjoyed living in the White House and partaking of the perquisites of her position, she wanted Grant to run for a third term.

When it came to the children, the Grants were indulgent to a degree rare in the second half of nineteenth century America. Never did they inflict physical punishment on them, and material wants were freely supplied. Both parents liked having the children at home, although Fred, the oldest, attended West Point during the early White House years (and had a most difficult time, academically and otherwise). Ulysses junior, or Buck, attended Harvard, which meant that only Nellie, and Jesse, the youngest, remained with their parents. Nellie spent a brief time at a girls' school in Connecticut but became homesick and was allowed to come home. Jesse had a similar experience at a boarding school in Pennsylvania three years later. He was homesick and complained of headaches. Fearing that he might be contracting typhoid, his mother had him return home. Jesse's schooling thereafter was of the informal variety. Nellie at the age of sixteen entered so enthusiastically into the social life of Washington that her parents deemed it wise to send her abroad. The device backfired, however, when on the return voyage she fell in love with an Englishman considerably her senior. In 1874, at a storybook White House wedding, Nellie, not yet nineteen, was married to Algernon Sartoris.[11]

Being President allowed Grant to indulge himself in his favorite diversion, travel, to the point where his political enemies criticized him for being away from Washington too much. The first summer of his presidency, Grant criss-crossed the northeastern part of the country, returning only briefly every few weeks to Washington to take care of necessary business. It was then that he began the practice of going to Long Branch, New Jersey, a custom which he and his family continued till the last year of his life. He was introduced to the shore resort by the wealthy Pennsylvanian, George W. Childs. There Grant would drive both morning and afternoon, sit on the porch, and converse with the many guests who frequented his "cottage." Other times he attended annual meetings of the Society of the Army of the Tennessee, or visited in St. Louis, Chicago, and other places around the northern part of the country. For some reason, he had a wanderlust, a trait noticeable from his youth, when he sought ways of avoiding work at his father's tannery.

As one who had experienced the depths of defeat and failure, Grant naturally liked being President. He enjoyed the praise of his fellow men and the laurels of victory, political as well as military. He seldom showed it, but he enjoyed possessing the power the President wields, and took it for granted that he would serve a second term.

Even so, he found it hard to take the bitter criticism and invective that increasingly were heaped on him as convention

time neared. Not only did a number of newspapers, such as
Charles A. Dana's *New York Sun*, turn from support to denunciation, but a good many erstwhile political supporters began to
come out against a second term for Grant. Among these, of
course, was Charles Sumner, but there were a great many more.
Such notables as Carl Schurz, Lyman Trumbull, Charles Francis
Adams, Horace Greeley, and Jacob Cox were frequently found
attacking Grant and his administration. By the fall of 1871 the
revolt within the Republican party, which coalesced into the
Liberal Republican movement, threatened to disrupt it completely.[12]

The number of defectors was actually not as great as their
clamor would lead one to believe, however, and, when the
showdown came, not only the bulk of the professionals stayed
with Grant, but so, too, did most of the rank and file. To the
professional politician of the day, with only a few exceptions,
civil service reform had little appeal. Some reformers like E. L.
Godkin wanted tariff reduction, others, like Horace Greeley,
did not. Most of the regulars supported the protective principle. The Liberal Republicans and, in particular the Missourians,
B. Gratz Brown and Carl Schurz, believed that the time had
come for general amnesty for all ex-rebels and a hands-off
policy toward the South now that the impracticality of Radical
Reconstruction had, they believed, been demonstrated by the
shortcomings of the carpetbag governments. The hard-nosed
politicians could hardly look with favor on the abandonment of
Southern Republicans, be they white or black, and it is always
possible that there was even a touch of altruism on the part of
those who refused to give up on the Republican party in the
South on the grounds that the former slaves deserved a better
fate than to be left to the tender mercies of their erstwhile
masters.

As for the average citizen in the North who had been in the
Republican party from before the attack on Fort Sumter or who
had supported Lincoln during the war, there was no thought of
deserting Grant, the savior of the Union. All might not be exactly as it should be, but Grant, for the loyal thousands who had
seen the war through to the finish, was blameless. When so
many had failed, Grant had given the supporters of the Union
hope. It was he, more than any other man, who had suppressed
the hated rebellion. To the countless thousands of Union veter-
ans, Grant was their beloved commander who could count on
their support under any circumstances. This rock-ribbed devo-

tion is well expressed in a letter from a Toledo businessman, John W. Fuller, the former colonel of the Twenty-seventh Ohio Volunteer Infantry, to the regiment's chaplain, John Eaton, Grant's wartime supervisor of freedmen's affairs and, in 1872, United States Commissioner of Education.

... I tell you General [wrote Fuller], this 'old soldier' feeling is the very essence of fealty & honor—I would rather trust it than any other sentiment you can appeal to—It is a something which forms *a part of* every man who feels it—& which leads him to consider, that with the party which represents the patriotic feelings called out by the war, is bound up, not only a successful sequel to the war, but also to a great extent, the status & reputation of the men who served in our army[.]

Strike down Grant, & you strike down us— Uphold him, & we are recognized as sharing indirectly in the honor conferred—And so true is this, that whenever you find an old soldier who *has* turned his back upon the party which sustained him during the war, you find *about* the meanest & most malignant 'cuss' extant—

If loyalty to Grant proved insufficient, loyalty to the Republican party frequently filled the void. Richard Yates, former governor of Illinois, who had given Grant his first wartime commission and who later served in the United States Senate, told a correspondent in June 1872 that he would support Grant and the Republican party. "It is true, perhaps," he wrote, " ... that I cannot expect any thing from Grant. It is for the cause, the Republican party that I shall struggle. ... "[13]

Finally, in the election of 1872, the voter had to choose between Grant, the Republican, and Horace Greeley, candidate of the Liberal Republicans and Democrats. The Liberals had nominated Greeley, editor of the *New York Tribune* at their Cincinnati convention early in May passing over more logical choices such as Charles Francis Adams and Lyman Trumbull. Greeley was seen as something of an eccentric and was thus an easy target for ridicule. Besides, not only did he favor tariff protection when so many of the reformers wanted drastic reduction in duties, but as an ardent Republican before, during, and after the war, had had a long record of open hostility toward the Democrats, and especially slave-holding Democrats. Yet, the only hope of defeating Grant lay in an alliance between the Liberal Republicans and the Democrats. And although the Democrats did nominate Greeley, they were not enthusiastic, especially in the South. Grant and his followers could hardly have asked for a more satisfactory opposition candidate.

Grant, of course, was the unanimous choice of the Republican convention meeting in Philadelphia on June 5. For Vice President the convention nominated Henry Wilson, of Massachusetts, in place of Schuyler Colfax. Replying to the official notice of his nomination, Grant promised "the same zeal and devotion to the good of the whole people, for the future of my official life, as shown in the past." Then he made the candid confession that "Past experience may guide me in avoiding mistakes, inevitable with novices in all professions and in all occupations."

Grant's part in the campaign was negligible. Much of the time he stayed at Long Branch. The usual mud-slinging went on and this meant the oft-repeated charges against Grant of drunkenness, nepotism, and corruption. Despite a certain degree of vulnerability on the corruption issue (for the Republicans in Congress had not been overly eager to investigate charges of wrong doing), the Republicans had much in their favor. Especially was this true of the economic condition of the country. Boutwell's debt reduction policies continued popular, and at the last session of Congress in the spring of the year, the Republican majority had repealed the income tax. In response to the demand for tariff reform, the same Congress had adopted a measure, which, while adhering closely to the protection principle, did call for an overall ten percent reduction as well as an extension of the free list. Also, at this time, the civil service reforms Grant and the commission had promoted were being implemented to the point where it became difficult to convince the voters that the administration had not taken this reform seriously.

Fish's triumphs in foreign policy matters also added luster to Grant's record. In September came word of the Geneva awards in the case of the *Alabama* and other Confederate cruisers, Great Britain being obliged to pay $15,500,000 to the United States. The following month the German Emperor decided the San Juan Islands (Puget Sound) boundary dispute in favor of the United States.

Other elements entered into the picture: the superior organization of Republican chairman, William E. Chandler, unsettled conditions in the South, Ku Klux atrocities, farmer and workingman unrest, the business community's concern over the prospects of Democratic victory and willingness to give generously to Grant's campaign, and what went under the general name of Grantism. But undoubtedly the election would hinge on the issues of Grant versus Greeley, and the Republican party, savior of the Union, versus the Democratic party, party of rebels and copperheads. In other words, the Civil War, the "Bloody Shirt," remained a potent influence in American politics and Grant would be its beneficiary.

Republican triumphs in October elections in Ohio and Pennsylvania foretold Grant's victory in November. Even Indiana, where the popular Democrat, Thomas A. Hendricks, won the governorship, but by a reduced margin, showed the basic Republican strength and the fundamental weakness of the Liberal Republican-Democratic combination. Fish, following these victories, displayed unwonted venom when he wrote to Badeau, in England, "Was there ever a more barefaced, profligate unprincipled coalition! or a more shameless sacrifice of principles. ... The Republican party is stronger as well as purer by reason of the men who have gone out from it."[14]

Purer it may not have been, but it most certainly proved stronger. Grant carried all but six states and these were either in the South or on the border. His popular vote was 3,597,000 to 2,834,000 for Greeley, in what appeared to be a dramatic personal triumph for the President. Greeley, overcome by the death of his wife, crushed by his overwhelming defeat, and exhausted from the strenuous campaign, died a few weeks after the election. Reform, as presented by the Democrats and Liberal Republicans, had proven unequal to the popular appeal of the hero of Appomattox and a nation riding the crest of economic prosperity.

CHAPTER X

Second-Term Troubles

GRANT INTERPRETED THE OUTCOME OF THE ELECTION OF 1872 as a personal vindication. Stung by the many charges of failure, ineptitude, and corruption, he would naturally see Republican votes as votes of endorsement for him. He said as much in his brief but revealing second inaugural address. Emphasizing that he had given faithful performance of his duty, he deplored the fact that from the start of the war through the recent campaign he had been "the subject of abuse and slander scarcely ever equaled in political history, which to-day I feel that I can afford to disregard in view of your verdict, which I gratefully accept as my vindication."[1]

The glow of victory had, unfortunately, already begun to dim, for, between the election and the inauguration, there had broken the Credit Mobilier scandal involving a number of Congressmen as well as Vice President Colfax and Vice President-elect Wilson. To add to the embarrassment of the Republicans, Ben Butler engineered what quickly came to be known as the salary grab. The Credit Mobilier affair stemmed entirely from the Johnson administration and only the fact that the revelations came while Grant was President and several prominent Republicans, as well as Democrats, were implicated has made it traditionally one of the Grant administration scandals. Yet the stench of corruption hung over Washington. It increased as the years passed, and, unfortunately, Grant did not act vigorously to dispel it. Herein lies the source of the verdict of failure so frequently applied to these late Reconstruction years.

The salary grab, or the back pay steal, was neither illegal nor totally without merit. The move to raise the salaries of President, cabinet officers, justices of the Supreme Court, and members of Congress was wholly justified in the light of the low level of pay these public officials were obliged to accept. Totally unwarranted, however, was the provision to make the pay increase for Congressmen, even for those who had been defeated in the previous election, retroactive for two years. This amounted to each Congressman receiving a bonus of $5,000. Since the measure was attached to a general appropriation bill and came at the end of the session, Grant had little choice but to sign it. He was obviously relieved that his own salary would henceforth be $50,-000 instead of $25,000. The public outcry against the pay increase for Congressmen was so great that the new Congress which met in December at a time of deepening depression repealed those provisions applying to themselves. Scandal this may have been, but the blame was as much with Democrats as Republicans. Yet Grant and his party were injured more than the opposition, and since the signing of the bill virtually coincided with the start of the new administration, it made an unfortunate beginning.[2]

The second Grant administration has little to commend it, and much to place it far down the list of presidential terms ranked according to respectability and freedom from scandal. Some of the unhappy events that established this reputation were not the President's responsibility but belong rather to the times themselves. For this was an era of low standards of public and private morality, for which no single individual can be held responsible. The unhappy truth, however, is that Grant brought some of the misfortune on himself, not only by some ill-advised and downright risky appointments, but also by his blindness in defending those appointees who were under attack and who in most cases scarcely deserved defense. Fortunately for Grant, he had built up such a large bank account of devotion amongst the people of the country (in the North especially) that even huge withdrawals in the form of a series of disasters still left a tidy sum remaining when it was all over in 1877.

A major problem for Grant throughout his presidency was in making suitable appointments and in facing the pressures of friends and relatives who asked for places in the government. Grant tried in most cases to satisfy their requests, even when this meant subjecting himself to the severest criticism. Two appointments in 1873 bear this out. Grant had given his brother-in-law, James F. Casey, the collectorship of the port of New Orleans, a job which carried with it much patronage and hence political importance. In the years of the Grant administration there was considerable gossip about Casey's custom house gang and his association with some of the more disreputable characters in the long, sordid history of Reconstruction in Louisiana. Yet, despite a damaging report of a Congressional investigating committee, Grant reappointed him in March 1873 for another four years, and it was with considerable difficulty that the appointment received the necessary Senate confirmation.[3]

Another appointment of questionable propriety was that of Alexander R. Shepherd, more commonly known as "Boss," who as director of public works for the territorial government of the District of Columbia had launched an ambitious program of physical improvements for the city of Washington. Despite the fact that Shepherd had introduced paved streets and other modernizations to the District and had sought to make L'Enfant's plan a reality, he had piled up an enormous debt and had brought charges against himself and friendly contractors for carrying on a corrupt ring in the style of "Boss" Tweed in New York City. When the territorial governor, Henry D. Cooke, resigned, Grant bucked public disapproval of Shepherd by naming him in September 1873 Cooke's successor. The President had taken the charges against Shepherd in the same way in which he considered the accusations against himself during the presidential campaign. Indeed it was not always easy to distinguish between the valid and the spurious charges that were bandied about so frequently in Washington, in the press especially. In the face of this, Grant built up a wall of indifference which nothing could penetrate once he had given his friendship and trust to a subordinate. More and more it seemed as if he believed the attacks upon his friends were attacks upon him.[4]

In another instance, the administration suffered embarrassment because of an ill-advised appointment by the President. It was a relatively minor matter, but just such an incident as would tend to undermine confidence in Grant's judgment. Early in 1873 Congress had appropriated funds for an American exhibit at the Vienna exposition to be held that year. Grant's appointment for the head of the American commission was a General T. B. Van Buren, a New York politician with no particular qualifications for the post. It was not long beforeVan Buren had a run-in with the American minister to Austria, John Jay, grandson of the famous statesman and jurist. On April 11, 1873 Fish read to the cabinet Jay's cable relating rumors of scandal in connection with the commission and urging an impartial investigation. The outcome was an unseemly washing of dirty linen in public, and the revelation of mismanagement on the part of Van Buren and of corruption on the part of some of his subordinates. Grant was more concerned with the airing in public of these matters than with the possibility of dishonesty on the part of the commission for which he was ultimately responsible. The initial mistake, of course, was in appointing Van Buren, but the President seemed unwilling to make that admission.

The worst example of bungling an appointment, however, was his attempt to find a replacement for Chief Justice Salmon P. Chase who died in May 1873. Not until November did Grant make a choice, and then he made a characteristic move in asking Roscoe Conkling to take the position. With the administration already under attack, Grant would have done better to have found a more suitable man. Fortunately Conkling declined the offer. Then the President went to the opposite extreme and asked Hamilton Fish to accept the position. The secretary would almost certainly have made a superb chief justice, but he doubted his own abilities and declined.

When the cabinet next day showed no enthusiasm for Caleb Cushing, the Massachusetts lawyer, statesman, and diplomat, Grant next turned to his Attorney General, George H. Williams, and actually sent his name to the Senate. But it turned out, as Grant ought to have anticipated, that Williams, even as Attorney General, lacked the qualifications for high office and, worse, had allowed government money to be used to supply him and his wife with an expensive carriage and the services of two liveried servants.

With some hesitation, Grant withdrew Williams' name, but only after Senate Republicans had bluntly told him that the nominee could not be confirmed. Despite the disclosures about, at best, injudicious behavior on the part of his Attorney General, Grant retained him in that position until the following year.[5]

With Williams no longer available, Grant, returned to Cushing and submitted his name. A lawyer of considerable ability and experience, Cushing in some respects was not an impossible choice, but the nomination made no sense politically since Cushing had a record as a prominent pro-Southern Democrat. Moreover, there were defects in temperament which might have caused Grant to steer clear of him even if he had been admirably suited from a political standpoint. The Cushing appointment elicited from one discouraged Republican the lament, "What a sad pity it is that our poor President has not some one to guide him. Heaven knows where he will land the party."

The Senate quickly ended Cushing's chances by discovering

a letter he had written in March 1861 to Jefferson Davis, recommending a clerk for a position in the Confederate service. Grant promptly withdrew Cushing's name. He finally found a winner in Morrison H. Waite of Ohio, a noncontroversial but respected lawyer who was promptly confirmed and then went on to serve ably for the next fourteen years. The search had taken nine months, and the nation had been treated to an amusing spectacle of the President making one misstep after another.[6]

What linked the second Grant administration to failure was not solely the scandals; the term had scarcely begun when the Panic of 1873 struck and then lingered on for the rest of the four-year period and even beyond. The Panic of 1873 has been variously attributed to delayed reaction from economic disturbances carrying over from the Civil War, worldwide conditions rocked by various disrupting events in Europe, especially the Franco-Prussian War, over expansion of American railroads, too rapid industrial and agricultural growth, and, in the eyes of some, declining confidence in the soundness of the American economy, exacerbated by the uncovering of scandal in national, state, and local government. The immediate precipitating factor was the failure of Jay Cooke & Company, September 18, 1873, although signs of trouble had been evident some weeks earlier.

In the pre-Civil War period the government could do little to control the economy of the nation in times of depression, nor was it expected to do so. It so happened, however, that during the Civil War the Treasury had issued, with Congressional authority, $400,000,000 in greenbacks, or currency not redeemable in coin. During the Johnson administration some $44,000,000 had been retired, contributing to a deflationary tendency. Some interests, however, opposed this trend, and during the first Grant administration, despite the Public Credit Act, neither Congress nor the Secretary of the Treasury had seen fit to retire any more greenbacks. But the $44,000,000 were available (although the law was not clear on this), and, over the objections of conservative bankers, Secretary of the Treasury William A. Richardson, who had succeeded Boutwell in March, had reissued $26,000,000 of these during the fall of 1873 to meet current expenses. Without admitting the fact, the administration was engaging in a mild form of inflation, but it was far too little for the true inflationists. Many of these were active after the start of the depression, especially Westerners, some of them in Congress, others even in the cabinet. They put much pressure on Grant at least to reissue the remaining $18,-000,000 of greenbacks in the Treasury, but beyond that to sponsor a far more extensive inflationary policy. It was necessary to make a decision.

Aside from a visit to New York soon after Jay Cooke's failure, and the tacit approval of Richardson's expenditure of the Treasury's greenbacks, Grant did nothing except listen to the desperate and gratuitous advice of anyone who thought he had a solution for the nation's financial ills. Even in his annual message to Congress in December, Grant's recommendations could be interpreted in more than one way. He did state his basic belief in specie payment, but left the door open for an expanded currency.

Spurred on by the inflationists, Congress proceeded to pass a currency bill on April 14, 1874, authorizing the issuance of $400,000,000 in greenbacks, or only $18,000,000 more than were then in circulation, and scarcely an extreme inflationary measure. Grant now had to decide. Many of his own party supported the bill, and he could easily justify signing it. On the other hand, in principle it went contrary to the sound money promises he and his party had made, and conservatives made dire predictions as to the consequences of inflation. Their fear was that this bill would open the door to more and more inflation as Congress bent to the insistent demands of the soft-money men.[7]

Grant agonized over the problem, first deciding to sign and even writing out his reasons for doing so. But, according to his own confession, he knew in his heart that these reasons were not how he really felt, and that in good conscience he could do nothing but veto the bill. His veto message, given on April 22, 1874, was hardly an example of financial acumen, but it struck a responsive chord with the solid people of the nation who believed in fiscal responsibility. Having nothing but praise for Grant, Hamilton Fish wrote to a fellow New Yorker,

... you must give the President the undivided credit for what he did. Never did a man more conscientiously reach his conclusions than he did in the matter of that bill, and this in the face of the very strongest and most persistent influences brought to bear upon him; .... He has a wonderful amount of good sense, and when left alone is very apt to follow it, and to 'fight it out on that line.' He did so in this recent matter, and astounded some who thought they had captured him.

Perhaps nothing else quite won the approval of so many Americans as did this one act, and yet from the vantage point of a later era, it is difficult to appreciate the depth of feeling it excited. Still what Grant had done was to reaffirm his and his party's determination not to take the easy way out, to maintain a principle, and to keep the way open for the return of specie payment. In the light of what Richardson had already done in reissuing the $26,000,000 in greenbacks, Grant did not deserve to be hailed as the unwavering friend of sound money, but his veto, in addition to previous assertions, gained him that reputation during the remainder of his presidency.

In his annual message that December, the president persisted in his hard money course, and on January 14, 1875, Congress passed Senator John Sherman's Specie Resumption Act, which set January 1, 1879, as the date on which the Treasury would redeem greenbacks in coin.[8] The Specie Resumption Act did not end the agitation for inflation, either in the form of greenbacks or silver; in fact the controversy between the soft and hard money interests would continue until the end of the century. Yet Grant's veto of the inflation bill in 1874 and his administration's adherence to a sound money policy established the standard to which the country remained committed until the New Deal period.

Another positive achievement of the early part of the second administration was the peaceful settlement of the *Virginius* affair, which for a period of a few days in November 1873 threatened war with Spain. The *Virginius*, engaged in aiding the Cuban rebels, and flying the American flag, was captured by the Spaniards near the coast of Cuba on October 31, 1873 and shortly thereafter fifty-three persons were summarily shot. Eight of these were American citizens. Both Grant and Fish took a firm stand, made stiff but reasonable demands of Spain, all the while holding back those who cried for war. The result was an apology and an indemnity from Spain and an avoidance of a needless conflict. But the administration's success was overlooked as the depression worsened.[9]

Had economic conditions been normal, it is conceivable that Grant's financial policies might have carried the Republican party to victory in the mid-term elections of 1874. A sudden reversal from the results of two years earlier could hardly have come had the nation enjoyed the same prosperity it did in 1872. But no administration can remain acceptable to the electorate in the face of hard times. Besides, the incumbent party usually has to expect the loss of some Congressional seats in a mid-term election.

The Democrats in the elections of 1874 won a stunning victory, gaining, for the first time since 1860, control of the House of Representatives with a majority of upwards of seventy seats (a number of independents were elected to the new Congress), and winning several state elections, notably in New York, Indiana, Illinois, Missouri, and Alabama. Such scandals as had already become public knowledge, reaction to affairs in certain parts of the South, the revelation of improper behavior in the government of the District of Columbia, and the salary grab surely added to Republican woes, as possibly did undenied rumors that Grant would accept a third term. Measuring the relative importance of each of these factors is patently impossible, and the only certainty is that the Republicans suffered a shocking defeat. Postmaster General Marshall Jewell said, "We have met the enemy and we are theirs." In view of Grant's enormous victory in 1872 in the face of all sorts of charges much the same as those of 1874, Grant could hardly be blamed for failing to take the election results as a rebuff to himself. This is not to say, of course, that the Republicans did not suffer at all from criticism of the administration, but the explanation for Democratic victory has to be found in the unfavorable economic conditions stemming from the Panic of 1873.[10]

That Grant's Southern policy ran into difficulties in the second term cannot be denied, and in some instances the President did show a degree of stubbornness and ill-considered judgment in his handling of the problems that arose in those Southern states which still had Republican administrations in 1873.[11] With Reconstruction officially ended, Grant would have preferred to pursue a policy of non-interference. Hoping that the Republican regimes could maintain themselves, he did not intend to intervene should, in the normal course of events, the Democrats regain political control. Unfortunately for him, carpetbag governments could not survive for any length of time because of inherent weaknesses, internal factional quarrels, sometimes inept or corrupt leaders, and most telling, because of the resort to intimidation and violence by white, conservative elements, determined to wrest political control from the Republicans at virtually any cost. Had it been possible for Grant, as President, to act in a clear-cut fashion either in response to calls from governors obviously in the right who were trying to suppress disorders instigated by criminal elements, or in support of laws of Congress being violated in such fashion that he had no choice but to intervene to uphold the federal authority, then his Southern policy would have received the wholehearted endorsement of reasonable men. But Grant never had that luck.

Instead, more often than not, he found himself intervening (always with legal justification) on behalf of an administration that was unworthy of his support, or refereeing a quarrel between two factions each of which was undeserving of federal assistance, either because it was corrupt or unrepresentative, or because it had gained what authority it enjoyed by trampling on the rights of the colored citizens. Grant continually found himself in the unhappy dilemma of either supporting an unworthy, unpopular (with the white population), and a too often corrupt Republican administration, or seeing a purer, more respectable, Democratic regime take over and deny to the Negro any meaningful share in the political life of the state. Indeed, it became evident that wherever the Republicans lost power in the South, the blacks were threatened with not just the loss of political power but the civil rights they had enjoyed during the brief period of Radical Reconstruction. The many instances of violence toward Negroes made it impossible not to be aware of what was happening. But the Southern question was becoming a political liability to the Republican party, and much of the white population of the North, tired of the continuing unsettled state of affairs in some parts of the South, disgusted by the apparent corruption of the carpetbag regimes, and overwhelmed by their own problems stemming from the depression, lost interest in a policy of intervention. Grant shared most of these feelings, although his sense of duty, both to the office of President and to the colored population of the South, and his concern for the future of the Republican party caused him to pursue a vacillating course of action. Consequently, in some instances, he responded positively to calls for aid from hard-pressed Republican governors; in others, he flatly turned them down. It could be argued that while in certain cases he showed unnecessary stubbornness in supporting some of the carpetbaggers, and in others he seemed to support the wrong faction, he nonetheless had the correct instinct. Sensing what was evolving in the South, he sought to prevent it, even though his heart was not always in the struggle.

Undoubtedly, the most troublesome state was Louisiana, which had had its full share of misgovernment from one of the least enlightened of the carpetbag governments. Grant in the disputed gubernatorial election of 1872 had tried to keep out by simply ordering the military to maintain order if called on to act. He desperately wanted Congress to assume the responsibility for deciding which of the competing state governments was the legitimate one. This the Congress refused to do. In order to keep the peace in Louisiana, the Grant administration, tacitly or otherwise, upheld the legality of the William Pitt Kellogg faction of Republicans, of which Grant's brother-in-law, James F. Casey, was a leading member. This was a questionable policy from the standpoint of many in the North who saw the Kellogg regime as unrepresentative of the people of Louisiana. Yet that support for the regular Republican faction which had the backing of the Negroes, was at least partially justified which was borne out by the Colfax massacre on April 13, 1873. This incident, occurring in a remote part of northwest Louisiana, resulted in the deaths of some sixty persons, mostly black, in a riot whose origins are obscured by conflicting reports. There is no question, however, about the ruthlessness with which the blacks were killed even after many had tried to surrender. In response to this and other evidence of disorder, Grant, on May 22, 1873, issued a proclamation formally announcing his recognition of the Kellogg government, and commanding "turbulent and disorderly persons to disperse" within twenty days. A period of relative calm settled on Louisiana, broken the following summer by the Coushatta massacre, on August 28, 1874. This time, six white men, Republicans from the North who were office holders in a rural Louisiana parish, having been forced to resign, were murdered as they were on the point of quitting the region permanently. This in turn was followed on September 14 by an attempted coup on the part of the opposition, Democrats supported by armed White Leagues, similar in purpose to the Ku Klux Klan. Kellogg, temporarily unseated, appealed to the President for assistance in suppressing domestic violence. Grant responded with a proclamation calling for an end to the disturbances within five days. He did this with great reluctance, for he had come to detest the whole controversy and distrusted Kellogg as a weak and foolish man. But Grant, Fish, and the rest of the cabinet all agreed that there was no choice but to support his government and to suppress what Fish called "a well matured & carefully organized scheme." On September 17, General William H. Emory took charge of the situation and deposed the McEnery government, which for three days had been in control of the state. Trouble resumed at the time of the November election, which ended with each party claiming victory. At first it appeared that the Democrats had elected a majority of the legislature, but the Kellogg-dominated returning board threw out enough Democratic votes to end up with an even split in the lower house of the legislature with five contested seats to be decided by the membership.[12]

Between the time of the election and the meeting of the legislature in January, Grant took two steps in regard to the Southern question, and particularly Louisiana. In his annual message to Congress, he called attention to the lawlessness that prevailed in Louisiana as well as elsewhere in the South, and which deprived legal voters of their privileges. White Leagues and other organizations intimidated the colored citizens by threatening them with the loss of their jobs should they dare to exercise their rights as voters. Worse, the violence that accompanied elections in the South contributed to a reign of terror in defiance of the authority of the government of the United States. The federal executive by virtue of the Enforcement Acts was charged with the protection of all citizens in the exercise of the franchise, and, he told Congress, "While I remain Executive all the laws of Congress and the provisions of the Constitution, including the recent amendments added thereto, will be enforced with rigor, but with regret that they should have added one jot or tittle to Executive duties or powers."

Grant took one other step. Sending Sheridan with secret orders to Louisiana, he authorized him to take command of the troops in that area and to use his authority to preserve order if necessary. Feigning a pleasure trip, Sheridan journeyed south and reached New Orleans early in January 1875. By the time of his arrival the opposing factions had become ensnared in a most serious tangle. In the first meeting of the legislature the Democrats moved swiftly to take control, but in a matter of a few hours General Philip De Trobriand, local troop commander, had, under direction of Governor Kellogg, ousted certain of the Democrats and permitted the Republicans to organize the House. For the military to preserve order was one thing; for it to interfere physically with the proceedings of the house of a state legislature was quite another, for the governor constitutionally would have no authority or right to interfere with the legislative branch of the government.

Sheridan had little time for such technicalities and gave his approval to De Trobriand's actions. Taking a quick look at this complicated situation, Sheridan sent a telegram to Grant.

I think [he told the President] that the terrorism now existing in Louisiana, Mississippi, and Arkansas could be entirely removed and confidence and fair-dealing established by the arrest and trial of the ringleaders of the armed White Leagues. If Congress would pass a bill declaring them banditti, they could be tried by a military commission. ... It is possible that if the President would issue a proclamation declaring them banditti, no further action need be taken, except that which would devolve upon me.

Grant was now placed in a difficult dilemma. He trusted and believed in Sheridan as in no other man. He would defend him to the last extremity. Yet, De Trobriand's action and Sheridan's message created, for the most part, a violently adverse reaction in the North. Public meetings denounced behavior which smacked of militarism and dictatorship. Furthermore, within his own cabinet, Grant encountered the severest kind of condemnation of the two army officers. Hamilton Fish, in particular, urged Grant to disclaim De Trobriand's action and to make it perfectly clear that the administration had no intention of carrying out Sheridan's suggestion. Fish had little confidence in the general and thoroughly disapproved of his actions in Louisianna, but convincing Grant was no easy task.[13]

A practical solution offered itself when Congress called on the President for information concerning the recent events in Louisiana. Under heavy pressure from Fish and Benjamin Bristow, the Secretary of the Treasury, Grant, with the aid of Attorney General George H. Williams, framed a message which went as far as anyone could wish in repudiating De Trobriand's action. For instance he stated that "I can conceive of no case, not involving rebellion or insurrection, where such interference by authority of the General Government ought to be permitted or can be justified. ... I have no desire to have United States troops interfere in the domestic concerns of Louisiana or any other State." But Grant, revealing his true feelings, said more. Going out of his way to defend Sheridan, he also tried to show that the trouble originated with the white people of Louisiana who were lawless and guilty of terrible atrocities. He cited the Colfax massacre and the failure of the civil authorities to bring the perpetrators to justice.

... it is a lamentable fact [he wrote], that insuperable obstructions were thrown in the way of punishing these murderers; and the so-called conservative papers of the State not only justified the massacre, but denounced as Federal tyranny and despotism the attempt of the United States officers to bring them to justice. Fierce denunciations ring through the country about office holding and election matters in Louisiana, while every one of the Colfax miscreants goes unwhipped of justice, and no way can be found in this boasted land of civilization and Christianity to punish the perpetrators of this bloody and monstrous crime.

The President went on to mention the Coushatta murders and other crimes in which no one was ever punished or even apprehended. He called attention to the suppression of Negro voting by the White Leagues, something which those who were urging him to renounce the Kellogg government and allow the Democrats to regain power in the state, conveniently overlooked largely because they had come to the conclusion that Negro voting was no longer desirable or at least no longer worth trying to defend. But he had that strong sense of duty forcing him to continue executing an unpopular policy. Accordingly, he wrote:

that to the extent that Congress has conferred power upon me to prevent it neither Kuklux Klans, White Leagues, nor any other association using arms and violence to execute their unlawful purposes can be permitted in that way to govern any part of this country; nor can I see with indifference Union men or Republicans ostracized, persecuted, and murdered on account of their opinions, as they now are in some localities.

In taking this stand, Grant had the support of a few persons in the North, as, for instance, the old abolitionist leader Wendell Phillips. But time was running out for the abolitionists, and the President found himself obliged to bend to the Congressional demand that he compromise the issue. So it turned out that a House committee was able to persuade both sides to accept an arrangement permitting the Democrats to control the lower house, the Republicans the senate, and Kellogg to retain the governorship until the expiration of his term. This was the so-called Wheeler compromise. The sub-committee of the House which worked out this scheme severely criticized the political manipulations of the Kellogg group in Louisiana, and at the same time exonerated the white population from the charge of intimidation of Negroes. But the other members of the committee, headed by George F. Hoar, gave a different report, one of atrocities committed against blacks, and intimidation of Republican voters generally. This, however, became lost in the general rejoicing over the relatively satisfactory solution to the impasse. Accounts of atrocities had lost their impact by this time, and a certain ennui had set in to the extent that there was not great pressure on the Congress to intervene on behalf of the colored population. Grant suffered a set-back in this instance because he supported an outworn policy. What he wanted to do and what he sensed ought to be done simply could not be carried out effectively in the mid 70s. Grant did not err; faint hearted Republicans in the North in following a policy of expediency were the ones who were responsible for the abandonment of the colored people of the South.[14]

Other trouble spots in the second administration were Arkansas, Mississippi, and South Carolina. Grant pursued a course in these states similar to the one in Louisiana. That is, he leaned toward intervention in pursuance of what he believed was his duty, but with dwindling enthusiasm as Northern resistance continued to build up, and as he, himself, realized the political liabilities associated with such a policy.

Arkansas proved to be almost as confusing in its politics as Louisiana and presented Grant with similar dilemmas. In the 1872 gubernatorial election, Joseph Brooks, a carpetbagger who was supported by the liberal faction of the Republican party, vied with Elisha Baxter, scalawag, backed by the regular Republicans and many Democrats. Despite charges of fraud and corruption coming from the Brooks camp, Baxter was declared the winner and was inaugurated without opposition in January 1873. For over a year, Baxter administered the executive office with increasing approval of the Democrats and conservatives in Arkansas, but with growing apprehension on the part of the Republican carpetbaggers. Suddenly, on April 15, 1874, a state judge ruled that Brooks had rightfully been elected in 1872 and should take over the governorship. This Brooks did, as far as he was able. The Baxter partisans refused to recognize Brooks and there ensued, for the space of a month, what is known as the Brooks-Baxter war.

Both sides appealed to Washington for official recognition and support, but Grant wanted no part of a factional dispute within a state. Between 1872 and 1874 the sides had become reversed with the regular Republicans no longer supporting Baxter, but, rather, trying to seat his 1872 rival, Brooks; while the opposition switched allegiance from Brooks to Baxter. So all Grant consented to do was order the military commander in Little Rock "to take no part in the political controversy ... unless it should be necessary to prevent bloodshed or collision of armed bodies."

Then Arkansas' two senators, supporters of Brooks, appeared

at the cabinet meeting and pleaded for interference, still no action was taken. Again on April 21, a delegation of Brooks adherents tried to persuade the Grant administration to interfere and prevent the Baxter supporters from disturbing the peace. But, according to Fish, Grant told them that all necessary measures for preserving the peace had been taken, within the limits of the powers of the government. Here is ample evidence to prove that Grant deplored having to resume involvement in the Southern states long after Reconstruction had been concluded. When it was a question of recognition of one of two rival state governments, he believed it was Congress' responsibility to make a decision. Only when there seemed to be no other choice did he see fit to act. Thus, in the case of Arkansas, when the so-called war threatened to develop into something really serious, George Williams, Grant's Attorney General, ruled that since the state legislature had decided in favor of Baxter, Baxter would have the legal backing of the United States government, in spite of the fact that both Grant and Williams privately believed that Brooks had received a majority of votes in the 1872 election. On May 15, Williams made a public announcement of his decision, and Grant followed it up on the same day with a proclamation sustaining the Baxter government and ordering armed resistance to cease. The Brooks-Baxter war was over, and Baxter resumed his unchallenged position as governor.[15]

Now, however, the obviously conservative legislature moved to abandon the existing ultra-liberal constitution and replace it with something more befitting a post-Reconstruction Southern state. In the ensuing months a new constitutional convention was held, not in conformity to the amending procedures provided for in the existing constitution, and the new document was overwhelmingly approved by the voters in a referendum in October. In elections for state offices, the Republicans, unwilling to recognize the legality of the new regime, refused to participate, and a Democrat, Augustus H. Garland, was easily elected. He was inaugurated on November 13, 1874. When Volney V. Smith, lieutenant-governor under Baxter, challenged Garland's right to the office, the usual appeals were made to Washington, especially by the anti-Baxter forces. At the cabinet meeting, November 17, 1874, there was discussion of the legality of Arkansas' new constitution. Grant noted that since a House committee was then making an investigation of conditions in Arkansas, it would be best to await the committee's report before taking any action. This is how the matter was left.

The committee, headed by Luke Poland of Vermont, impressed by the steady hand of the Garland administration in contrast to the turmoil of the previous regimes, reported on February 6, 1875 in favor of Garland, and recommended that there be no interference by the federal government. Senator Powell Clayton, Arkansas Republican, and once a powerful influence in the state during the heyday of Radicalism, still hoping that Grant would come to the rescue, now pushed through a resolution calling on the President for information on affairs in Arkansas. In all likelihood influenced by Babcock, and Babcock's friends, "Boss" Shepherd, and carpetbag Senator Stephen W. Dorsey, Grant replied that it was the responsibility of Congress to determine such matters, but that in his opinion Brooks had legally been elected in 1872, and the new constitution had been fraudulently foisted on the state in violation of legal procedures. The House, however, paid no attention to this surprising pronouncement, and on March 2, 1875, adopted the Poland report as an expression of its wishes. There was no attempt at interference, and Arkansas remained in the ranks of "redeemed" states. This meant that the results of Radical Reconstruction failed to become permanent in Arkansas; expediency had won out. It was comforting for white Northerners to know that the intelligent leaders of Arkansas were now in control, that peace and order would prevail, and that the colored population would be restrained from being too active in politics. Some would regret the passing of the state from the Republican to the Democratic column and the unfortunate fate of the Negroes, but the price was worth it in return for peace and stabilitiy. Grant's actions in this episode indicate that he, too, had mixed feelings about what had been happening in Arkansas. He, too, preferred stable government to anarchy, hence his belated support for Baxter in May 1874. But he was uneasy over undoing the results of the war insofar as this meant the reseating of old secessionists who would be defiant of federal authority and callous concerning the political rights of the colored population. Hence, his apparently inconsistent denunciation of the Garland government in February 1875. In the end, Grant did what at the time had to be done; he went along with the Poland committee and recognized a *fait accompli*.[16]

The ranks of carpetbag governments were growing thin by early 1875. Throughout most of the old Confederacy, Democratic, or redeemer administrations dominated the state capitals with the Republicans thoroughly crushed or in full retreat. They maintained a precarious existence only in South Carolina, Florida, Louisiana, and Mississippi. Alabama and Texas had been redeemed in 1874 along with Arkansas. Asked to intervene in Texas in behalf of the Republicans, Grant, consistent with his policy of non-intervention, refused.

The story of Mississippi was not unlike that of Arkansas in that factionalism within the Republican party contributed to the restoration of conservative government. Thus in 1873 the carpetbagger Adelbert Ames defeated the scalawag James L. Alcorn, both ostensibly Republicans. Ames' administration, drawing most of its support from the Negro population, frequently ran into difficulties and often appealed to Washington for help. In December 1874, when there were disturbances in Vicksburg, Grant did issue a proclamation calling for an end to the disorders. The most important request for aid came at the time of the state elections in 1875. Once again, Grant faced a dilemma. To abandon Ames was to see the Democrats gain control of Mississippi, and that meant loss of civil and political rights for the colored population, for the so-called Mississippi Plan of the native whites was simply a plan of intimidation to keep Negroes from voting. Once the Democrats should gain political control of the state there could be little doubt as to the future of Negro suffrage there. The President, however, disliked interfering in the affairs of the state, because he was well aware of the damage this was doing to the Republican party in the North. A delegation of Ohio Republicans told him that intervention in Mississippi would bring defeat to Rutherford B. Hayes, candidate for governor, in the fall election. Members of the cabinet advised against intervention. So, for instance, William W. Belknap, Secretary of War, suggested to Grant that he inform Ames that the emergency was not such as to justify the employment of federal troops. Grant knew full well how Hamilton Fish felt about such things. Accordingly, he turned down Ames' request. His dilemma is well expressed in the telegram he sent to Attorney General Edwards Pierrepont at the time of the refusal:

The whole public are tired out with these annual autumnal outbreaks in the South, and the great majority are ready now to condemn any interference on the part of the Government. I heartily wish that peace and good order may be restored without issuing the proclamation, but if the proclamation must be issued I shall instruct the commander of the forces to have no child's play; the laws will be executed and the peace will be maintained in every street and highway of the United States.

The only intervention, however, was in the form of a peace mission by George K. Chase, representing the Attorney General, who worked out a settlement between the opposing factions whereby open fighting was avoided. Sporadic outbursts of violence did occur, but the principal tactic of the Democrats was non-violent intimidation, so as to avoid provoking the interference which Ames so desperately wanted. The result was a sweeping Democratic victory, as thousands of Negroes stayed away from the polls, and one more state was redeemed. The following year, Grant had occasion to comment on the situation in Mississippi, saying that that state "is governed to-day by officials chosen through fraud and violence such as would scarcely be accredited to savages, much less to a civilized and Christian people." More clearly than many other Northern Republicans, Grant sensed what was happening in the South. His efforts to stem the tide brought him little but denunciation from those who could only see what damage was being done to the party, or who preferred orderly white-controlled government in the Southern states to seemingly unrepresentative, sometimes corrupt, and frequently inept carpetbag regimes. That the Negro would be stripped of most of what gains he had achieved during Reconstruction was merely seen as a price that had to be paid.[17]

CHAPTER XI

Some of the Guilty Escape

DURING GRANT'S SECOND ADMINISTRATION, DESPITE CERTAIN dramatic instances of intervention cited above, relatively little attention was given to what was called the Southern question. Monetary matters loomed as the most pressing problems the administration had to face. This was only to be expected in a period of economic depression. But the outstanding feature of these years was the series of scandals which unfolded one after the other in frightening regularity. Although the actual events may have occurred at an earlier date (as was the case with the Credit Mobilier), the impression left was one of almost total disintegration, at least until the fall elections of 1876. Dismayed as he must have been by the series of events which brought so much discredit to his administration, Grant displayed no sign of discouragement as he lived out the closing years of his term. Conscious of his own rectitude, as he saw it, accustomed for years to sniping and abuse, and convinced that his detractors were selfishly motivated, he found it possible to carry out his duties as President almost as if nothing were happening around him.

One visible sign of possible trouble in the second Grant administration, true also of the first, was the excessive number of changes within the cabinet. Here, as before, Grant made some excellent appointments, but apparently this resulted from chance rather than from an ability to attract good men because of the comparable number of poor or mediocre choices.

In the late summer of 1875, Columbus Delano was all but forced out of the cabinet after rumors of corrupt practices in the Interior Department had freely circulated. Grant appointed Zachariah Chandler to the office. Nothing could have more positively signified the President's preference for the professional politician than this appointment. While Chandler gave a satisfactory administration of his department, he made no pretense at being anything other than a practical spoilsman.

One of the more questionable selections was that of William A. Richardson as Boutwell's successor in the Treasury Department.

Richardson, a Massachusetts man, had served as assistant secretary under Boutwell, but had alienated the hard money men in the country by his reissuance of several millions in greenbacks in the fall of 1873. But Richardson is best remembered for his association with the Sanborn contract affair, one of the scandals connected with the Grant administration.

John D. Sanborn, associate of Ben Butler, had entered into contracts with the Treasury Department for the recovery of delinquent taxes, according to the terms of a rider to an appropriation bill continuing, in this one instance, the old moiety principle, now generally discarded. Under the terms of the contract, Sanborn would retain one half of all sums collected. On its face, this arrangement cast no discredit on Richardson, but a House committee later reported that the secretary had connived at some of Sanborn's tactics which made it possible for him to pocket large sums of money which he never could have done had Richardson been more willing to face Butler's ire. Condemning the secretary and some of his subordinates, the report made it embarrassing for him to remain in the cabinet. Grant, unwilling to give in to his critics, had supported his subordinate during the investigation, even though Richardson's usefulness had already ended. The President's responsibility for the Sanborn affair is one of those which a man in a high executive position automatically must assume. Yet he was culpable only in his tardiness in ridding himself of a subordinate of questionable integrity. If only he had not appointed Richardson to the Court of Claims he would not have looked so bad in the eyes of conscientious citizens appalled at the goings-on in Washington.

At about this same time, Grant again showed how great Butler's influence was with the administration. When the collectorship of the port of Boston became vacant, Butler asked that one of his chief lieutenants, William A. Simmons, be appointed. Against strong opposition from the "better" elements in Massachusetts, including E. R. Hoar, his brother George, and Sumner, Grant made the appointment and refused to withdraw it. The very fact of Sumner's opposition was enough to make Grant unyielding, but he also had no desire to disappoint Butler. Simmons' confirmation by the Senate proved to be a major triumph for the Massachusetts congressman.

When Elihu Washburne declined the Treasury post, Grant turned to a young Kentuckian, war veteran, and the nation's first Solicitor General, Benjamin H. Bristow. A hard-money

tow was in complete sympathy with Grant's fiscal
nd hence fully acceptable to the economic conserva-
had earned the President's praise in his earlier posi-
brought to the Treasury Department a strict integrity,
conscientious devotion to duty, and a high degree of intelligence so necessary for his demanding assignment. The Kentuckian was one of the best appointments Grant made. Pity that
the President came to distrust him to the point where Bristow
found it expedient to resign in June 1876.[1]

Trouble between them developed after Bristow had proceeded quite far in his investigation of the whiskey frauds. This,
the most famous of the Grant administration scandals, had its
origins in the first administration, when distillers in the west,
and especially St. Louis, leagued with internal revenue officers
to cheat the government out of several millions of dollars in
excise taxes. Head of the ring in St. Louis was General John A.
McDonald, who owed his position as collector of internal revenue in St. Louis to Orville Babcock, Grant's secretary. Becoming quite friendly with McDonald, Grant himself entertained
him in Washington, and was entertained, in turn, in St. Louis.

Bristow's predecessors, Richardson and Boutwell, had failed
to pay attention to strong rumors and even positive evidence of
the existence of a ring which was defrauding the government.
Not so with Bristow, who wanted to run an honest department.
It is also said that Bristow had ambitions for the presidency,
and a successful prosecution of criminals would increase his
chances of attaining the goal. It is impossible to tell just where
desire to serve the public good gave way to personal ambition,
but Bristow's presidential ambitions were perfectly legitimate,
especially after Grant had disclaimed, on May 30, 1875 in a
letter intended for public consumption, any desire to seek a
third term.

The secretary collected evidence over a long period of time
and in the face of the most determined opposition, for the
Internal Revenue Bureau, both in its field offices and in Washington headquarters, was shot through with dishonest agents in
the pay of the ring. Investigations were thwarted before they
could be fairly started. Aware of this, Bristow finally worked
only through trusted lieutenants, some of whom were not officially a part of the Treasury Department.[2]

During the early stages of Bristow's behind-the-scenes investigation, Grant gave him full cooperation. At one point, in September 1875, Bristow offered Grant his resignation but the

President urged him to stay on and even intimated that he was in line for the presidency. When Bristow had obtained the evidence he needed, on May 10, 1875, he staged simultaneous raids in St. Louis, Chicago, Milwaukee, and other distilling centers in the west, which resulted in wholesale arrests of Internal Revenue agents as well as distillers. Early the next month indictments were brought against 350 distillers and government officials. One of these was John A. McDonald, who just two days before the raid had written Babcock that he was in no way implicated with the whiskey ring.

McDonald, however, was directing his denials to the wrong party, because it was not long before Babcock himself came under suspicion. On May 22, 1875, Bristow had come to Fish to tell him that Babcock was deep in the whiskey ring and that he had the most positive evidence, not necessarily of fraud "but of intimate relations and confidential correspondence with the very worst of them." Bristow went on to tell Fish about McDonald's position at the center of the plot. The secretary related how Grant, in about as naive a statement as he ever made, had assured him that McDonald could be relied on as an honest man because he was Babcock's intimate friend. The fact that McDonald within a few months was tried and convicted is proof of Grant's gullibility. The young secretary had so established himself in Grant's affections and trust that nothing could convince the President that he was anything but upright and honest. Unfortunately, in this case, Babcock's associations with members of the ring were indiscreet at best and damagingly incriminating at worst. For several years he had maintained a close relationship with men who subsequently were found guilty of fraud against the government as members of the whiskey ring.[3]

Hamilton Fish mentioned Babcock frequently in his diary. In particular he resented Babcock's meddling in the affairs of the State Department, but more than once he wrote of his positive attributes. Thus he could say in September 1874 that Babcock, "has brains & very many excellent & gentlemanly qualities, but is spoiled by his position. . . . " He also, at this time, was unwilling to listen to the rumors of Babcock's involvement in dishonest dealings for, he wrote, "I have not seen anything that justified a doubt of Babcock's personal integrity. . . . " The next year in a moment of pique, Fish confided to his diary, "the truth is Babcock fancies himself President of the United States."

Babcock had been able to protect himself from suspicion by his own prudence and by his closeness to the President. But Bristow, at about the time of the raids, uncovered a telegram from "Sylph" to McDonald, written in December 1874, which read, "I succeeded, they will not go I will write you." Bristow suspected that Babcock sent this at a time when investigators were about to leave Washington for St. Louis to give McDonald the chance to prepare for them. Later, in September, Bristow extracted from Babcock an admission of authorship of the telegram, but Babcock insisted that the message had reference to some other matter. Grant gave Bristow the same explanation. The only trouble was that the event Babcock and Grant referred to had occurred two months after the sending of the telegram.[4]

In the summer of 1875, while Grant was at Long Branch, he received a letter from a St. Louis banker, W. D. W. Barnard, who noted that several Treasury officers in St. Louis had asserted that Grant would sustain them, because, if he did not, Babcock would be ruined. Sending the letter on to Bristow, Grant endorsed it with ringing words:

I forward this for information and to the end that if it throws any light upon new parties to summon as witnesses they may be brought out. *Let no guilty man escape if it can be avoided.* Be specially vigilant—or instruct those engaged in the prosecution of fraud to be—against all who insinuate that they have high influence to protect—or to protect them. No personal consideration should stand in the way of performing a public duty.

At a later date Grant testified that Babcock had never tried to influence him in any way, and in the absence of any contrary evidence this positive statement deserves consideration. For, if Grant was telling the truth, his belief in Babcock's innocence was not the result of brain-washing by his secretary, but, if at all, from others, or from the conviction he held all along that his secretary was an honorable man.

Babcock, under suspicion by Bristow and Fish, still was not in really serious trouble until November 1875, when the trial of the principal suspects began in St. Louis. First John A. Joyce and then McDonald were found guilty and sentenced. Their testimony, particularly McDonald's, revealed the close relationship between members of the ring and Babcock. These revelations became public knowledge, and the evidence was such that it was easy to assume Babcock's guilt.

Under such circumstances, Babcock asked Grant for a military court of inquiry, with the obvious intention of avoiding a civil trial. The question was brought up at a cabinet meeting on December 2, 1875, and, according to Fish, it was agreed that Babcock, as an army officer, had the right to have a court of inquiry. Soon after, the grand jury in St. Louis indicted him, so when the military court requested the papers relating to the case, the government legal officers in St. Louis refused to give them up on the grounds that they were needed for the civil trial. Also, Attorney General Edwards Pierrepont declared that for the military court of inquiry to take over the case from the civil court would be ruinous to Babcock, Grant, and the administration. So the idea was abandoned and Babcock subsequently was tried by the civil court.[5]

Meanwhile, Grant, perhaps unknowingly, had aided Babcock by ordering Pierrepont not to grant immunity to any of the distillers who might give evidence against the principal offenders, some of whom were politically important. While this conceivably could have been done to protect Babcock or John A. Logan in Illinois, Grant's motive, as Attorney General Pierrepont expressed it was

to have these prosecutions so conducted that when they are over the honest judgment of the honest men of the country—which is sure in the main to be just—will say that no one has been prosecuted from malice, and that no guilty one has been let off through favoritism, and that no guilty one who has been proved guilty or confessed himself guilty, has been suffered to escape punishment.

Babcock's trial began on February 8, 1876 in St. Louis with the defense attorneys doing everything possible to keep damaging evidence from being admitted. Surely, their conduct of the case was such as to lend credence to the suspicion that Babcock was guilty of having in the first place known about the activities of the ring, and second, having benefitted monetarily from it.

On that very day, at a special cabinet meeting called by the President to take up the question of Babcock's trial, Grant stating his belief that the prosecution was aimed at him, and reasserting his conviction that Babcock was innocent, made the astounding announcement that he would go himself to St. Louis, starting either that evening or the next morning, to testify in Babcock's defense. The cabinet all agreed that this would never do, Fish pointing out that Grant, as the head of the government and hence ultimately responsible for the prosecution of the case, could not with propriety assist a person who was being prosecuted by the government.

Instead of going in person, Grant settled on a deposition given four days later to Chief Justice Waite, with Bristow and Pierrepont present. It is hard to see how the deposition, in principle, was much of an improvement over a personal appearance in court. For several hours Grant answered questions and testified to Babcock's good character. He stated that he never had any inkling of his secretary's involvement with the whiskey ring. As already noted, he insisted that Babcock had not tried to influence him in any manner, indeed, had not even talked with him about the whole affair.[6]

Whether or not Babcock would have been found guilty without Grant's deposition is a debatable point. It is perfectly possible that there was insufficient evidence for conviction. Still, for the President of the United States to go so far in injecting himself into a legal proceeding such as this must have had some bearing on the outcome.

Despite his persistent belief that Babcock was the victim of an intrigue directed against himself, Grant realized that it would no longer be possible to have Babcock remain as his private secretary. During the trial, Grant had his son, Buck, act as secretary, but as soon as Babcock secured his acquittal, he was back at his desk in the White House. Fish was astounded, and when he asked Grant about it, the President replied that Babcock "felt aggrieved at not being allowed to occupy the next room," but that he was about to depart.

Babcock did finally leave, apparently with some reluctance, and yet he retained for the time his position as superintendent of buildings and grounds for the District of Columbia. Not long after, Grant named him inspector of lighthouses, an office which he occupied until his accidental death by drowning at Mosquito Inlet, Florida in 1884. When Grant was on the point of leaving the White House, he wrote an endorsement on Babcock's 1869 orders, which assigned him to duty with the President, according his thanks "and the assurance of my confidence in his integrity and great efficiency."

The sequel to this bizarre story is the unhappy fate of Bristow, who was, in Grant's eyes, responsible for all the misfortunes inflicted not only on himself and Babcock but also on the administration and the Republican party. To make matters worse, this was an election year. For that reason, Grant had refrained from dismissing Bristow at the time of Babcock's trial, although he told Fish that he could not see how Bristow could long remain in the cabinet. But Grant clearly held Bristow responsible and was convinced that the secretary believed the President implicated in the affair, and, according to Fish, "was using his office for the purpose of annoying him [Grant]. . . . He didn't think Bristow so much at fault as those around him who wanted to make him President."[7]

That Bristow had admirers who were promoting his candidacy is not to be denied. Still, he would have been a logical choice for the nomination had he not antagonized so many Republicans by his relentless pursuit of the criminals in the whiskey frauds, no matter what the political consequences might be. Bristow had much to commend him and emerges from the sordid accounts of this period with an unsullied reputation. He insisted that he did not want the nomination, and even if that were not a truly candid admission, he conducted himself as Secretary of the Treasury with perfect propriety.

Grant, however, could see Bristow in no other light than as an enemy and thus had no hesitancy in accepting his resignation dated June 17, 1876, just a few days after the Republican convention. Although he wrote a correct acceptance letter, a few months later Grant confided to Fish that Bristow "was the only person who had been associated with him in his Cabinet who on parting had left an unpleasant impression who he said had been treacherous in the Cabinet." Grant went on to describe Bristow as a man endowed with a nature of "intense selfishness and ambition and of extreme jealousy and suspicion." Fish found the conversation "sad and painful" because he liked Bristow but significantly added, "although I think that he has given the President much ground for his present feelings."[8]

Grant's appointment of Belknap to succeed the deceased Rawlins soon after the beginning of his first adminstration seemed to be satisfactory, at least for almost seven years. Then the country was treated to a War Department scandal, which, coming on top of the Babcock episode, gave the Grant administration an even worse reputation than it already had.

Belknap came to his post well-recommended. Son of a high-ranking regular army officer, he had attended Princeton, studied law in the District of Columbia, and then settled in Keokuk, Iowa, where he established a legal practice. A Douglas Demo-

crat at the outbreak of the war, he entered the army as a volunteer officer, achieved a distinguished record under Sherman,
and emerged a major-general of volunteers. Sherman thought so
highly of Belknap he recommended him for a commission in
the regular army. Instead of continuing his military career, Belknap accepted the position of collector of Internal Revenue in
Iowa, receiving his commission from Andrew Johnson in July
1866.

When Grant sought a replacement for Rawlins, Sherman suggested Belknap, since the President was looking for a western
man. Grant had had only a slight acquaintance with the Iowan,
but having faith in Sherman's judgment, he sent Belknap's
name to the Senate for confirmation.

Belknap's administration of the War Department attracted
relatively little notice, but his inability to get along with Sherman was not a healthy sign. Sherman, who commanded the
army following Grant's elevation to the presidency, resented
the secretary's practice of bypassing him, and was unable to
find a sympathetic ear with Grant. One of the sad features of
this period was the estrangement between Sherman and Grant,
brought on, in part by a difference of opinion on Reconstruction policy. Also, because Grant failed to back up Sherman in
his dispute with Belknap, Sherman began to think that he was
no longer wanted. To his father-in-law, Thomas Ewing, Sherman wrote in 1871, "I feel everyday the growing jealousy of
Genl Grant & his Cabinet, who think I do not blow their trum-
pet loud enough." In the same letter he complained of the
treatment he received from Belknap. Shortly before, he had
moved his headquarters to St. Louis in an obvious attempt to
get away from the Secretary of War.[9]

If Sherman found Belknap to be coarse and unfeeling, this
side of the secretary seemed not to show up in his private life.
He had had more than his share of personal tragedy. The tall,
blond, and bearded Belknap had lost his first wife in 1862, his
second in 1870, one child in 1871, and another in 1874. His
third wife, the sister of the second, was the lovely and vivacious
"Puss" Bower. Their home and family life, at least to outsiders,
appeared to be happy. Yet all the while a dreadful scandal was
brewing because of Belknap's unwise, if not dishonest, handling
of certain desirable positions at his disposal, and because of his
second wife's greed for money.[10]

One of the duties of the Secretary of War was to appoint post
traders to the various army posts located near Indian reserva-

tions in the West. These private dealers sold a variety of goods to the general public as well as to army personnel and were in a position to make large profits. Belknap's policy was to hand out these lucrative places to friends and relatives including Grant's brother Orvil. If the original appointee chose to make some arrangement with a third party for the actual operation of the trading post, with a monetary consideration for the privilege, he did not object. Any conscientious administrator would never have permitted such practices, and both Belknap and Grant showed grave shortcomings by condoning the sale of these post traderships.

A friend of the second Mrs. Belknap, Caleb P. Marsh, a New York merchant, at her suggestion, received the post tradership at Fort Sill, Indian Territory. Marsh had no intention of manning the post himself and willingly entered into an arrangement with the incumbent, one John S. Evans. Belknap himself told Evans about Marsh and let Evans know that whatever arrangement Evans could make with the merchant was entirely his business. This was bad enough, but in Marsh's case the arrangement was that he would pay to Mrs. Belknap half of the money he received from Evans. This all took place in October 1870, and Marsh continued to make the payments even after Mrs. Belknap's death in December of that year. Within a year or two Belknap married his deceased wife's sister. The Belknaps led a gay social life and lived beyond the modest salary of a cabinet officer. Surely, with Belknap's easy ethics concerning the farming out of post traderships it is conceivable, indeed likely, that he could find some way to rationalize Marsh's payments. It is also conceivable, and probable, that once having allowed his wife to accept money from Marsh without unpleasant consequences, Belknap became deadened ethically. The explanation that the secretary believed the money to be income from the property belonging to his second wife is not credible.[11]

The secretary's sudden resignation on March 2, 1876, actually came after several months of public notice of his questionable handling of the post traderships. Representative Heister Clymer of Pennsylvania, Belknap's Princeton classmate, informed the secretary on March 1 that at a meeting of the Committee of Expenditures in the War Department, the day before, "testimony of a character important to yourself was taken," and Belknap was invited to appear to cross-examine the informant. The secretary did not attend the committee meeting, but on the following day, March 2, accompanied by Zach Chandler, he hurried to the White House to submit his resignation. The committee investigation had progressed to the point where Belknap saw the expediency of getting out fast.

It was mid-morning when Belknap and Chandler encountered Grant in the White House. Belknap somewhat incoherently told Grant that he had to resign and that in some way his wife's honor was at stake. Always ready to defend a man under attack, especially when the good name of a female was involved, Grant quickly had an acceptance written which he forthwith signed.[12]

Coming just as the Babcock trial was nearing its end, this latest eruption might well have given Grant pause. Unable to comprehend that a trusted advisor might have betrayed him, Grant unwisely neglected to find out just what specifically had happened and to withhold judgment until he could determine whether or not legal steps should be taken. The next day Fish related how Grant explained his hasty action to the members of his cabinet.

The President spoke of Belknap's defection [Fish recorded in his diary] saying that yesterday he had really, in the first part of the day been unable to comprehend its magnitude & importance the surprise was so great, that it was really not until evening that he could realize the crime, and its gravity. He spoke of his long continued acquaintance with Belknap in the Army, of his having known his father as one of the finest officers of the Old Army, when he himself was a young lieutenant. . . . He said that he had accepted the resignation on its being tendered and under the wrong impression, as he did not fully understand the statements of Belknap, who was very much overcome and could scarcely speak: he did not know that acceptance was not a matter of course.

The House on the afternoon of March 2 voted to impeach Belknap. The trial before the Senate eventually hinged on whether or not Belknap's resignation removed him from the jurisdiction of that body.

As with Babcock, Grant soon was convinced of Belknap's lack of guilt. On March 7 at a cabinet meeting which took up the case, Grant asserted his belief that Belknap was entirely innocent. The cabinet's silence on hearing this speaks volumes. Because 1876 was an election year and the House controlled by the Democrats, he would naturally conclude, as he had in Babcock's case, that the sole motive for the investigation was political, and that it was directed at him. His feelings were tacitly expressed by permitting his wife to receive Mrs. Belknap at the

White House. Later, Belknap wrote to his sister that the Grants were treating him and his wife "with exceeding kindness."[13] The early weeks of the trial were taken up with an effort to get the case dismissed on the grounds that the Senate lacked jurisdiction in view of Belknap's prior resignation. The taking of testimony did not begin until July 6. The case centered on the question of Marsh's motive in sending the money to Mrs. Belknap, because the fact that money was sent and delivered was well established. Marsh asserted that the motive was simply for the pleasure of it. "I sent him the money as a present always, gratuitously," he testified. "That is the only reason I had." Belknap's lawyers insisted that the mere giving of money by Marsh was no crime; it would be such only if it had been given with the intent to influence. Always, in the background, was the veiled hint that Belknap was shielding his wife. In the vote on August 1, Belknap was acquitted, but it could hardly be said he was fully vindicated. The vote was 37 to convict and 25 for acquittal, not the two thirds needed for conviction.

Not long after the trial's end, Belknap, his wife, and son, called on President and Mrs. Grant and according to his account, "No reception could have been more cordial." This was Grant's way of letting the country know that he believed Belknap worthy of his confidence.

The evidence against Belknap, read with any degree of objectivity, can be regarded as nothing more than reasonably conclusive proof of his guilt. Yet the civil suit that was contemplated was dropped, and in the one attempt to bring him to justice he was acquitted. He never admitted to any guilt; Montgomery Blair, one of his counsel, and a man of national prominence, proclaimed his innocence. The President of the United States, stated in a cabinet meeting and indicated by his personal attentions his belief in Belknap's integrity. He lived many years in Washington as a prominent lawyer and received military honors at his death in 1890.[14]

One by-product of the Belknap affair was the death of General George A. Custer, who had been a principal witness against the Secretary of War. Custer had the courage, and the temerity, to speak out against evils which, he believed, existed in the handling of post traderships, and for this Grant had seen to it that he did not command the expedition against the Sioux in the summer of 1876. Instead, he was relegated to a subsidiary role, and, in a desperate attempt to redeem himself, showed unwise boldness in the presence of the Indians. This proved to be his undoing.[15]

With the Belknap affair coming directly on top of the Babcock trial, the reputation of the Grant administration had sunk to depths from which it would never recover. Unfortunately, the President himself had brought discredit on the administration by his ill-advised and foolish interference in the efforts to root out evil in national political life. Had he, from the start of his first administration, taken a firm stand against any and all wrong-doing he could have won a name for himself as a stern upholder of integrity and honesty in government even if he had never sponsored a statesman-like act. But he stubbornly sided with those being attacked by men who considered themselves reformers, but whom he considered trouble-makers and persons eager to make him look bad. He had seen many of these in his lifetime and had built up a strong hostility to them. How much of the hostility was the product of a sense of inferiority and sensitivity to criticism from those whom he believed were behaving toward him in a condescending way is impossible to determine with accuracy. Yet a man who himself so frequently suffered from what he believed to be unfair charges, and from persons who might be patronizing him, would be inclined to feel sympathy toward those whom he had known and trusted and who had stood by him when he had been under attack. For a man holding the highest office in the land to be guided by such principles, based as they were on emotion and feeling rather than reason and sound thinking, could only convince the intelligent citizen that the President lacked the basic requisites for strict, impartial administration. Even if Babcock and Belknap had been innocent, Grant still should not have behaved as he did. At the least, he can be charged with a lack of sense of propriety, of the fitness of things, a shortcoming which was imbedded deep in Grant's upbringing and early associations.

Unfortunately, the Babcock and Belknap affairs were not the only scandals in 1876. A lesser stir came as a result of a House committee investigation (the Democrats in this election year overlooked no opportunity to embarrass their rivals) into the conduct of General Robert C. Schenck, who was Motley's successor as minister to Great Britain.

Contrary to some accounts, General Schenck was not a buffoon whose sole claim to fame was his book on poker. Rather, he was an educated man, a former teacher of French and Latin, and, for two years before the war, minister to Brazil. He served creditably in the army during a part of the war and then was elected to Congress as a representative from Ohio. In the House he rose to the chairmanship of the Ways and Means

Committee. Grant held him in respect, as did Fish. In fact, one of the most interesting aspects of the affair is the degree to which the incorruptible Secretary of State befriended and praised Schenck.

On Motley's removal from his post as minister to Great Britain, Grant, after failing to obtain the services of either Oliver P. Morton, Frederick Frelinghuysen, and several others, sent Schenck's name to the Senate. At about this time the negotiations that culminated in the Treaty of Washington were about to get under way, and Grant named Schenck to be one of the members of the American delegation. Thus the general did not assume his duties in England until June of 1871. From all accounts, he appears to have done an excellent job as minister, and won the warm commendation of Hamilton Fish. One difficulty, however, did arise which brought discredit on Schenck, and, indirectly on Grant.

Schenck was not a wealthy man, and although he coveted the ministerial post, his private means were not sufficient to maintain himself in the accustomed manner in London. It was true then, as it always has been, that the salary of the American representative in several of the European capitals does not begin to cover the cost of maintaining a proper diplomatic establishment. Schenck was aware of this when he accepted the post, but he apparently believed he could make ends meet through some timely investments. In particular, he had stock in the Emma silver mine in Utah, an enterprise typical of the day, which, if all went well, could pay a rich return on a modest investment. In November 1871, Grant and Fish first became aware of Schenck's involvement with the Emma mine, not simply as a stockholder, but also as a director. His name appeared in some promotional advertising of the stock, and the American press seized on this in highly critical fashion. Fish immediately instructed Schenck to resign the directorship. Schenck complied, although not until after a month had passed during which time friends and associates of his could, if they desired, unload their investment before any drop in the price might occur because of Schenck's withdrawal. Also, in publicly announcing his resignation, he gave a final endorsement of the stock, an action hardly in keeping with Fish's instruction.

The matter languished for about a year but erupted again in early 1873, when English investors began to complain because the mine gave out, and the stock plunged from £ 33 a share to £ 4. It now appeared that the prospectus which Schenck had endorsed contained false and misleading statements. In England feeling against Schenck was running high. At a cabinet meeting on August 6, 1873, the plan to send the minister a letter demanding an explanation was dropped on the assumption that Schenck would deny the charges, assert that he had acted legally and within his rights, and that the administration would either have to accept his denial or conduct an embarrassing investigation. In full agreement, Grant added significantly, "I will not become the accuser of General Schenck."

Had the Democrats not won control of the House, it is likely that the whole affair would have been forgotten. Not even the revelation of the fact that Schenck had written and published the book on poker would have made any appreciable difference. When Grant learned of the book in March 1875, he determined that Schenck would have to go. But Fish came quickly to his rescue, reminding Grant "that he had done good service to the country, and the Republican party, and that his removal at this time might disappoint a great many, and certainly would make an enemy of him; . . . ." Fish went on to say that, since Schenck was a good friend and a poor man, he would prefer not to write the letter of dismissal. The President remarked sarcastically about Schenck's connection with the Emma mine. Thus it was that against Grant's wishes the minister remained at his post through the intercession of Hamilton Fish. Then early in February of 1876 the Democratic House called for an investigation of the affair, and a committee, headed by Abram S. Hewitt, exposed the unsavory relationship between Schenck and the Emma mine. There was now no choice but to remove the general and this Grant and Fish proceeded to do, Fish still trying hard to save Schenck's feelings.

Undoubtedly, Schenck had misbehaved and his conduct was censurable. One cannot, however, help but feel sympathy for the bluff Ohioan, who commented on leaving for home, "Don't send anybody here who is not rich." The culmination of this affair, it will be noted, came simultaneously with the Babcock trial, and only a short time before the Belknap scandal broke.[16]

A House investigation of George Robeson's administration of the Navy Department uncovered some hard-to-explain facts concerning contracts with a certain A. G. Cattell & Co. of Philadelphia, friendly relations between Robeson and members of the Cattell firm, and a rapid increase in the size of Robeson's bank account. Though the committee found no specific evidence of corruption, the impression left was decidedly unfavorable to Grant's Secretary of the Navy. This report appeared in the midst of the Belknap impeachment trial. Then, to top everything, another House committee looked into the manner in which the whiskey ring trials had been conducted, and revealed how Grant had committed several improprieties on behalf of Babcock.

Congress, this election year, went out of its way to embarrass the President. In addition to the actions already noted, there was passed, in April, a bill to reduce the President's salary to $25,000. Unwilling to see this occur even though the reduction would not apply to him, Grant vetoed the measure. Then the House called for the facts on the amount of time Grant had spent away from Washington, an obvious reference to his lengthy summer vacations at Long Branch, and his frequent trips to other parts of the country. Grant's way of handling this was to detail the absences of every President from Washington to Lincoln.[17]

That the Democrats would resort to this kind of tactics is understandable in the light of their overwhelming desire to gain victory in the 1876 elections, after so many years in the wilderness. Much seemed to be going for them: the depression lingered; opposition to Grant within the Republican party seemed as rife as in 1872; and the revelation of scandal raised hopes that the voters in 1876 would demand a change.

Yet, inexplicably, the Democratic triumph of 1874 was not repeated in 1875 or in the spring elections of 1876. Apparently enough voters either dissociated the scandals from the Republican party, or the contests were primarily local in character and thus unrelated to the national political picture. In any event, the party showed signs of being very much alive. Even so, the chance of the Republicans selecting a candidate identified with honest government and reform increased proportionately to the number of scandals linked to the Grant administration.

Grant did not control the Republican convention that met in Cincinnati on June 14, 1876. Indeed, the nomination of Rutherford B. Hayes of Ohio implied a repudiation of the President in that Hayes' principal claim on the delegates was his reputation as an honest administrator during two terms as governor of Ohio. At least, Grant had the satisfaction of seeing Bristow fail in his bid for the nomination and of having the convention dutifully endorse his administration.

Grant had mixed feelings about the election of 1876. Naturally he wanted a Republican victory, and he sent a congratula-

tory telegram to Hayes when the convention decision was
known. Yet he could hardly be enthusiastic about Hayes' candidacy. For one thing, the whole tone of the Republican campaign was one of repudiation of the sordid past and a promise
for more honesty and uprightness for the future. In addition,
Hayes' acceptance speech contained assurances that he would
serve only one term and made a bid for the reformers' support
with a strong endorsement of civil service reform. Grant could
only see this as a slap at himself. Hayes, learning of Grant's
reaction, felt obliged to write a letter of explanation.[18]

Despite his misgivings about Hayes, Grant was a good
enough politician to support the party ticket. Hayes and the
platform strongly backed a sound money policy, which the
Democrats, who nominated Samuel J. Tilden of New York, did
not do (although Tilden was a hard money man), and Grant, as
so many other Americans, could still see the Democratic party,
influenced by ex-rebels, as a threat to the safety of the nation.
Somehow it would mean a repudiation of the results of the war
should the Democrats gain control of the presidency and the
Congress. Consequently, Grant, while preserving proper deco-
rum, did use his office to help the Republican party's cause. So,
for instance, he offered no objection to his Secretary of the
Interior, Zach Chandler, filling the position of Republican party
chairman. Nor did he hesitate to fill various offices with an eye
to strengthening the party in certain areas. Thus, when Marshall Jewell, able and conscientious Postmaster General, resigned at Grant's request, the President appointed James N.
Tyner of Indiana, Second Assistant Postmaster General, with an
eye to helping the party in that doubtful state. Grant called
Tyner to the White House and told him bluntly, "I have decided, Mr. Tyner, to ask for your resignation." Tyner, dismayed,
was ready to accept his fate, when Grant added, "And to appoint you Postmaster General." He asked for the resignation of
the collector and deputy collector of the port of Baltimore, and
of the United States Marshall, District of Maryland. He even
bowed to the wishes of Illinois' senators to oust his friend, and
Orville Babcock's uncle, J. Russell Jones, as collector of customs
in Chicago.[19]

Grant strengthened his party in Pennsylvania by appointing
Simon Cameron's son to the post of Secretary of War to replace
Alphonso Taft of Ohio. Taft, who had been Belknap's successor
became Attorney General when Edwards Pierrepont went to
England as a replacement for Schenck. When Bristow resigned

as Secretary of the Treasury immediately after the Republican convention, Grant appointed a senator, Lot M. Morrill of Maine, a known sound money man who would reassure the eastern financial community.

As the outlook for victory in November grew murky, Republican papers such as the *New York Tribune*, which had earlier not hesitated to castigate Grant and his administration, saw good in him after all. It was beginning to be realized that Grant still had a large measure of popularity with the voters of the country and that he was a valuable political asset. Late in August the *Tribune* conceded that "Unpopular as the later years of his administration have been, he will thus go out of office amid general good will."

Congressman James A. Garfield, two months later in the closing weeks of the campaign, wrote in his diary,

Today I was again impressed with the belief that when his Presidential term is ended, General Grant will regain his place as one of the very foremost of Americans. His power of staying, his imperturbability, has been of incalculable value to the nation, and will be prized more and more as his career recedes.

Grant's handling of Southern affairs in this election year also had a bearing on the outcome of the Hayes-Tilden contest. He might well have indirectly saved South Carolina for the Republicans, thus contributing enormously to Hayes' victory, and by his stubborn refusal to respond to the urgent appeals of the Republicans in Louisiana strengthened his reputation for impartiality in dealing with matters pertaining to the South. When the crisis of the disputed election threatened the internal stability of the nation, it was Grant's great reputation for honesty, firmness, and strength of character which helped avert a renewal of civil strife.[20]

Southern tactics for recovering political control had grown more sophisticated since the early days of the Ku Klux Klan, but the basic device, that of intimidation, was still being employed. The so-called Mississippi Plan of intimidation without physical violence had proved effective in that state in 1875, and it was currently being applied in South Carolina. To refrain completely from violence was not always possible, however, and in July at Hamburg, South Carolina, a serious racial conflict erupted, in which an indeterminate number of Negroes were killed. Another outbreak of even more serious proportions occurred at Ellenton in September. The danger to the Negro population and to those whites who supported the Republican party was such that Governor Daniel H. Chamberlain, carpetbagger from New England, appealed to Grant for federal assistance. So once more, but in one of the infrequent instances in which the Southern question had come to the fore in recent years, Grant had to decide what his duty was. Though the political motive for intervention was so obvious that Grant could not escape the charge of taking advantage of convenient racial trouble to win election votes for the Republican candidate, his reluctant decision to help preserve order in South Carolina, and his unwillingness to intervene at all in Louisiana proves conclusively that he did not use the Southern situation for partisan advantage in the 1876 election. To him, it was clear that the appeal of Governor Chamberlain and the obviously unsettled and lawless conditions prevailing in South Carolina could not be ignored. That he felt revulsion over the Hamburg massacre is indicated in his letter to Chamberlain. The incident he termed, "cruel, bloodthirsty, wanton, unprovoked, and ... uncalled for." He likened conditions in South Carolina to those in Mississippi and Louisiana. Elections in Mississippi he said had been marked by fraud and violence

such as would scarcely be accredited to savages, much less to a civilized and Christian people. ... There has never been [Grant continued] a desire on the part of the North to humiliate the South—nothing is claimed for one State that is not freely accorded to all the others, unless it may be the right to kill negroes and republicans without fear of punishment. ... Government that cannot give protection to the life, property, and all guaranteed civil rights ... to the citizen, is in so far, a failure, and every energy of the oppressed should be exerted to regain lost privileges or protection.

Though additional troops were not thrown into South Carolina at this time, continued disorder in the state led Chamberlain to renew his request for military assistance. On October 17, Grant issued a proclamation ordering the rifle clubs, which were believed to be the cause of the disturbances, to disperse within three days. At the same time he ordered General Sherman to send reinforcements to the troubled state.

Federal troops at polling places in South Carolina made it possible for Chamberlain to run a close race with the Democratic candidate, Wade Hampton, and for Hayes to claim the state's electors in the national election. South Carolina was only one of the three Southern states where the election result was in doubt until shortly before inauguration day.

Grant was in Philadelphia visiting his friend George Childs on election day. As the returns came in, doubts began to rise as to the outcome. Grant took the position that Tilden had won. At Fish's urging, three days after the election, when the Republican leadership was claiming the three states of South Carolina, Florida, and Louisiana, he issued orders to Sherman:

> Instruct General [C. C.] Augur in Louisiana and General [T. H.] Ruger in Florida to be vigilant with the force at their command to preserve peace and good order. . . . No man worthy of the office of President should be willing to hold it if counted in or placed there by fraud. Either party can afford to be disappointed in the result. The country cannot afford to have the result tainted by the suspicion of illegal or false returns.

Prompt action of this sort indicated Grant's primary concern with preserving the peace. Nowhere did he try to swing the election toward Hayes, despite urgings from Zach Chandler, Secretary of War Cameron, and Attorney General Taft. A wide-open opportunity existed in South Carolina, but Grant refused to allow himself to be drawn into a partisan intervention.[21]

Election day did not bring any relief from the tensions in South Carolina, for the result of the gubernatorial election between Chamberlain and Wade Hampton remained in doubt for months. With violence threatening to erupt, Grant insisted only that the federal troops maintain order. But the more partisan members of the cabinet, realizing that for Hayes to win the disputed election he must carry South Carolina (as well as the other disputed states), tried to commit Grant to a policy of intervention on the side of Chamberlain. Cameron and Taft wanted Grant to order General Ruger to control the membership of the state legislature, but, according to Fish, "The President objected saying that the troops were not there to act under the orders of Chamberlain but were there to preserve peace and order and he did not think that he (the President) had any right to say who should or should not be excluded from the Chamber."

The next day's cabinet meeting saw a repetition of the previous debate with Grant standing firm against the proddings of Cameron and Taft. Noting what the country's reaction was to the Louisiana episode of two years before, the President denied that the federal government had any authority "to interfere in the organization of a state legislature."

The weeks immediately following the election saw no solution to the election disputes either on the state or the national level. While frantic efforts on both sides were being made to gain an advantage, Grant sent to the Congress his annual message on the state of the Union. The factual content held few surprises. There was no reference to the request he had made the previous year for a constitutional amendment requiring each state to maintain a system of public education on the condition there be no public support of church-related schools, nor to his suggestion that Congress tax church property not used for religious purposes. The most unusual part of the message was a return to the Santo Domingo matter which could be accounted for in no other way than as a sign that Grant hated to admit failure and wanted vindication. But the message had a unique feature in the form of a confession, the like of which has never before or since appeared in a presidential message to Congress. Looking back over the past eight years, Grant obviously wanted to make some explanation for the scandals that were still fresh in everyone's mind. Thus he began,

It was my fortune, or misfortune, to be called to the office of Chief Executive without any previous political training. ... Under such circumstances it is but reasonable to suppose that errors of judgment must have occurred. Even had they not, differences of opinion between the Executive, bound by an oath to the strict performance of his duties, and writers and debators must have arisen. It is not necessarily evidence of blunder on the part of the Executive because there are these differences of views. Mistakes have been made, as all can see and I admit, but it seems to me oftener in the selection made of the assistants appointed to aid in carrying out the various duties of administering the Government —in nearly every case selected without a personal acquaintance with the appointee, but upon recommendations of the representatives chosen directly by the people. I have acted in every instance from a conscientious desire to do what was right, constitutional, within the law, and for the very best interests of the whole people. Failures have been errors of judgment, not of intent.

Grant, an intensely sensitive man, must have suffered agonies while setting those thoughts down on paper.

The President's problems would continue, however, right down to the day his successor was inaugurated. As the weeks passed, the possibility of inauguration day arriving without a decision about the election increased. Rumors of impending violence circulated. Louisiana presented one of the most diffi-

cult problems because of the patently fraudulent character of
the election in that unhappy state. The Republicans controlled
the returning board, but the Democrats appeared to have won
the election, both in the presidential contest and the race for
governor. The only way the Republicans could claim the state
and seat Stephen B. Packard, the Republican candidate for governor, would be for the returning board to throw out enough
Democratic votes to give the Republicans a majority.[22]

The Louisiana Republican leaders, carpetbaggers for the
most part, counted on the help of the federal government.
Without that help it was hardly likely that Packard could be
inaugurated and the Republican-dominated legislature assemble. A request for troops from the incumbent governor, William
Pitt Kellogg, received on January 2, 1877, was so vaguely
worded that Grant decided to ignore it. But on January 7, a
new call for help demanded some kind of decision, and Grant
hastily summoned the cabinet. On arrival at the White House,
Fish asked Grant the reason for the meeting, as Fish recorded
in his diary, and Grant replied that—

it was 'again the Louisiana trouble,' adding with some manifestation of
impatience, 'they are always in trouble there and always wanting the
U. S. to send troops. They want me to inaugurate their governor and
legislature.' He handed me a paper which he said was the answer he
intended to give them—it was a peremptory refusal to comply with their
request.

Unfortunately for Grant, he was subjected to a great deal of
contrary advice. While Fish applauded his decision not to intervene on behalf of the Kellogg-Packard faction, Cameron, Taft,
and Chandler urged him to reconsider. Grant had little use for
the Louisiana Republicans, but he could not ignore the urgent
pleas of three influential men in his cabinet. On January 17, he
called in Hamilton Fish on whom he could rely for sound advice. Confessing that the Louisiana troubles and the importuni-
ties of such leading Republicans as John Sherman and Eugene
Hale had cost him sleep, he denounced the Louisiana carpetbaggers as incompetents, men who would leave the state as
soon as they lost office. Then came an admission which revealed the depths of Grant's conservatism on the race question,
and, since it undoubtedly coincided with views of countless
white Americans in the year 1877, helps to account for the
abandonment of the Negro to the control of the Southern

whites. "He says," wrote Fish, "he is opposed to the XV amendment and thinks it was a mistake; that it had done the Negro
no good, and had been a hinderance to the South, and by no
means a political advantage to the North."

The comment on Negro suffrage was in the nature of an
aside. The immediate question was whether or not to support
the Louisiana Republicans with the military, and Grant successfully resisted all efforts to persuade him to do more than simply
to direct that the peace should be maintained. Although he did
not want to admit it publicly, he believed that the Democratic
claimaint of the governorship, Francis R. T. Nicholls, would
give better service to the people of Louisiana than Packard.
Right down to the end, Grant, declaring on February 23 that he
would not sustain legislatures with military force, and on March
1 that troops would "not be used to establish or pull down
either claimant for the control of the State," continued to stave
off the interventionists. And on March 3, in a letter to Cameron, he wrote, "I would let the two Governors work out their
own precedence for Executive recognition in the same manner
as any Northern state would have to do under like circumstances."[23]

Meanwhile, the greater crisis, that involving the future of the
presidency, moved on without solution into the new year. Finally, the Congress came up with a compromise proposal for an
electoral commission made up of five representatives each from
the House, Senate, and Supreme Court to give a decision on the
disputed vote in the four states of Louisiana, Florida, South
Carolina, and Oregon. At first the Democrats backed the plan
more enthusiastically than did the Republicans since they expected the decisions to go in their favor. Grant, however, believing it to be the best way to arrive at a peaceful way out of
the dilemma, supported it. At Fish's suggestion, he sent a message to the Senate, on January 29, directly after the passage of
the bill creating the Electoral Commission, voicing his support
of the plan and urging his countrymen to accept its verdict.
This might well have had a salutary effect and led to a greater
feeling of confidence in this unique device for determining the
election of the president. At least, this is what Adam Badeau,
watching these events from London, believed. And there is no
question but that Grant's reputation for firmness and respect
for the law, plus his known determination to maintain the
peace, with force if necessary, contributed to a lessening of the
tension.[24]

It was, however, a behind-the-scenes maneuver by certain Republicans working for Hayes and some Southern Democrats, most of whom were more in sympathy with Whig (or, in this instance, Republican) economic views that brought a peaceful ending to the electoral crisis. Grant had nothing to do with these schemes. The Electoral Commission found for Hayes in each instance; Congress accepted the findings, and the way was finally clear for Hayes' inauguration.

Hayes arrived in Washington March 2, and the next evening dined at the White House. Since March 4 fell on a Sunday and the public inauguration was scheduled for Monday, the fifth, there loomed the prospect of an interregnum. With all that had gone before, with all the rumors of force being used to place Tilden in office, or of his taking the oath in New York, it is hardly surprising that leaders of both the outgoing and incoming administrations should have looked with some trepidation on the prospect of no president being legally installed for even as brief a period as one day. On Saturday afternoon, Fish gained Hayes' consent to take the oath that evening in private, at the White House. Just before dinner, Chief Justice Waite administered the oath to Hayes in the Red Room with only one or two witnesses attending. As it turned out, the precaution was unnecessary, for the public ceremony went off without incident on Monday. When it was over, the Grants entertained the new President and his wife at a luncheon at the White House, after which they departed from the house they had lived in for eight years and went to stay at the home of Hamilton Fish for several weeks.[25]

CHAPTER XII

Last Years: Tragedy and Triumph

FOR THE FIRST TIME IN SIXTEEN YEARS GRANT WAS A PRIVATE citizen, and he now occupied that most awkward of positions, ex-president of the United States. Being an inveterate traveler, and never having been abroad, he and Mrs. Grant decided to take a trip to Europe. Fortunately, the money was available for an extended tour; Grant had $25,000 and his son Buck had made some investments for him in mining stock, which, in the course of the trip, happened to pay off handsomely, thus providing additional funds.[1]

Following a hurried visit to St. Louis and to the general's boyhood home in Georgetown, Ohio, the Grants sailed from Philadelphia on May 17, 1877. With them went their youngest son, Jesse, Grant's first Secretary of the Navy, Adolph E. Borie, and a writer for the *New York Herald*, J. Russell Young.

Grant's last years in office had seen a marked decline in overt demonstrations of his popularity. Not that his countrymen no longer respected his services to the nation; but the misfortunes of his presidency, the ill-feeling generated by some of his policies, actions, and appointments sharpened by the debilitating effects of a lengthy depression had seemingly lessened that exuberant enthusiasm and affection so evident at the close of the war. How gratifying then to experience an outpouring of admiration at the moment of departure from his homeland. A round of receptions, parties, and public demonstrations preceded his departure from Philadelphia and then, as the ship moved down the Delaware River toward the open sea, it was escorted by a fleet of attendant vessels, which showed by their festive decorations and crowded decks that Grant still retained a favored place in the hearts of his fellow Americans. It was as if they were willing to look backward to the dark days of the war and recall his heroic services to the Union. As Sherman wrote to Badeau soon after Grant's arrival in England,

Now that he is untrammeled by the personal contests of partisans, all men look upon him as *the* General Grant, who had the courage, with Lee at his front and Washington at his rear, to undertake to command the Army of the Potomac in 1864, to guide, direct, and push it through sunshine and storm, through praise and denunciation, steadily, surely, and finally to victory and peace; and *afterwards, though unused to the ways and machinery of civil government, to risk all in undertaking to maintain that peace by the Constitution and civil forms of government.*

The reception he received in England equalled in enthusiasm the send-off from America and for the same reasons. The London *Times* was even ready to praise him for his services as President especially for "having brought his country through a very critical period." Englishmen, said the *Times*, will forget his faults and remember only his virtues, and "he will be welcomed as one of the most distinguished men whom the United States have yet produced. . . . "[2]

The enthusiastic welcome from the English people of all classes can only be accounted for by their conviction that Grant truly was a great man, probably the greatest living military figure and someone worthy of their accolades. Especially gratifying to him was the warmth of the reception by the working people of England; they seemed to grasp instinctively that here was a man who understood them, who could be reached, whose hand could be grasped. He was the embodiment of the democratic ideal.

In England, Grant associated with persons of all ranks. For the aristocrats, he was the great attraction who had to be called upon and entertained. This included the Queen and the most prominent peers. The American minister, Edwards Pierrepont, arranged matters so that Grant was accorded the same treatment as an ex-sovereign, and no embarrassment insofar as etiquette was concerned occurred, except at a dinner given by the Prince of Wales. On that occasion, neither Grant nor his wife was given much recognition, and they were seated well down from the head of the table. Grant gave no notice of the incident, although when Queen Victoria entertained him and Mrs. Grant at Windsor, he asked that his son Jesse be included in the invitation, instead of having to eat with the household.[3]

It was not long before Grant became adept at public speaking. He was forced into it from necessity, and once having demonstrated his facility at the task he had so resolutely avoided all during his presidency, he developed into a polished, graceful speaker, always coming up with just the right words for the occasion.

Having visited the sights in Britain, the Grant party moved on to the continent, and eventually, over a period of many months, visited every country of western Europe. Everywhere the enthusiasm was as pronounced as in England, except perhaps in France, where it was thought Grant had been partial to the Germans during the Franco-Prussian War.

Of course, Grant was obliged to do an enormous amount of sightseeing, most of which he did not enjoy. Especially was he bored by art museums and churches. He preferred engineering works and natural sights such as the Alps. Stoically, though, he did his duty, regardless of the point of interest he was asked to observe, only occasionally balking at having to walk through another gallery. And he avoided reviewing troops whenever possible.[4]

On his travels, which incidentally were random, unplanned, and subject to his or Mrs. Grant's whim, he met with virtually every ruler and statesman of note and was accorded all the dignity and ceremony befitting an honored representative of the highest rank of a friendly power. Bismarck, Gambetta, and Disraeli especially impressed him.

Having covered most of Europe rather thoroughly, and still unready to return directly home, Grant, at the end of 1878, decided to complete the circuit of the globe by way of Egypt, India, China, and Japan. China intrigued Grant, but he particularly liked Japan. He noticed and disapproved of the over-bearing ways of westerners toward orientals. "The course of the average minister, consul & merchant in this country & China towards the native," he remarked to his daughter, "is much like the course of the former slave owner towards the freedman when the latter attempts to think for himself in matters of choice of candidates."[5]

Japan proved the last stop on the journey home, although Grant confessed to Badeau that were there a steamship line running between Japan and Australia he would postpone his return still further. The truth was he did not want to return. He told Badeau that after the first year of absence from home he was quite homesick. "Now," he confessed, " ... I dread going back. ... " His plan was to return to Galena, stay there until winter, and then travel, possibly to Cuba and Mexico.

Grant did not elaborate on why he dreaded returning home. It may have been that he had no plans and had no desire to live out the rest of his life in Galena. More probably, he was referring to the forthcoming presidential election. Already, he was being mentioned as the candidate for the Republican party in 1880, and he knew that whenever he set foot on American soil, he would be the center of political maneuvering and at the mercy of the party leaders.

His presence abroad, the reports of his welcome by peoples of foreign lands, and his enthusiastic acceptance by royalty and leading statesmen, made his fellow Americans realize, if they needed reminding, how important a person Ulysses S. Grant was in the eyes of the world. A surge of affection and an outpouring of devotion thus greeted the wanderer on his return to the United States. No one could deny that he was still the great hero to multitudes of Americans, who showed it by giving him a tumultuous reception from San Francisco, where he landed on September 20, 1879, to Chicago and Philadelphia. Had the Republican convention met in the fall of 1879 instead of the spring of 1880, Grant might very well have been nominated by acclamation, so high was the tide of Grant's strength at that time. This is why the Grant supporters wanted him to remain out of the country for another six months. His nomination, however, was never a certainty, for the same people who hailed Grant as their hero could well have been thinking of the war years, and not to his career as President.[6]

One thing seemed certain: Hayes would not be the Republican nominee in 1880. He had announced that he did not want another term, but, in addition, he had made powerful enemies within the party. All those, such as Conkling, who had been closely associated with the Grant administration, could not accept with good grace several of Hayes' appointments, especially that of Carl Schurz, Grant's implacable foe, to a cabinet position. The whole manner in which Hayes handled the patronage was distasteful to the hardcore spoilsmen who had no sympathy with Hayes' reforming tendencies. From Scotland, Grant had written Fish that in his opinion Hayes would "find out that there were two great humbugs influencing him now; namely, reform and reformers." Nor had Hayes enjoyed much success in his administration, especially in his attempt to win over conservative Southerners to the Republican party. In making the effort, he had alienated those remaining Radicals who believed the party owed the freedmen something and that it was a crime to abandon them.[7]

Grant professed to be terribly worried over the possibility of a Democratic victory in the election. To Washburne he wrote from Havana in February that all he wanted was "that the gov-

ernment rule should remain in the hands of those who saved
the Union until all the questions growing out of the war are
forever settled." Yet, despite many protestations to the contrary, he was also interested in being elected President for a
third term. In the same letter while he stated flatly that he was
"not a candidate for anything," he nonetheless refused to state
that he would not accept a nomination. On the contrary, he told
Washburne that because of his obligations "to the Union men of
the country that if they think my chances are better for election
than for other probable candidates ... I cannot decline if the
nomination is tendered without seeking on my part."[8]

While Grant did not actively seek the nomination, he did, on
his way back from a trip to Cuba and Mexico that winter, return via New Orleans, Vicksburg, and Memphis, and of course
he had a full share of publicity with every move. His friends
proceeded on the assumption that he would accept the nomination, and Badeau believed Grant to be "extremely anxious" for
it. This was also Garfield's conclusion shortly after he had assumed office. On June 21, 1881 he wrote in his journal: "It is
now evident (what I had not supposed) that Grant had his heart
fully set on the nomination at Chicago and was deeply hurt at
his failure."

Grant seemed not to be aware of a strong anti-third term
movement, or if he was, his friends, especially Conkling, Cameron, Boutwell, and Logan, reassured him. Instead, they led
him to think that there would be no serious opposition to his
nomination. Had he known of what was to happen, it is most
unlikely he would have allowed his name to be presented to the
convention. The movement to stop Grant was so powerful,
however, it is strange that he failed to appreciate its strength.
For one thing, several other men had designs on the nomination
and quite naturally believed that Grant had had his turn. Furthermore, the reform element in the party simply could not
tolerate another Grant administration, with the spoilsmen once
more assuming control. Finally, there were experienced politicians who frankly did not believe Grant could win. Thurlow
Weed, for instance, told Washburne in April that Grant could
not carry New York, and that his friends should persuade him
not to accept the nomination.[9]

On the first ballot in Chicago Grant received 304 votes, to
284 for Blaine with the rest scattered. Another major rival was
Senator John Sherman, and even Grant's old friend Washburne
had some votes. Grant's vote in the numerous ballots that were

taken never fell below 302, but it climbed no higher than 313, well under the 370 needed. Conkling kept his forces well in hand, but he had antagonized so many people and the opposition to Grant was so determined it was inevitable that the hero of Appomattox would never get the nomination.

On the second day of the balloting and on the thirty-sixth ballot there occurred a sudden rush to James A. Garfield, but on that last ballot 306 loyal men recorded their votes for Grant. It was a remarkable demonstration of fidelity and stubbornness as well as a testimonial to Conkling's ability as a disciplinarian.

Grant was at the office of General William R. Rowley, a Galena neighbor and wartime staff member, along with a few friends when he learned of Garfield's victory and his own defeat. As usual, he showed no emotion, remarked that Garfield was a good man, and went home. Julia, who had wanted to return to the White House, was manifestly disappointed.[10]

Though Grant took his defeat without a murmur so far as the general public was concerned, he nonetheless felt the humiliation deeply and harbored resentment against those whom he believed had betrayed him. He was especially bitter about Washburne who had outwardly supported Grant, but had neither worked actively for him, nor withdrawn from the race when his name was presented to the convention. Grant never again met with Washburne, and a few years later, when the general was seriously ill in New York, and Washburne arrived in the city hoping that Grant would ask for him, the call never came. This tendency to turn against friends without any attempt at reconciliation was not one of Grant's more praiseworthy traits, and in this instance he was unnecessarily unkind toward a man who had done so much to enable him to achieve success.

For a time, Grant made no move to support the ticket of Garfield and Chester A. Arthur. He sent no message of congratulation to the nominee and not until September did he openly indicate that he would campaign for the party. Meanwhile he had visited Colorado to investigate the possibility of becoming president of a mining company.

What brought Grant out of his peeve was the possibility that the Democrats, with his old comrade Winfield S. Hancock their standardbearer, might win the election. He then entered wholeheartedly into the campaign, even though his critics declared this was undignified for an ex-president.

But [he wrote his friend General E. F. Beale] our sacrifice of blood and treasure has been too great to loose [sic] all the good results now to save a little dignity. I sincerely believe that a democratic success now would be almost as disastrous as a war, and that disaster would be no less to our section, or to our party, than to the other.[11]

Political campaigning meant speaking before crowds, something which for Grant was, in his words, "a terrible trial," but he had developed a degree of proficiency in this art during his two years abroad, and in a month of speaking in New England, New York, and New Jersey contributed immeasurably to Garfield's ultimate success. Because of his help, Grant believed it proper to give advice to the new President-elect, especially in regard to appointments and to Southern policy. When Garfield failed to heed the proffered advice in all particulars, Grant reacted strongly. He went so far as to remark to Badeau that "Garfield has shown that he is not possessed of the backbone of an angle-worm."

The shooting and subsequent death of Garfield brought Arthur to the presidency, and this colleague of Conkling could have been expected to get along well with Grant. Generally, however, this was not the case, largely because Arthur wanted to be his own master and not do things Grant's way. What the general asked for and expected to receive was compliance with his wishes, especially in the matter of favors for his friends. He had a good many patronage requests to make, but Arthur did not honor them all, nor did the two men agree on all phases of policy.

At the time of Garfield's assassination, Grant was in Mexico to see about some railroad matters with which he was then concerned. Having lost the nomination, he had been obliged to look to his financial situation and decide how he was going to maintain his family's social and economic position. Shortly after the election of 1880, in an effort to assure himself an income, Grant invested most of his liquid assets in a Wall Street financial partnership in which his son, Buck, was involved. This arrangement made no demands on the general, and for a few years he simply enjoyed the profits which came in quite handsomely. He even became a silent partner in the firm, Grant and Ward, on the understanding that his name would never be involved in any deal involving government contracts. Having complete faith in his son's financial ability, Grant was content to leave the active management of the firm to him and his two youthful colleagues, Ferdinand Ward and James D. Fish.

Meanwhile, Grant sought some occupation that would be remunerative and at the same time allow him an outlet for his energies. His interest in Mexico and his friendship with Don Matias Romero, long-time minister of Mexico to the United States, led him into accepting the presidency of a company planning to construct a railroad from Mexico City to the Guatemala border. The venture proved unsuccessful, but since Grant's position as president was mostly nominal, he apparently did not suffer any financial loss.[12]

President Arthur, in 1882, appointed Grant and William H. Trescot, a South Carolinian and former Confederate official, commissioners to negotiate a commercial treaty with Mexico. Because of Grant's strained relations with the administration, his acceptance of the position proved somewhat awkward, but he had such a strong interest in furthering good relations with Mexico that he consented. Although a treaty favorable to both countries was signed in January 1883, it was never implemented because Congress failed to pass the necessary enabling legislation.

During these years, except for an occasional visit to Mexico, the West, and, of course Long Branch in summers, Grant and Mrs. Grant lived in a house on 66th Street, near Fifth Avenue in New York City. A group of friends had raised $100,000 for the purchase of the mansion, and other well-to-do friends had raised $250,000 to serve as a trust fund for Mrs. Grant. Through 1883 and 1884 the financial picture seemed unclouded. In fact, Grant wrote to his daughter Nellie on November 24, 1883, "we are all well, your brothers are all doing well and are happy. As a family we are much better off than ever we were before. The necessity for strict economy does not exist, or is not so pressing, as it has heretofore been."

At this time, Grant had, it seemed to him, an assured income from Grant and Ward. He would ride down each day to the office in the financial district, read mail, talk with callers, and enjoy the company of some of the big names in the business world. All the while he had little idea of what was happening in the firm to which he had lent his name and in which he had invested virtually all his liquid assets. As the financial picture brightened, however, his popularity dimmed. The image of the hero who had saved his country could not somehow be reconciled with the Wall Street investor whose closest friends and associates were the wealthiest men in the country.[13]

None of this troubled Grant, who seemed to enjoy freedom

from financial care and the companionship of the rich. No doubt he would have continued in this same pattern through the remainder of his days had not adversity struck once again. From the heights of financial security and success, overnight Grant and his whole family were plunged into almost total disaster with the failure of Grant and Ward.

Ferdinand Ward, hailed as the Napoleon of Wall Street, had succeeded, through brazenness and nerve, in convincing not only Grant but also men who had wide experience in the business world that he was something of a financial wizard whose magic touch would produce huge profits from the most modest investments. Grant believed this as did his wife, his sons, and other members of the family. The general might have been suspicious of the ease with which Ward produced dividends for the firm's investors, but his trusting soul and unbounded confidence in his son's business knowledge allowed no trace of doubt to cross his mind.

Ward, however, was not a magician; instead he had misused other people's money, and had built up the false image of a sound firm. When he reached the inevitable end of the road he compounded his crime by deliberately playing on Grant's goodwill and tricking him into providing thousands more for his own dishonest purposes. On a Sunday evening, early in May of 1884, Ward came to Grant's home with a tale that the bank, with which the firm did business and where his father-in-law was president, had immediate need of $150,000 to tide it over a temporary crisis. Having no reason to doubt the young man who for four years had done so well by him, Grant agreed to find the money. He went to the home of William H. Vanderbilt and arranged for a personal loan (the only kind Vanderbilt would make since he did not have confidence in Ferdinand Ward). Grant turned over the funds to Ward, but that was the last he saw of the youthful financier. The firm had failed completely; the loan, his investments, everything was gone. As Grant entered his office on Tuesday, May 6, 1884, he was met by his son, Buck, who related the disaster.

The financial loss was bad enough, indeed had it not been for some real estate owned by Mrs. Grant and the $250,000 trust fund, which was tied up in legal red tape at that time, the family fortunes would have been all but wiped out. But Grant felt the humiliation most of all, and he also knew how he was responsible, be it all indirectly, for the losses of friends and relatives who had invested in the firm simply because he had a share in it.

With scarcely enough cash on hand to pay ordinary household

expenses, Grant was saved from embarrassment by two gifts, equalling $1500. One came from Grant's Mexican friend, Romero, the other from a stranger, Charles Wood of Lansingburg, New York, who sent the money "on account of my share for services ending April, 1865." Mrs. Grant's two houses brought in some additional cash, but for several months Grant wallowed in the depths of financial despair.[14]

To add to his woes, his health was not the best. The previous Christmas Eve, he had slipped on the ice in front of his home and suffered a severe leg injury. Rheumatism settled in this leg and became very painful, so that it became necessary for him to use crutches. In fact, from this point to the end of his life Grant never again enjoyed good health.

Fortunately, an opportunity came along early that summer to enable him partially to recoup his fortunes. *Century Magazine* at that time was publishing a series of articles by Civil War participants, and the editors asked Grant if he would contribute one or more. He had turned down the offer in January but when the editors returned in June to ask again and made him an attractive offer, Grant, in his need, agreed to write two articles. Guided by Badeau, who taught him to enliven his terse narrative with human interest stories, geographical descriptions, personal experiences, and the like, the general wrote his first article on Shiloh, and his second one in the summer at Long Branch, on Vicksburg. Writing perked him up; becoming deeply interested in what he was doing, that summer he decided to write his memoirs after completing the two additional articles for which he had contracted. The receipt of five hundred dollars for the first and a thousand for each of the three succeeding articles made it possible for him to discharge his most pressing debts.[15]

Grant asked Badeau to help him with the memoirs and, in October, the former secretary went to live at the Grant house, where he stayed until the following May. One problem was that of choosing a publisher. *Century* of course had first claim, but Mark Twain, visiting Grant in the fall of 1884, told him that the magazine's offer was grossly inadequate and that he could do much better. At that time the famous author was associated with the C. L. Webster Company of Hartford. Believing that Grant's memoirs would have a wide sale, he offered exceedingly generous terms, which early in March 1885 Grant at length accepted.

The C. L. Webster offer came just about the time that Grant's financial problems again became acute. Minor creditors threatened to attach his war trophies, gifts from foreign governments collected during his trip around the world, and other personal possessions. Knowing this, Vanderbilt, in an attempt to save them from loss, offered to take them as payment of the debt and deed them to Mrs. Grant, with the understanding that after her death they would become the property of the national government. Cyrus W. Field and other men of means now began to raise the money Grant needed to discharge his debt to Vanderbilt, but, hearing of it and not wanting to suffer this well-meant but degrading offer of help, the general wrote to Field that he must decline his generosity.[16]

These were months of serious mental depression for Grant. The humiliation of his financial collapse must have revived memories of the lean days in St. Louis before the war. This was bad enough, but much worse was the realization sometime during the fall that he had a serious cancerous condition in his throat. Grant had been troubled that summer by a sore throat but had largely ignored it until October, when he consulted a specialist, Doctor J. H. Douglas, in New York. While some attempt was made to minimize the serousness of his sickness, Grant knew well what the trouble was and that he would probably get progressively worse. In December he wrote his friend, General Edward F. Beale,

I am now a great sufferer from my throat. It is nearly impossible for me to swallow enough to sustain life, and what I do swallow is attended with great pain. It pains me even to talk. I have to see the doctor daily, and he does not encourage me to think that I will be well soon.

Grant's mental anguish increased when on February 16, 1885 a bill to restore him to his army rank was defeated in Congress. The reason was political, the result of a difference between President Arthur and the Democrats, but it pained the general since passage of the bill would have solved his financial difficulties which were still acute. It was not until the very end of the session that Congress acted favorably on a bill acceptable to Arthur, but Grant's commission had to be signed by the incoming President, Grover Cleveland. This naturally pleased Grant, although by this time his physical condition was such that it could do little to relieve his anguish.

Congress acted out of sympathy for Grant in his distress, both economic and physical, and the senators and representatives simply reflected the sentiments of the country at large. As word spread of the general's suffering, expressions of sympathy and concern poured in from all sections of the land and from all classes of people. No reference was made to the political past or to the recent business debacle; memories went back to the hope that Grant brought in the dark days of the war, to Fort Donelson and unconditional surrender, to Pemberton's surrender at Vicksburg on the great national holiday, to the sweep of Thomas' men up Missionary Ridge, to the grim fighting of the Wilderness, and to the drama of Appomattox. When toward the end of March and early in April, Grant passed though a crisis, and when virtually everyone, including Grant himself, believed that he was on the point of death, the expressions of sympathy grew in number. It was at this time that he received baptism at the hands of a Methodist clergyman.[17]

When Grant learned that his countrymen still thought well of him and were ready to overlook his recent humiliation, he recovered sufficiently to resume work on his memoirs. And when he realized that if he worked quickly he could finish the job, he took up the task with renewed effort sustained and inspired by the knowledge that the completed memoirs could mean financial security for his wife and children.

A Philadephia friend, Joseph W. Drexel, offered Grant the use of his summer home in the Adirondacks, and so, on June 16, Grant left New York by train, went up the Hudson, past West Point on to Saratoga and beyond to Mount McGregor. The clear, cool air helped, but there was still more work to do on his memoirs. By this time Grant could scarcely use his voice, and so would write out what he wanted to say on sheets of paper.

One of the remarkable sources for information about Grant's last days is the large number of these notes which he wrote to Doctor Douglas, telling in detail of his state of health, the pain he was feeling, the food and the drugs he had taken, his comments on matters mentioned in the papers, and his chances of survival. On June 17, for instance, he informed the doctor that his system was in a state of dissolution, because of hemorrhages, strangulation, and exhaustion, that all the doctor could do would be to lessen the pain. He would rather not have another physician, but conceded that if Douglas wanted to consult with a colleague he should be called in. "I dread them however," wrote Grant, "knowing that it means another desperate effort to save me, and more suffering." On July 2, he told Douglas that he was then ready to go "without a murmur. . . . I should prefer going now to enduring my present suffering for a single day without hope of recovery."

Not until July 5 could Grant really feel that his task was completed. On that day he wrote, "I feel much relieved this morning. I had begun to feel that the work of getting my book together was making but slow progress. I find it about completed, and the work now to be done is mostly after it gets back in gallies. ... "[18]

Grant clearly recognized what had been going on, and just a week before he died confessed that

there never was one more willing to go than I am. I know most people have first one thing and then another to fix up, and never get quite through. I first wanted so many days to work on my book so the authorship would be clearly mine. It was graciously granted to me, after being apparently much lower than since, and with a capacity to do more work than I ever did in the same time. My work had been done so hastily that much was left out and I did all of it over from the crossing of the Rapidan River in June/64 to Appomattox. Since then I have added as much as fifty pages to the book, I should think. There is nothing more I should do to it now, and therefore I am more likely to be more ready to go than at this moment.[19]

The last days were relatively quiet. Drugs kept down the pain, but the general continued to fail and he died on the morning of July 23, 1885. People around the nation knew of his condition, and when the end came there was a sense of relief that the old soldier would suffer no more. But the response of a grief-stricken people and the outpouring of sentiments of respect from all around the globe attest to the tremendous grip he had on the affections of millions of people. These last months of illness had made it clear that the man who had seen so much adversity, so much success, was never as great a hero to his fellow men as when he struggled with this cruelest of illnesses fraught with pain and suffering.

The funeral rites befitted a fallen hero and the nation's mourners, thousands of whom had been his old soldiers in the armies of the Union, turned out to show that they revered his memory. The body lay in state in the capitol at Albany, and later at City Hall in New York. There was a majestic funeral procession to the temporary tomb in Riverside Park. And on April 27, 1897, on what would have been his seventy-fifth birthday, the body was re-entombed in the grandiose mausoleum overlooking the Hudson.[20]

In the years after his death the memoirs, appearing in two large volumes, had such a wide sale that Mrs. Grant quickly was restored to a comfortable financial position. But the money was only one result of Grant's final, strenuous efforts. More important for the world at large was the literary product, a strong, clear account of Grant's life through the Civil War with the emphasis on his campaigns. Seldom has a work received such undeviating praise as has this work.[21] Here the reader will find the true Grant: modest, tough, kind, reticent but not silent, and, above all, honest. But Grant the enigma remains and it will always be that way, simply because Grant defies reasoned analysis. His was a unique character, a mass of contradictions, yet he was a leader who more than once in his life reached upward to greatness.

Notes and References

CHAPTER I

1. Bruce Catton in Ulysses S. Grant, *The Papers of Ulysses S. Grant*, ed. John Y. Simon (Carbondale and Edwardsville, 1967, 1969), I, xiv. Henry Adams once wrote about Grant, "One seemed to know him so well, and really knew so little." *The Education of Henry Adams* (Boston, 1918), 263.

2. Lloyd Lewis, *Captain Sam Grant* (Boston, 1950), 17–18; U. S. Grant, *Personal Memoirs of U. S. Grant* (2 vols., N.Y., 1885), I, 17–24; Albert D. Richardson, *A Personal History of Ulysses S. Grant* (Hartford, 1868), 49–50; Hamlin Garland, *Ulysses S. Grant: His Life and Character* (N.Y., 1920), 5–6.

3. Grant, *Memoirs*, I, 24–31; Lewis, 22–48.

4. Grant, *Memoirs*, I, 32; Lewis, 51–59.

5. Grant, *Memoirs*, I, 38. For Grant's own views on his name, Grant to Julia Dent, Aug. 31, 1844, March 31, 1853, Grant, *Papers*, I, 36, 298; Garland, 43. For Grant's affection for West Point, Grant to Julia Grant, July 13, 1851, Grant, *Papers*, I, 219.

6. Grant, *Memoirs*, I, 43–47; Ishbel Ross, *The General's Wife: The Life of Mrs. Ulysses S. Grant* (N.Y., 1959), 13–16.

7. Grant, *Memoirs*, I, 47–51; Grant to Julia Dent, July 11, 1845; Grant, *Papers*, I, 50.

8. Grant to Julia Dent, June 4, 1844, Sept. 14, Nov. 11, 1845, Feb. 7, 1846, Grant, *Papers*, I, 23–25, 53–55, 61–62, 74; Grant, *Memoirs*, I, 53–56.

9. Grant to Julia Dent, May 3, 11, 1846, Grant, *Papers*, I, 83, 84–86.

10. Grant to Julia Dent, Aug. 14, 1846, *ibid.*, 106, and note.

11. Grant to Bvt. Col. John Garland [Aug. 1846], *ibid.*, 106–107; Grant to Julia Dent, Sept. 6, Oct. 3, 1846, *ibid.*, 108–109, 112; Grant, *Memoirs*, I, 105–107, 110–112, 115–118, 180; Grant to Julia Dent, Sept. 23, Oct. 3, Dec. 27, 1846; to unknown addressee, Dec. 1846, Grant, *Papers*, 110–113, 118–119, 122.

12. Grant to Julia Dent, April 3, 24, 1847, Grant, *Papers*, I, 129, 131; Grant to John W. Lowe, May 3, 1847, *ibid.*, 136–137; Grant to unknown addressee, April 24, 1847, *ibid.*, 134; Grant to Julia Dent, May 17, 26, Aug. 4, 1847, *ibid.*, 138–143.

13. Lewis, 232–237; Grant, *Memoirs*, I, 151–153, 157–159; Bvt. Col. Francis Lee to Bvt. Maj. Gen. Roger Jones, Jan. 16, 1849, Grant, *Papers*, I, 381–382; Lewis, 259, 261; Grant, *Memoirs*, I, 162–163.

14. Grant, *Memoirs*, I, 175–190; Grant to Julia Dent, May 7, 1848, Grant, *Papers*, I, 155–157; Grant, *Memoirs*, I, 192–193; Lewis, 281; Grant to Julia Dent, June 4, 1848, Grant, *Papers*, I, 160.

15. Lewis, 283–287, 291; Grant to Bvt. Maj. Oscar F. Winship, Feb. 10, 23, March 9, 1849, Grant, *Papers*, I, 173, 175, and note, 177–178, 181, and note; Grant to Julia Grant, May 20, 1849, *ibid.*, 188–190.

16. Lewis, 289–291; Grant to Julia Grant, June 7, 1851 [July 5], Aug. 16, 1852, Grant, *Papers*, I, 206, 247, 254.

17. Grant to Julia Grant, Aug. 9, Oct. 26, 1852, Grant, *Papers*, I, 251–253, 270–271; Grant to Board of Survey, Sept. 3, 1852, *ibid.*, 261–262.

18. Grant to Julia Grant, Aug. 20, Dec. 3, 1852, *ibid.*, 256–258, 274–276.

19. Grant to Julia Grant, March 31, 1853, *ibid.*, 297; Oct. 7, 1852, June 28, July 13, 1853, *ibid.*, 267–268, 304–306; Dec. 3, 1852, March 4, 19, June 15, 1853, *ibid.*, 275, 291, 294–295, 301; Lewis, 312; Grant to Julia Grant, June 15, 28, 1853, Grant, *Papers*, I, 301, 305.

20. Grant to Julia Grant, Jan. 18, Feb. 2, 6, March 25, 1854, Grant, *Papers*, I, 315, 316–318, 320–322, 327.

21. William C. Church, *Ulysses S. Grant and the Period of National Preservation and Reconstruction* (N.Y., 1897), 52–54; Richardson, 149.

22. Grant to Julia Grant, March 25, 1854, Grant, *Papers*, I, 326. For a full discussion of the drinking matter see Lewis, 324–325, 327–331. See also, John Eaton, *Grant, Lincoln, and the Freedmen* (N.Y., 1907), 100, 102.

23. Grant to Col. S. Cooper, April 11, 1854, Grant, *Papers*, I, 329–330; Grant to 1st Lt. Joseph B. Collins, April 11, 1854, *ibid.*, 331; Lewis, 331–332.

24. Grant to Jesse R. Grant, Dec. 28, 1856, Feb. 7, 1857, Grant, *Papers*, I, 334–337; Grant to Mary Grant, Aug. 22, 1857, *ibid.*, 338; Pawn ticket, Dec. 23, 1857, *ibid.*, 339.

25. Lewis, 355; Grant to Mary Grant, March 21, Sept. 7, 1858, *ibid.*, 340–341, 343; Manumission document [March 29, 1859], *ibid.*, 347–348; Grant to Jesse R. Grant, March 12, 1859, *ibid.*, 345–346, and note.

26. Lewis, 363–364; Grant to Board of County Commissioners, Aug. 15, 1859, Grant, *Papers*, I, 348–349, and note; Grant to Jesse R. Grant, Aug. 20, 1859, *ibid.*, 350–351; Grant to Simpson Grant, Oct. 24, 1859, *ibid.*, 353–354; Lewis, 370; Grant to Julia Grant, March 14, 1860, Grant, *Papers*, I, 355–356.

CHAPTER II

1. Grant to Jesse R. Grant, April 21, 1861, Ulysses S. Grant, *The Papers of Ulysses S. Grant*, II, 6–7; Lewis, *Captain Sam Grant*, 375, 377; Church, *Ulysses S. Grant*, 63; Grant, *Memoirs*, I, 229–231; Lewis, 396–406; Grant, *Memoirs*, I, 230–232; John Y. Simon, "From Galena to Appomattox: Grant and Washburne," *Journal of the Illinois State Historical Society*, LVIII (Summer 1965), 165–189.

2. Grant to Julia Grant, May 1, June 1, 10, 17, 1861, Grant, *Papers*, II, 15–16, 37–38, 40–43; Lewis, 407, 409, 415–418; Grant, *Memoirs*, I, 239–240; John Russell Young, *Around the World with General Grant* (2 vols., N.Y., 1879), II, 214–215; Lewis, 426–428; Grant, *Memoirs*, I, 244–246; Lewis, 429–430.

3. Grant to Julia Grant, July 7, 13, Aug. 3, 10, 31, Sept. 3, 8, 1861, Grant, *Papers*, II, 59–60, 69–70, 82–83, 96–97, 159–161, 180–181, 213–214; Grant, *Memoirs*, I, 246–247; Bruce Catton, *Grant Moves South* (Boston, 1960), 16–17; Grant, *Me-*

moirs, I, 257–266; *The War of the Rebellion: The Official Records of the Union and Confederate Armies* (128 vols., Washington, 1880–1891), series I, vol. 3, p. 150. Hereafter referred to as O. R. All references are to series I. Volume, part, and page number will be in that order. O. R., 4, 196–197; Grant, *Memoirs*, I, 269–280; O. R., 3, 267–272.

4. A. L. Conger, *The Rise of U. S. Grant* (N.Y., 1931). Conger's theme is this progressive development and growth through various grades. Rawlins to Washburne, Dec. 30, 1861 in James H. Wilson, *The Life of John A. Rawlins* (N.Y., 1916), 68–71; Grant, *Memoirs*, I, 285–293; O. R., 7, 121–122, 140.

5. O. R., 7, 124; Grant, *Memoirs*, I, 298–299, 302–303, 305–307; O. R., 7, 269; Lew Wallace, "The Capture of Fort Donelson," *Battles and Leaders of the Civil War* (4 vols., N.Y., 1884–1888), I, 422; Catton, *Grant Moves South*, 166–169; O. R., 7, 618; Grant, *Memoirs*, I, 310–313.

6. Catton, *Grant Moves South*, 179–180, 188, 190; Grant to Julia Grant, Feb. 24, 1862, Grant Papers, CHS; O. R., 7, 679–680, 682–684; O. R., 10, 2, 15, 21, 62–63.

7. O. R., 10, 2, 55, 62.

8. O. R., 10, 1, 86, 89; O. R., 10, 2, 85, 90, 92, 94, 95; Grant, *Memoirs*, I, 336; O. R., 10, 1, 185.

9. Grant, *Memoirs*, I, 336–343; Catton, *Grant Moves South*, 236–238; Grant, *Memoirs*, I, 349.

10. O. R., 10, 2, 96–97, 99, 398, 400; Grant, *Memoirs*, I, 368–369.

11. O. R., 10, 1, 98, 99; *N. Y. Herald*, April 16, 1862; A. K. McClure, *Abraham Lincoln and Men of War Times* (Philadelphia, 1961), 193.

12. O. R., 10, 2, 144; William T. Sherman, *Personal Memoirs* (3d ed., 2 vols., N.Y., 1890), I, 283; Grant to Washburne, June 19, 1862, in Catton, *Grant Moves South*, 275.

CHAPTER III

1. Grant to Washburne, March 22, 1862, James G. Wilson, ed., *General Grant's Letters to a Friend, 1861–1880* (N.Y., 1897), 7; John Eaton, *Grant, Lincoln and the Freedmen*, 1–5, 9–15, 18–29; O. R., 17, 2, 424, 530, 544. See also Bertram W. Korn, *American Jewry and the Civil War* (Philadelphia, 1951), 122–155, also O. R., 17, 2, 330, 337, 421–422; O. R., 24, 1, 9.

2. Archer Jones, *Confederate Strategy from Shiloh to Vicksburg* (Baton Rouge, 1961), 70–71, 75; Grant, *Memoirs*, I, 404–420; O. R., 17, 1, 64–69, 155, 169–170, 387; Grant to Halleck, Oct. 26, 1862, O. R., 17, 2, 296; Grant to Washburne, Nov. 7, 1862, Wilson, ed., *General Grant's Letters to a Friend*, 18–22.

3. O. R., 17, 1, 477–478, 593–594, 605–610.

4. McClernand to Grant, Jan. 3, Feb. 17, 1862, copies in McClernand Papers, ISHL; McClernand's report of Shiloh, O. R. 10, 1, 114–122; Grant to Capt. A. C. Kemper, April 29, 1862; O. R., 10, 1, 114.

5. Catton, *Grant Moves South*, 324–327.

6. O. R., 17, 1, 469; O. R., 17, 2, 415, 420, 425, 461–462; Catton, *Grant Moves South*, 336–343.

7. Grant, *Memoirs*, I, 439–440; O. R., 17, 1, 699, 700–709; O. R., 17, 2, 545–547, 553, 555, 559.

8. O. R., 24, 3, 19; Grant's order, O. R., 24, 1, 11; Grant to McClernand, Jan. 31, 1863, O. R., 24, 1, 13; McClernand to Grant, Feb. 1, 1863, O. R., 24, 1, 13–14.

9. Grant, *Memoirs*, I, 443. (Italics in original.)

10. J. Russell Jones to Washburne, Jan. 29, Feb. 5 [1863], J. R. Jones Papers,

CHS; Grant to Halleck, March 7, April 13, 1863, Grant-Halleck Papers, ISHL; O. R., 24, 1, 19–20, 29; Catton, *Grant Moves South,* 377–387; Kenneth P. Williams, *Lincoln Finds a General* (5 vols., N.Y., 1949–1959), IV, 310–329.

11. John C. Pemberton, *Pemberton: Defender of Vicksburg* (Chapel Hill, 1942), 100–102; O. R., 24, 3, 631–632, 663, 668–669, 687, 689, 712; Grant, *Memoirs,* I, 446, 449, 458; Grant to Washburne, March 10, 1863, Grant-Washburne Papers, ISHL; Grant to Halleck, March 7, 1863, Grant-Halleck Papers, ISHL; O.R., 24, 1, 20; O. R., 24, 3, 127.

12. On Feb. 4, 1863 Grant had written Halleck indicating that the move down the west bank might have to be adopted as soon as the roads would permit. O. R., 24, 1, 14. See also, O. R., 24, 3, 188, 201, 211–214; Grant, *Memoirs,* I, 461, 463.

13. Grant, *Memoirs.* I, 473–478, 480–481; Catton, *Grant Moves South,* 422–425, 437; Pemberton, 123–127; Jones, 195, 225–227; O. R., 24, 1, 33–34.

14. Grant, *Memoirs,* I, 481–484, 490–491; O. R., 24, 1, 32–33.

15. Catton, *Grant Moves South,* 429, 435–436, 438–439; O. R., 24, 1, 50; Grant, *Memoirs.* I, 496–497; O. R., 24, 1, 36.

16. O. R., 24, 3, 300, 305, 307, 873, 876, 877, 882.

17. Grant, *Memoirs.* I, 512–520, 523–526, 528; O. R. 24, 1, 52–54, 149.

18. O. R., 24, 1, 37; Grant, *Memoirs,* I, 536–537; Catton, *Grant Moves South,* 468; O. R., 24, 3, 909, 917, 929–930, 953, 958, 963, 967, 980, 981, 987.

19. Sylvanus Cadwallader, *Three Years With Grant,* ed. Benjamin P. Thomas (N.Y., 1955), 102–111; *American Heritage,* VII, no. 5, pp. 106–111; K. P. Williams, IV, 402, 439–451; U. S. Grant, III, "Civil War: Fact and Fiction," *Civil War History,* II, no. 1 (1956), 29–40; Catton, *Grant Moves South,* 464; Louis A. Coolidge, *Ulysses S. Grant* (2 vols., Boston, 1924), I, 126.

20. Grant, *Memoirs,* I, 546–547, 555–570; Catton, *Grant Moves South,* 466–467; O. R., 24, 1, 164; O. R., 24, 3, 460, 470, 484.

21. Grant to Lincoln, July 20, 1863, O. R., 52, 1, 416; Gideon Welles, *Diary of Gideon Welles,* ed. H. K. Beale (3 vols., N.Y., 1960), I, 386–387; Bruce Catton, *Grant Takes Command* (Boston, 1968), 3–6.

CHAPTER IV

1. July 13, 1863, Roy P. Basler, ed., *The Collected Works of Abraham Lincoln* (7 vols., New Brunswick, 1953), VI, 326.

2. Sherman to Grant, July 12, 1863, O. R., 24, 2, 523; Grant to Halleck, July 18, 24, 1863, O. R., 24, 3, 529, 546–547; Banks to Halleck, July 30, 1863, O. R., 26, 1, 661–662; Banks to Grant, July 18, 1863, O. R., 24, 3, 527–528; Lincoln to Grant, Aug. 9, 1863, Basler, ed., *Works of Lincoln,* VI, 374.

3. Bruce Catton, *Never Call Retreat* (Garden City, 1965), 258, 496; John A. Rawlins to Emma Hurlbut, Nov. 16, 1863, Rawlins Papers, CHS.

4. O. R., 30, 4, 404; Grant, *Memoirs,* II, 17–19.

5. O. R., 31, 3, 26, 34, 38–39, 48, 54, 60, 65, 122.

6. O. R., 31, 2, 31–34; Grant, *Memoirs,* II, 75.

7. O. R., 31, 2, 314–318; Catton, *Grant Takes Command,* 77; O. R., 31, 2, 35–36, 67, 573–575, 722; Grant, *Memoirs,* II, 83. The order to Thomas read, "Your command will either carry the rifle-pits and ridge directly in front of them or move to the left, as the presence of enemy may require." O. R., 31, 2, 44; Catton, *Grant Takes Command,* 76, 79–80. For the attack on Missionary Ridge not being a spontaneous unordered feat by the soldiers see *ibid.*, 81–84; also, Grant, *Memoirs,* II, 78–80.

8. O. R., 31, 2, 36, 49–50; O. R., 31, 3, 341; Basler, ed., *Works of Lincoln*, VII, 53.

9. *Congressional Globe*, 38th Cong., 1st sess., part 1, 9, 21, 428–431, 586–594, 850–851; Catton, *Grant Takes Command*, 120–121; T. H. Williams, *Lincoln and His Generals* (N.Y., 1952), 297; B. Burns to Grant, Dec. 7, 1863, Grant to Burns, Dec. 17, 1863, Grant Papers, ISHL.

10. C. A. Dana to Stanton, Nov. 29, Dec. 12, 1863, O. R., 31, 2, 71–72; Grant to Halleck, Dec. 7, 1863, O. R., 31, 3, 349–350; Dana to Grant, Dec. 21, 1863, O. R., 31, 3, 457–458; Halleck to Grant, Jan. 18, 1864, O. R., 32, 2, 126–127.

11. Halleck to Grant, Jan. 8, 1864, O. R., 32, 2, 40–42; Grant to Halleck, Jan. 19, 1864, O. R., 33, 394–395; Halleck to Grant, Feb. 17, 1864, O. R., 32, 2, 411–413; T. H. Williams, 291–297.

12. Catton, *Grant Takes Command*, 121; Grant, *Memoirs*, II, 114.

13. Grant, *Memoirs*, II, 115–116; Catton, *Grant Takes Command*, 124–127.

14. T. H. Williams, 300–301.

CHAPTER V

1. O. R., 32, 3, 245–246; O. R., 33, 794–795; Bruce Catton, "The Generalship of Ulysses S. Grant," in Grady McWhiney, ed., *Grant, Lee, Lincoln and the Radicals: Essays on Civil War Leadership* ([Evanston], 1964), 19, 29; Adam Badeau, *Military History of Ulysses S. Grant* (3 vols., N.Y., 1885), II, 9–10.

2. Catton, *Grant Takes Command*, 145–146, 155–157; George Meade, *The Life and Letters of George Gordon Meade* (2 vols., N.Y., 1913), II, 178, 183; Hans L. Trefousse, *Ben Butler: The South Called Him BEAST!* (N.Y., 1957), 136–137, 147; J. F. C. Fuller, *The Generalship of Ulysses S. Grant* (London, 1929), 218.

3. O. R., 32, 3, 245–246; Grant to Meade, April 9, 1864, O. R., 33, 827–829.

4. O. R., 33, 1009; O. R., 36, 2, 331–334; Grant, *Memoirs*, II, 130, 160, 177–203; Bruce Catton, *A Stillness at Appomattox* (Garden City, 1953), 59–91; O. R., 36, 1, 2, 18.

5. William T. Sherman, "The Grand Strategy of the Last Year of the War," *Battles & Leaders*, IV, 248; O. R., 36, 2, 481; Catton, *A Stillness at Appomattox*, 91–92; Catton, *Grant Takes Command*, 212–242.

6. O. R., 36, 2, 627; Grant, *Memoirs*, II, 226–238; O. R., 36, 1, 20; O. R., 36, 2, 840–841; Catton, *Never Call Retreat*, 352.

7. Catton, *Grant Takes Command*, 248–255; O. R., 36, 2, 910; Andrew A. Humphreys, *The Virginia Campaign of '64 and '65* (N.Y., 1883), 124–125; O. R., 36, 1, 997–998; O. R., 36, 3, 285; O. R., 36, 1, 21–22; O. R., 36, 3, 477–478; Catton, *A Stillness at Appomattox*, 153.

8. O. R., 36, 3, 524–526; Grant, *Memoirs*, II, 276; Catton, *Grant Takes Command*, 267–269; O. R., 36, 3, 526; *N. Y. World*, June 8, 1864; Benjamin P. Thomas, *Abraham Lincoln* (N.Y., 1952), 423–424.

9. O. R., 33, 827–829, 904, 1017–1018; O. R., 36, 3, 598, 599; O. R., 34, 4, 514–515; Catton, *A Stillness at Appomattox*, 177–178.

10. Lee to Beauregard, June 16, 1864, O. R., 40, 2, 659; Catton, *Grant Takes Command*, 280–282, 285–293; O. R., 40, 1, 313–314; O. R., 40, 2, 59–61, 86, 88–89, 93, 117–118, 156, 167, 179, 205.

11. O. R. 36, 1, 33; Edward Steere, *The Wilderness Campaign* (Harrisburg, 1960), 18; Badeau, *Military History*, II, 456–457; Catton, "The Generalship of Ulysses S. Grant," 28.

12. O. R., 36, 1, 22, 24, 26, 796–797; Catton, *Grant Takes Command*, 297–298;

George E. Pond, *The Shenandoah Valley in 1864* (N.Y., 1883), 37–38; O. R., 37, 1, 98–100.

13. "That Maryland raid upset my plans. . . ." Grant to Washburne, July 23, 1864, Wilson, ed. *General Grant's Letters to a Friend*, 37; O. R., 36, 1, 27–31.

14. O. R., 40, 1, 13–14; Catton, *Grant Takes Command*, 296; O. R., 42, 2, 244, 292, 442, 469–470; T. S. Bowers to G. K. Leet, in Leet to W. R. Rowley, Aug. 23, 1864, Rowley Papers, ISHL.

15. Catton, *Grant Takes Command*, 240–241, 248, 352, 370–374; Badeau, *Military History*, II, 314–315.

16. O. R., 40, 3, 334, 577; T. H. Williams, *Lincoln and His Generals*, 321–324; William F. Smith, *From Chattanooga to Petersburg Under Generals Grant and Butler* (Boston, 1893), 32–59, 174–178; Clarence E. Macartney, *Grant and His Generals* (N.Y., 1953), 212–218; Catton, *Grant Takes Command*, 326–335.

17. O. R., 40, 1, 45, 170, 524, 526–529; O. R., 40, 3, 424, 438, 458, 459, 590–591; Grant, *Memoirs*, II, 315; Catton, *Grant Takes Command*, 321–325.

18. O. R., 39, 2, 355, 364; Grant, *Memoirs*, II, 348–350; O. R., 39, 3, 202, 222.

19. O. R., 42, 3, 620, 995; O. R., 36, 1, 41–42; O. R., 45, 2, 97, 115, 143, 171, 194, 195, 265; Grant, *Memoirs*, II, 359–374, 379–386.

20. Catton, *Grant Takes Command*, 362–363, 416; Horace Porter, *Campaigning with Grant* (N.Y., 1897), 325–326, 329–332; Badeau, *Military History*, III, 135–136, 141.

21. O. R., 44, 636, 740, 797, 820; O. R., 36, 1, 43–45; O. R., 42, 1, 965–975; O. R., 46, 2, 29, 60; J. G. Randall and Richard N. Current, *Lincoln the President: Last Full Measure* (N.Y., 1955), 289–293; O. R., 46, 1, 394–399.

22. Grant, *Memoirs*, II, 403–405; O. R., 47, 2, 101–102; O. R., 45, 2, 609–610; O. R., 48, 1, 580; O. R., 46, 2, 365, 495.

23. O. R., 49, 1, 342, 344; Grant, *Memoirs*, II, 411; O. R., 36, 1, 50–52; Catton, *Grant Takes Command*, 425–427.

24. O. R., 36, 1, 48; Grant, *Memoirs*, II, 412–413, 418; Catton, *Grant Takes Command*, 433–434; Badeau, *Military History*, III, 137–138; Porter, 402, 406–410.

25. O. R., 46, 3, 112–113; Porter, 405–406; Alfred H. Burne, *Lee, Grant and Sherman* (N.Y., 1939), 180–182; O. R., 36, 1, 54; O. R., 46, 3, 109, 196, 224, 243.

26. O. R., 46, 3, 234; George R. Agassiz, ed., *Meade's Headquarters, 1863–1865: Letters of Colonel Theodore Lyman from the Wilderness to Appomattox* (Boston, 1922), 329–330; D. S. Freeman, *R. E. Lee* (4 vols., N.Y., 1935), IV, 31–32; O. R., 46, 3, 341, 381.

27. O. R., 46, 3, 342, 381, 397–399; Humphreys, 356; O. R., 46, 1, 1103–1105; Porter, 442–443.

28. O. R., 46, 3, 528–529; Porter, 452–453; O. R., 46, 3, 610; Basler, ed., *Works of Lincoln*, VIII, 392.

29. O. R., 46, 3, 619, 621, 633, 641; Freeman, IV, 94; Grant, *Memoirs*, II, 477–478.

30. O. R., 46, 3, 653–654, 664–665; O. R., 46, 1, 1181, 1215; Freeman, IV, 115, 119–120; Lyman, *Meade's Headquarters*, 354; Grant, *Memoirs*, II, 483–485.

31. O. R., 36, 1, 59–60; O. R., 46, 3, 663, 665–666; Porter, 479; Catton, *Grant Takes Command*, 463–468; Grant, *Memoirs*, II, 496.

32. Young, *Around the World with General Grant*, II, 355–356; Grant, *Memoirs*, II, 513–517.

CHAPTER VI

1. Garland, *Ulysses S. Grant*, 337; Grant to Stanton, Aug. 12, 1865, HQA, NA;

O. E. Babcock to Washburne, Oct. 2, 1865, A. Badeau to Washburne, Oct. 20, 1865, Washburne Papers, LC; William B. Hesseltine, *Ulysses S. Grant. Politician* (N.Y., 1935), 62, 63; Daniel Butterfield to Grant, Feb. 15, 1866, Grant Papers, ISHL: Badeau to Washburne, Nov. 9, 1865, Washburne Papers.

2. Grant to Sheridan, Oct. 22, 1865, Sheridan Papers, LC; Grant to Halleck, Nov. 13, 1865, Grant to Sheridan, Dec. 19, 1865, HQA.

3. Badeau to Washburne, Oct. 20, 1865, Washburne Papers; Grant to Stanton, Nov. 29, 1865, Grant to Johnson, Dec. 18, 1865, HQA; H. S. Commager, ed., *Documents of American History*, 7th ed. (2 vols., N.Y., 1963), I, 460–461; Welles, *Diary*, II, 396–397.

4. June 24, 1868, Sherman Papers, LC.

5. Grant to G. H. Thomas et al., Dec. 25, 1865; to Johnson, Feb. 17, March 14, 1866, HQA; Benjamin P. Thomas and Harold M. Hyman, *Stanton: The Life and Times of Lincoln's Secretary of War* (N.Y., 1962), 476.

6. Thomas & Hyman, 478, 490, 498–499; G. K. Leet to Sheridan, Oct. 17, 1866; Grant to Stanton, Nov. 22, 1866, HQA; James E. Sefton, *The United States Army and Reconstruction, 1865–1877* (Baton Rouge, 1967), 80–81.

7. On July 25, 1866 Congress passed a bill establishing the grade of general. Johnson immediately appointed Grant to the higher grade. Hesseltine, 69; Adam Badeau, *Grant in Peace* (Hartford, 1887), 47.

8. Welles, II, 593, 595; Benjamin C. Truman, "Anecdotes of Andrew Johnson," *Century*, LXXXV (1913), 438. See also *The Diary of Orville Hickman Browning* (2 vols., Springfield, Ill., 1925, 1933), II, 115.

9. Grant to Johnson, Oct. 21, 24, 1866, HQA; Sherman to Thomas Ewing, Senior, Jan. 25, 1867, Thomas Ewing Family Papers, LC; Cyrus B. Comstock, Diary, Oct. 23, 24, 1866, LC; Grant to Stanton, Oct. 27, 1866, HQA; C. B. Comstock to Sheridan, Oct. 31, 1866, Sheridan Papers.

10. Browning, Jan. 4, 1867, II, 122; Grant to General [Ord], Dec. 6, 1866, Porter Papers, LC; Grant to Howard, Jan. 18, 1867, Bureau of Refugees, Freedmen and Abandoned Lands, NA; Grant to Stanton, Feb. 8, 1867, HQA; Welles, III, 42.

11. Grant to Washburne, March 4, 1867, Wilson, ed., *General Grant's Letters to a Friend*, 52–53; Badeau, *Grant in Peace*, 59–60; Welles, III, 62, 63; Hesseltine, 83, Sefton, 115.

12. Grant to Washburne, April 5, 1867, Wilson, ed., *General Grant's Letters to a Friend*, 55.

13. Grant to Pope, April 21, 1867, to Ord, June 23, 1867, HQA; Grant to Sheridan, April 21, May 26, June 7, 24, 1867, Sheridan Papers; *N. Y. Tribune*, June 6, Aug. 13, 1867; Allan Nevins, *Hamilton Fish: The Inner History of the Grant Administration* (2 vols., N.Y., 1936), I, 93; Grant to Stanton, Aug. 12, 1867, HQA; Horace White to Washburne, Aug. 13, 1867, Washburne Papers; Thomas Ewing, Jr. to his father, Oct. 19, 1867, Thomas Ewing Family Papers; Grant to President, Feb. 3, 1868, 40th Cong., 2d sess., House Ex. Docs., no. 149 (serial 1337), 8; Rawlins to Mrs. Rawlins, Aug. 19, 1867, in James H. Wilson, *The Life of John A. Rawlins*, 344; Garland, 366; Badeau, *Grant in Peace*, 90; Thomas & Hyman, 550.

14. Welles, III, 169; Grant to Johnson, Aug. 1, 17, 1867, HQA.

15. Welles, III, 234; Thomas & Hyman, 560; Browning, II, 162, 167–168; Sherman to [John Sherman], Sept. 12, 1867, Sherman Papers; Sherman to T. Ewing, Sr., Oct. 18, 1867, Thomas Ewing Family Papers; *N. Y. Tribune*, Sept. 13, Dec. 5, 1867; John Sherman to W. T. Sherman, Nov. 1, 1867, Sherman Papers; O. O. Howard to Joseph Bycroft, Dec. 12, 1867, Howard Papers, Bowdoin College.

16. W. T. Sherman to Grant, Jan. 27, 1868, Sherman Papers; Hesseltine, 104–105.

17. Grant to President, Jan. 14, 1868, Johnson Papers, LC; Thomas & Hyman, 569–571; Sherman to Grant, Jan. 27, 1868, Sherman Papers; W. S. Hillyer to Johnson, Jan. 14, 1867, Johnson Papers.

18. Hesseltine, 105–107; Badeau, *Grant in Peace*, 110–114; James Ford Rhodes, *History of the United States from the Compromise of 1850* (7 vols., N.Y., 1893–1906), VI, 100–102; Thomas & Hyman, 570; Browning, II, 174–175; Welles, III, 259–262.

19. Browning, II, 179–180; Browning to Johnson, Feb. 6, 1868, Browning Papers, ISHL; Welles, III, 262–263, 266–274; Grant to Johnson, Feb. 3, 1868, 40th Cong., 2d sess., House Ex. Docs., no. 149 (serial 1337), 8; Badeau, *Grant in Peace*, 114.

20. Sherman to Johnson, Jan. 31, Feb. 14, 1868; to John Sherman, Feb. 14, 1868, Sherman Papers.

21. Grant to Sherman, Jan. 19, 1868, Sherman to Johnson, Jan. 18, 1868, Sherman Papers; T. Ewing, Jr. to Gen. Hugh Ewing, Oct. 5, 1867 (typed copy), Thomas Ewing Family Papers; Grant to Sheridan, March 31, 1868, Sheridan Papers; *N. Y. Tribune*, April 3, 1868; Badeau, *Grant in Peace*, 136.

22. Horace White to Washburne, March 12, 1866, Washburne Papers; Badeau, *Grant in Peace*, 144; Grant to Sherman, June 21, 1868, Sherman Papers; Church, *Ulysses S. Grant*, 364.

23. Badeau, *Grant in Peace*, 145–146; L. S. Felt to Washburne, July 20, 1868, Washburne Papers.

24. E.g., Hesseltine, 131; Coolidge, *Ulysses S. Grant*, I, 271.

25. All Southern and border states have been excluded in this count. Mississippi, Texas, and Virginia did not take part in the election.

26. Grant got 49.5% of the vote in New York. *The Statistical History of the United States from Colonial Times to the Present* (Stamford, Conn., 1965), 688.

27. Badeau, *Grant in Peace*, 149.

CHAPTER VII

1. Babcock to Washburne, Oct. 9, 1867, Washburne Papers, LC; Browning, *The Diary of Orville Hickman Browning*, II, 103.

2. James D. Richardson, ed., *A Compilation of the Messages and Papers of the Presidents, 1789–1897* (10 vols., Washington, 1896–1899), VII, 6–8.

3. Harry E. Resseguie, "Federal Conflict of Interest: The A. T. Stewart Case," *New York History*, XLVII (1966), 287–288.

4. Boutwell, William W. Belknap, Columbus Delano, John A. J. Cresswell, and George W. Williams had relatively long tenures.

5. Nevins, *Hamilton Fish*, I, 100–101.

6. Hesseltine, *Ulysses S. Grant, Politician*, 150–153.

7. He referred to the Ku Klux outrages in S. C. in the Third Annual Message, 1871 (Richardson, ed., VII, 150), and offered some general remarks about conditions in the South (*ibid.*, 153). There was a reference to enforcement of the law against the Klan in the 1872 message (*ibid.*, 199); a one-sentence request in 1873 for a law to better secure the civil rights of the freedmen (*ibid.*, 255); and a reference to the political troubles in Arkansas in 1875 (*ibid.*, 298–299).

8. *Ibid.*, 8; Hesseltine, 186–187; Richardson, ed., VII, 55–56; Fish to J. Meredith Read, March 30, 1870, Fish Papers, LC.

9. C. Vann Woodward, "Seeds of Failure in Radical Race Policy," *New Frontiers of the American Reconstruction*, ed. Harold M. Hyman (Urbana, 1966), 145–146.

10. Ralph L. Peek, "Election of 1870 and the End of Reconstruction in Florida," *Florida Historical Quarterly*, XLV (1967), 352–368; Hesseltine, 240.

11. Hesseltine, 244–245; Hamilton Fish, Diary, Feb. 24, 1871, LC; Grant to Blaine, March 9, 1871, Grant Papers, LC; Richardson, ed., VII, 127–128; George S. Boutwell, *The Lawyer, the Statesman and the Soldier* (N.Y., 1887), 171.

12. Richardson, ed., VII, 134–138, 212–213; Grant to W. W. Belknap, Feb. 19, 1871, Jan. 5, 1873; to H. J. Dawes, Jan. 12, 1872, Grant Papers, LC; Fish, Diary, Dec. 1, 1871, Jan. 12, 1872.

13. Richardson, ed., VII, 163–164.

14. Robert S. Henry, *The Story of Reconstruction* (N.Y., 1938), 468; Nevins, I, 293; Fish, Diary, April 15, 1870; Richardson, ed., VII, 153; Coolidge, *Ulysses S. Grant*, II, 376–378.

15. Fish, Diary, April 15, 1870.

16. Richardson, ed., VII, 153; Coolidge, II, 376–378.

17. Fish to Edward G. Baker, Oct. 26, 1872, Fish Papers, LC; Paul H. Buck, *The Road to Reunion* (Boston, 1937), 96–97; Woodward, "Seeds of Failure in Radical Race Policy, " 125–147.

CHAPTER VIII

1. Walter T. K. Nugent, *Money and American Society, 1865–1880* (N.Y., 1968), 11, 107, 126, 128, 130, 138–139; Nevins, *Hamilton Fish*, I, 288; George S. Boutwell, *Reminiscences of Sixty Years in Public Affairs* (2 vols., N.Y., 1902), II, 126, 138; Grant to Washburne, Sept. 7, 1869, Grant-Washburne Papers, ISHL; Hesseltine, *Ulysses S. Grant, Politician*, 167.

2. Fish to J. Meredith Read, Jr., Sept. 4, 1869, Fish Papers, LC.

3. Henry Adams, "The New York Gold Conspiracy," *The Great Secession Winter of 1860–61, and Other Essays*, ed. George Hochfield (N.Y., 1958), 159–189; 41st Cong., 2d sess., House Reports, no. 31 (serial 1436), hereafter referred to as House Reports, no. 31; Hesseltine, 171, 173; *N.Y. Herald*, Oct. 25, 1869.

4. House Reports, no. 31, 6, 8, 13, 15, 17, 142, 155, 174, 231–232, 249, 251, 358–359, 444–445, 448; John A. Carpenter, "Washington, Pennsylvania and the Gold Conspiracy of 1869," *Western Pennsylvania Historical Magazine*, XLVIII (1965), 345–349. Washington, Pennsylvania was not an isolated community. Washington (Pa.) *Reporter*, Jan. 22, 1948; *N.Y. Tribune*, Oct. 25, 1869.

5. House Reports, no. 31, 15–17, 461–479; Boutwell, *Reminiscences*, II, 168; Hesseltine, 179.

6. Nugent, 45, 110; Irwin Unger, *The Greenback Era: A Social and Political History of American Finance, 1865–1879* (Princeton, 1964), 43, 68, 174–178; Rembert W. Patrick, *The Reconstruction of the Nation* (N.Y., 1967), 174–175; Nevins, I, 305–306.

7. Nevins, I, 156–157, 174–175, 183–184, 192–200, 203–207, 216–217, II, Appendix III; Badeau, *Grant in Peace*, 153; Hesseltine, 161–162.

8. Nevins, I, 247, 348, 362; Richardson, ed., *Messages and Papers of the Presidents*, VII, 31–32, 64–69; Fish, Diary, June 2, 17, July 10, 1870, LC.

9. Badeau, *Grant in Peace*, 213; Charles C. Tansill, *The United States and Santo Domingo, 1798–1873* (Baltimore, 1938), 244–245, 351; Samuel F. Bemis, *A Diplomatic History of the United States* (4th ed., N.Y., 1955), 404; Nevins, I, 275, 276, 318.

10. Fish, Diary, April 5, 6, 1869; Nevins, I, 264; Richardson, ed., VII, 128–131; Jacob D. Cox, "How Judge Hoar Ceased to be Attorney-General," *Atlantic Monthly* LXXVI (Aug. 1895), 166–167; Charles F. Adams, *Lee at Appomattox*

and Other Papers (Boston, 1902), 130 ff; Grant to James W. Nye, June 27, 1870, Grant Papers, LC.

11. Fish to Grant, Sept. 17, 1869, Fish Papers; Cox, "How Judge Hoar Ceased to be Attorney-General," 166–167; Fish, Diary, Oct. 19, Dec. 21, 1869; Tansill, 371, 384–388; *Congressional Globe*, Dec. 21, 1870, 41st Cong., 3d sess., p. 243.

12. Nevins, I, 273–275, 318, II, 501; Tansill, 404–406, 412; Fish, Diary, June 17, 1870; Richardson, ed., VII, 61–63.

13. Tansill, 395; Grant to Baez, Oct. 17, 1870, Grant Papers, LC; Fish, Diary, Nov. 25, 1870; Richardson, ed., VII, 100–101; Nevins, II, 453, 497; Fish to Washburne, Jan. 17, 1871, Fish Papers.

14. Tansill, 436–439; 42d Cong., 1st sess., Senate Ex. Docs., no. 9 (serial 1466), 3, 11, 31; Richardson, ed., VII, 130, 412–413; Fish, Diary, June 25, Oct. 21, 1870.

15. Fish, Diary, Jan. 8, March 5, 1871; Fish to [Schenck], Feb. 24, 1871, to D. Sickles, March 10, 1871, Fish Papers; Boutwell, *Reminiscences*, II, 251; George F. Hoar, *Autobiography of Seventy Years* (2 vols., N.Y., 1903), I, 211; Grant to A. G. Cattell, March 27, 1871, Grant Papers, LC.

16. Richardson, ed., VII, 102; Hesseltine, 224; Nevins, I, 443–447, II, 474, 486–489, 493.

CHAPTER IX

1. Fish, Diary, June 25, July 10, 1870, May 29, June 15, Dec. 5, 6, 1871, LC; Fish to Grant, July 7, 1870, to C. Hamilton, June 23, 1870, Fish Papers, LC; Grant to Colfax, Aug. 4, 1871 (copy), Grant Papers, CHS; Tansill, *The United States and Santo Domingo*, 340; Nevins, *Hamilton Fish*, II, 494–495, 515–516, 578; Badeau, *Grant in Peace*, 245.

2. Boutwell, *Reminiscences*, II, 211; Fish, Diary, April 6, Oct. 19, 1869, June 13, 14, 1870; Cox, "How Judge Hoar Ceased to be Attorney-General," 168–170; Nevins, I, 365; Grant to Hoar, June 15, 1870, Grant Papers, LC; Hesseltine, *Ulysses S. Grant, Politician*, 209.

3. Richardson, ed., *Messages and Papers of the Presidents*, VII, 8, 23–24; Leonard D. White, *The Republican Era 1869–1901: A Study in Administrative History* (N.Y., 1958), 184–185, 189, 190–192; Robert M. Utley, "The Celebrated Peace Policy of General Grant," *North Dakota History*, XX (1953), 121–142; R. Pierce Beaver, *Church, State, and the American Indians* (St. Louis, 1966), 126–152; Hesseltine, 161; Elsie M. Rushmore, *The Indian Policy during Grant's Administrations* (Jamaica, N.Y., 1914), 29.

4. Fish, Diary, June 17, Oct. 4, 1870; Grant to Cox, Oct. 5, 1870, Grant Papers, LC; Nevins, II, 467, 764–765; Coolidge, *Ulysses S. Grant*, II, 490–491.

5. Ari Hoogenboom, *Outlawing the Spoils: A History of the Civil Service Reform Movement 1865–1883* (Urbana, 1961), 13–32, 43, 68–69, 78–80; White, 279–281; Ari Hoogenboom, "Spoilsmen and Reformers: Civil Service Reform and Public Morality," in *The Gilded Age: A Reappraisal*, ed. H. Wayne Morgan (Syracuse, 1963), 74–79, 83–84; Boutwell, *Reminiscences*, II, 133–135.

6. Richardson, ed., VII, 109, 155; Hoogenboom, *Outlawing the Spoils*, 87, 95; Fish, Diary, Dec. 19, 1871, Jan. 23, Feb. 2, 1872; Fish to J. C. Bancroft Davis, Feb. 12, 1872, Fish Papers.

7. Fish Diary, Feb. 2, 1872, April 15, 1873; Nevins, II, 593–595; Hoogenboom, "Spoilsmen and Reformers," 84–87; Grant to Murphy, Nov. 20, 1871, to Curtis, March 26, 1873, to Medill, April 9, 1873, Grant Papers, LC; John G. Sproat, *"The Best Men": Liberal Reformers in the Gilded Age* (N.Y., 1968), 74–75, 261; Hoogenboom, *Outlawing the Spoils*, 122.

8. Donald B. Chidsey, *The Gentleman from New York: A Life of Roscoe Conkling* (New York, 1935), 142, 151, 184; Trefousse, *Ben Butler*, 208–212; Hoogenboom, *Outlawing the Spoils*, 125–130, 132–133; Young, *Around the World with General Grant*, II, 263–267; Richardson, ed., VII, 300–301; Fish, Diary, March 9, July 8, 1875.

9. Nevins, II, 573–576, 609; Badeau, *Grant in Peace*, 173–175, 245; Hesseltine, 294, 301–302; Charles King, *The True Ulysses S. Grant* (Philadelphia, 1914), 360; Howard to W. E. Dodge, Feb. 3, 1868, Howard Papers, Bowdoin College.

10. Nevins, II, 588, 781; Fish, Diary, Sept. 21, 22, Oct. 24, 1874, June 14, 1875.

11. King, 368; Badeau, *Grant in Peace*, 244, 259, 412–413; Horace Porter to J. H. Wilson, Oct. 13, 1870, J. H. Wilson Papers, LC; Hesseltine, 298–299.

12. George W. Childs, *Recollections of General Grant* (Philadelphia, 1885), 27–28; Badeau, *Grant in Peace*, 164; Fish, Diary, Feb. 9, 1870.

13. Fuller to Eaton, May 15, 1872, in Leroy P. Graf, ed., "Three Ohio Republicans Consider the Political Currents of 1872: A Document," Historical and Philosophical Society of Ohio, *Bulletin*, XII (1954), 301–303; Yates to Logan U. Reavis, June 3, 1872, Logan U. Reavis Papers, CHS.

14. Grant to Thomas Settle, et al., June 10, 1872, Grant Papers, LC; to Washburne, Aug. 26, 1872, Grant-Washburne Papers, ISHL; Nevins, II, 600, 605; Fish to Badeau, Oct. 9, 1872, Fish Papers.

CHAPTER X

1. Richardson, ed., *Messages and Papers of the Presidents*, VII, 223.

2. Coolidge, *Ulysses S. Grant*, II, 435–437; Hoogenboom, "Spoilsmen and Reformers," 70; William D. Mallam, "The Grant-Butler Relationship," *Mississippi Valley Historical Review*, XLI (1954), 272–274.

3. Nevins, *Hamilton Fish*, II, 657.

4. Hesseltine, *Ulysses S. Grant, Politician*, 321–322.

5. Fish, Diary, April 11, Nov. 30, Dec. 1, 30, 1873, Jan. 7, 1874, LC; Hesseltine, 362.

6. Fish, Diary, Jan. 9, 1874; C. H. Hill to B. Bristow, Jan. 10, 1874, Benjamin H. Bristow Papers, LC.

7. Hesseltine, 327, 329, 331–332; Unger, *The Greenback Era*, 235–246; Coolidge, II, 449–451.

8. Young, *Around the World with General Grant*, II, 153–154; Fish to Gen. L. Schuyler, April 25, 1874, in Nevins, II, 714; Fish, Diary, April 21, 1874; Richardson, ed., VII, 268–271, 285; Nugent, *Money and American Society*, 226–227; Hesseltine, 339–340.

9. Coolidge, II, 523–525; Nevins, II, 667–694; Fish, Diary, Nov. 7, 14, Dec. 7, 1873.

10. Hesseltine, 371; Nevins, II, 746–747.

11. Alabama, Arkansas, Florida, Louisiana, Mississippi, South Carolina, and Texas.

12. Richardson, ed., VII, 223–224, 276–277, 308; Hesseltine, 346; Henry, *The Story of Reconstruction*, 492, 519–520, 527; Kellogg to Grant, Sept. 14, 1874, Grant Papers, LC; Fish, Diary, Sept. 16, 1874.

13. Richardson, ed., VII, 296–299; Nevins, II, 749–751, 753; Henry, 534; Benjamin Bristow to E. D. Force, Jan. 11 [1875], Bristow Papers.

14. Richardson, ed., VII, 305–314; Phillips to Belknap, Jan. 7, 1875, Belknap Papers, Princeton University; Hesseltine, 354; Coolidge, II, 471–472; Kenneth M. Stampp, *The Era of Reconstruction* (N.Y., 1966), 204–211.

15. Henry, 492, 511; Babcock to Sec. of War, April 16, 1874, Grant Papers, LC; Fish, Diary, April 17, 21, May 5, 1874; Richardson, ed., VII, 272–273.

16. Fish, Diary, Nov. 17, 1874; Richardson, ed., VII, 298, 319; Coolidge, II, 461–463; Hesseltine, 356-357; Nevins, II, 757–760.

17. Henry, 505, 544–549; Richardson, ed., VII, 322–323; Hesseltine, 390; Belknap to Grant, July 30, 1874, Grant Papers, LC; Grant to Pierrepont quoted in Coolidge, II, 464–465; Grant's comment on conditions in Mississippi, quoted in Coolidge, II, 466. Grant had nothing to do with the passage of the Civil Rights Act of March 1, 1875 other than to sign it. The act forbade discrimination in hotels, eating places, public conveyances, and the like.

CHAPTER XI

1. Nevins, *Hamilton Fish*, II, 705–711, 714, 774–781; Trefousse, *Ben Butler*, 227–229; Hesseltine, *Ulysses S. Grant, Politician*, 363–365, 376–377; Grant to Bristow, Nov. 15, 1872, Grant Papers, LC.

2. Patrick, *Reconstruction of the Nation*, 188; Nevins, II, 764; Hesseltine, 376–378; H. V. Boynton, "The Whiskey Ring," *North American Review*, vol. 123 (1876), 280–307. Boynton had a strong prejudice against Grant, as did John McDonald who wrote a campaign tract for the election of 1880, *Secrets of the Great Whiskey Ring* (St. Louis, 1880). See also, 44th Cong., 1st sess., House Misc. Docs., no. 186 (serial 1706).

3. Boynton, 304; Fish, Diary, May 22, 1875, Feb. 6, 1876, LC; McDonald to Babcock, Jan. 24, 1874, May 18, 1875, Babcock Papers, Newberry Library; Babcock to Joyce, Jan. 20, 1872, Grant Papers, LC.

4. Fish, Diary, Sept. 21, 1874, June 14, July 26, Sept. 17, 1875; "Sylph" to McDonald, Dec. 1874, photo copy, Bristow Papers, LC.

5. Grant's endorsement on Barnard's letter quoted in Coolidge, *Ulysses S. Grant*, II, 479; *ibid.*, 484; Fish, Diary, Dec. 2, 3, 1875; Babcock to Grant, Dec. 2, 1875, Grant Papers, LC; *N. Y. Herald*, Dec. 4, 1875; Belknap's memorandum of cabinet meeting, Dec. 3, 4, 1875, Belknap Papers, Princeton University.

6. 44th Cong., 1st sess., House Misc. Docs., no. 186 (serial 1706), 8, 360, 366; Coolidge, II, 452, 483–484; Fish, Diary, Feb. 8, 1876; *N. Y. Times*, Feb 13, 1876.

7. *Nation*, March 2, 1876; Babcock to Mrs. Babcock, Feb. 23, 1876, Babcock Papers; Badeau, *Grant in Peace*, 494; Jesse R. Grant, *In the Days of My Father General Grant* (N.Y., 1925), 119–120; Fish, Diary, Feb. 22, 25, March 5, 6, 1876; Grant to Babcock, March 1, 1877, Babcock Papers.

8. John E. Harlan to Bristow, March 9, 1875, Bristow Papers; E. Bruce Thompson, "The Bristow Presidential Boom of 1876," *Mississippi Valley Historical Review*, XXXII (1945), 3–30; Bristow to Harlan, Jan. 22, 1876, to Grant, June 17, 1876, Bristow Papers; Grant to Bristow, June 19, 1876, Grant Papers, LC; Fish, Diary, Oct. 12, 1876.

9. Sherman to Stanton, Aug. 18, 1865, photo copy, Belknap Papers; Belknap's Internal Revenue commission, June 17, 1866, Belknap Papers; Sherman to Grant, Sept. 2, 1870, Sherman Papers, LC; Sherman to Thomas Ewing, Sr., July 8, 1871, Thomas Ewing Family Papers, LC.

10. A minor scandal in Belknap's administration of the War Department concerned the sale of government arms, via a private firm, to the French during the Franco-Prussian War. A Congressional investigating committee found that there had been no violation of the law. Hesseltine, 265–266.

11. Nevins, II, 805–807; Belknap to Hugh Belknap, March 21, 1876, Belknap Papers. For an assertion that Belknap's "household expenses were annually less

than his salary," see Philip D. Jordan, "The Domestic Finances of Secretary of War W. W. Belknap," *Iowa Journal of History*, LII (1954), 193–202. *Congressional Record*, 44th Cong., 1st sess., vol. IV, part 7, 328, 339; *Nation*, March 9, 1876.

12. *Washington Gazette*, Jan. 23, 1876, clipping in Belknap Papers; *N. Y. Herald*, Feb. 9, 10, March 3, 4, 7, 1876; Nevins, II, 805–806; *N. Y. Times*, March 3, 1876.

13. Fish, Diary, March 3, 7, 1876; *N. Y. Times*, March 3, 1876; 44th Cong., 1st. sess., House Reports, no. 791 (serial 1713) and no. 799 (serial 1715); Fish to G. W. Blunt, March 17, 1876, Fish Papers, LC; Nevins, II, 808–809; Belknap to Mrs. Clara Belknap Wolcott, May 21, 1876, Belknap Papers.

14. *Congressional Record*, 44th Cong., 1st sess., vol. IV, part 7, 237–238, 322–323, 327; Edward McPherson, *A Hand-Book of Politics for 1876* (Washington, 1876), 170; Belknap to Anna Belknap, Aug. 19, 1876, Montgomery Blair to Anna Belknap, Aug. 14, 1876, Belknap Papers. See also Jesse R. Grant, *In the Days of My Father*, 121–125.

15. Nevins, II, 821; Edgar I. Stewart, *Custer's Luck* (Norman, Okla., 1955), 120–139.

16. Nevins, II, 649–651, 814–815; Fish to Schenck, Nov. 4, 1872, Feb. 14, 1876, Fish Papers; Fish, Diary, Dec. 2, 1870, Nov. 24, 1871, Aug. 6, 1873, March 12, 1875, Feb. 11, 14, 1876.

17. Nevins, II, 815–818; Ellis P. Oberholtzer, *A History of the United States since the Civil War* (5 vols., N.Y., 1917–1937), III, 180–182; Fish, Diary, April 18, 1876; Hesseltine, 394; Richardson, ed., *Messages and Papers of the Presidents*, VII, 361–366.

18. Hesseltine, 391, 397, 407; Grant to Hayes, June 16, 1876, Grant Papers, LC.

19. Young, *Around the World with General Grant*, II, 269–270; *N. Y. Tribune*, July 12, 1876; Nevins, II, 824–825, 829, 840; C. C. Sniffen to Washington Booth, July 12, 1876, to George Small, July 28, 1876; Grant to E. Y. Goldsborough, Aug. 11, 1876, to J. Russell Jones, Aug. 13, 1876, Grant Papers, LC.

20. Hesseltine, 408–409, 411; *N. Y. Tribune*, Aug. 25, 1876; Theodore C. Smith, *The Life and Letters of James Abram Garfield* (2 vols., New Haven, 1925), II, 742; C. Vann Woodward, *Reunion and Reaction: The Compromise of 1877 and the End of Reconstruction* (Boston, 1951), 9–10.

21. Fish, Diary, July 26, Oct. 17, 1876; Grant to Chamberlain, July 26, 1876, Grant Papers, LC; Richardson, ed., VII, 396–397; Hesseltine, 413; Grant's comment on conditions in the South, quoted in James G. Blaine, *Twenty Years of Congress* (2 vols., Norwich, Conn., 1886), II, 581–582; Nevins, II, 845–849.

22. Grant to J. D. Cameron, Nov. 26, 1876, Grant Papers, LC; Fish, Diary, Nov. 30, Dec. 1, 1876; Richardson, ed., VII, 334–335, 399–400, 411–412; Woodward, *Reunion and Reaction*, 110–112; Patrick, 261, 269; Henry, *The Story of Reconstruction*, 579–581.

23. Nevins, II, 851; Fish, Diary, Jan. 7, 17, 26, Feb. 23, March 1, 1876; Grant to Cameron, March 3, 1876, Grant Papers, LC.

24. Fish, Diary, Jan. 20, 1877; Richardson, ed., VII, 422–424; Badeau, *Grant in Peace*, 250.

25. Woodward, *Reunion and Reaction*, 3–14; Badeau, *Grant in Peace*, 252, 258–260.

CHAPTER XII

1. Badeau, *Grant in Peace*, 316; Grant to Badeau, Dec. 18, 1877, *ibid.*, 494.

2. Young, *Around the World with General Grant*, 5–10; Sherman to Badeau, June 27, 1877, Badeau, *Grant in Peace*, 122–123; London *Times*, March 27, 1877, in James G. Wilson, *The Life and Public Services of Ulysses Simpson Grant* (N.Y., 1885), 90.

3. Grant to Fish, June 22, 1877, in Nevins, *Hamilton Fish*, II, 893–894; Badeau, *Grant in Peace*, 264–266, 269–271, 275–288.

4. Church, *Ulysses S. Grant*, 428–429; Young, I, 129; Badeau, *Grant in Peace*, 305–306. Grant felt obliged to attend reviews in Germany and Japan. Young, I, 132, 419–421, II, 533–534, 553.

5. He also included in this group, Li Hung Chang, the Chinese statesman. Badeau, *Grant in Peace*, 312; Young, II, 161; Grant to Washburne, Dec. 24, 1878, Grant-Washburne Papers, ISHL; Grant to Badeau, June 22, 1879, Badeau, *Grant in Peace*, 515–516; Grant to Nellie Sartoris, Aug. 10, 1879, Grant Papers, CHS.

6. Grant to Badeau, Aug. 1, 28, 1879, Badeau, *Grant in Peace*, 313, 517–518; to Badeau, March 22, 1878, Nov. 21, Dec. 27, 1879, *ibid.*, 497, 521, 524.

7. Grant to Fish, Sept. 9, 1879, in Nevins, II, 894; Vincent P. DeSantis, *Republicans Face the Southern Question: the New Departure Years, 1877–1897* (Baltimore, 1959), 102–103, 106.

8. Grant to Washburne, Feb. 2, March 25, 1880, Wilson, ed., *General Grant's Letters to a Friend*, 102–104, 105–107.

9. Badeau, *Grant in Peace*, 319–320; Smith, *Life and Letters of James Abram Garfield*, II, 1175; Augustus L. Chetlain, *Recollections of Seventy Years* (Galena, Ill., 1899), 182; Weed to Washburne, Feb. 27, April 30, 1880, Washburne Papers, LC.

10. Coolidge, *Ulysses S. Grant*, II, 544–547; Mrs. Madison Y. Johnson to Leslie Johnson, June 9, 1880, Madison Y. Johnson Papers, CHS; Chetlain, 181–182.

11. Chetlain, 183–185; Badeau, *Grant in Peace*, 322, 324, 350, 527; Grant to Beale, Oct. 22, 1880, Grant Papers, LC; to Sheridan, Oct. 25, 1880, Sheridan Papers, LC.

12. Grant to E. F. Beale, Oct. 22, 1880, Grant Papers, LC; Grant to Badeau, May 7, 1881, Badeau, *Grant in Peace*, 534; Coolidge, II, 554–556; Badeau, *Grant in Peace*, 418.

13. Church, 440; Nevins, II, 897, 898; Grant to Nellie Sartoris, Nov. 24, 1883, Grant Papers, CHS; Coolidge, II, 555.

14. Badeau, *Grant in Peace*, 418–419, 423; Church, 446–447; Grant to E. F. Beale, June 26, 1884, Grant Papers, LC.

15. Grant to Badeau, Jan. 21, 1884, Badeau, *Grant in Peace*, 554–555; *ibid.*, 424–425; Grant to Editor of the *Century*, June 30, 1884, Grant Papers, LC; Grant to Gen. William R. Rowley, Aug. 8, 1884, Rowley Papers, ISHL; Hesseltine, *Ulysses S. Grant, Politician*, 448–449; Coolidge, II, 561.

16. Badeau, *Grant in Peace*, 425, 432–433; 564–565; Albert B. Paine, *Mark Twain: A Biography, the Personal and Literary Life of Samuel Langhorne Clemens* (2 vols., N.Y., 1912), II, 800–805; Grant to Field, Jan. 6, 1885, Grant Papers, LC.

17. Grant to Nellie Sartoris, Nov. 18, 1889, Feb. 16, 1885, Grant Papers, CHS; Grant to E. F. Beale, Dec. 16, 1884, Grant Papers, LC. Mark Twain visited Grant in February and said to Dr. Douglas, Grant's physician, that he assumed the cancer "was probably due to smoking." Douglas replied that he did not think so. Paine, II, 803–804. Badeau, *Grant in Peace*, 443–444; Hesseltine, 452.

18. Badeau, *Grant in Peace*, 456–458; Grant's notes of [June 17], July 2, [5], 1885, typed copies in J. H. Douglas Papers, LC.

19. Horace Green, *General Grant's Last Stand: A Biography* (N.Y., 1936), 320–321.

20. Church, 454–455.

21. Edmund Wilson, *Patriotic Gore: Studies in the Literature of the American Civil War* (N.Y., 1966), 131–173; Matthew Arnold, *Civilization in the United States* (Boston, 1900), 6.

Bibliography

Any work dealing with Ulysses S. Grant must give due consideration to the general's own story, *Personal Memoirs of U. S. Grant* (2 vols., N.Y., 1885). Now, fortunately, two volumes of Grant papers have appeared and more are to follow in the near future. These will make the task for future biographers easier than has been the case in the past when the paucity of original Grant manuscripts has been a decided handicap. See, *The Papers of Ulysses S. Grant*, ed. John Y. Simon (2 vols. to date, Carbondale and Edwardsville, 1967, 1969).

Other sources of Grant material are: James G. Wilson, ed., *General Grant's Letters to a Friend, 1861-1880* (N.Y., 1897), Jesse G. Cramer, ed., *Letters of Ulysses S. Grant to his Father and his Youngest Sister, 1857-78* (N.Y., 1912), and M. J. Cramer, *Ulysses S. Grant: Conversations and Unpublished Letters* (N.Y., 1897). For Grant's presidential writings see, James D. Richardson, ed., *A Compilation of the Messages and Papers of the Presidents, 1789-1897* (10 vols., Washington, 1896-1899). The standard collection of Lincoln material is, Roy P. Basler, ed., *The Collected Works of Abraham Lincoln* (7 vols., New Brunswick, 1953).

The definitive biography of Ulysses S. Grant has not been completed. Almost two decades ago Lloyd Lewis, biographer of Sherman, published a first volume of a projected multi-volume work, his admirable, *Captain Sam Grant* (Boston, 1950). Following Lewis' untimely death, Bruce Catton took over the assignment and has given us two fine additional volumes, *Grant Moves South* (Boston, 1960), and *Grant Takes Command* (Boston, 1968). These take the story through the war years. Both Lewis and Catton are noted for their artistic writing style and their work is, in addition, scholarly and authoritative.

Of the numerous Grant biographies which have appeared over the years only a select few can be mentioned. General James G. Wilson produced a campaign document for the 1868 election, *The Life and Campaigns of Ulysses Simpson Grant* (N.Y., [1868]), and later wrote, *The Life and Public Services of Ulysses Simpson Grant: General of the United States Army and*

Twice President of the United States (N.Y., 1885). Another 1868 biography, by Albert D. Richardson, a correspondent for the *New York Tribune*, was *A Personal History of Ulysses S. Grant* (Hartford, 1868).

Hamlin Garland, the distinguished novelist and literary figure, turned his talents to the writing of one of the most perceptive of the works on Grant, *Ulysses S. Grant: His Life and Character* (N.Y., 1920). This is a generally laudatory work as are those by George S. Boutwell, *The Lawyer, the Statesman and the Soldier* (N.Y., 1887), William C. Church, *Ulysses S. Grant and the Period of National Preservation and Reconstruction* (N.Y., 1897), Owen Wister, *Ulysses S. Grant* (Boston, 1901), and Charles King, *The True Ulysses S. Grant* (Philadelphia, 1914).

A more scholarly, but still friendly, work appeared in 1917. This was Louis A. Coolidge's, *Ulysses S. Grant* in the American Statesmen Series (2 vols., Boston, 1917, 1924). Somewhat more critical is *Meet General Grant* by W. E. Woodward, a Southern writer (Garden City, 1928). A brief work in the Library of American Biography is Bruce Catton's, *U. S. Grant and the American Military Tradition* (Boston, 1954).

A number of works deal specifically with Grant's career in the Civil War. Very thorough, and also friendly, is Adam Badeau, *Military History of Ulysses S. Grant* (3 vols., N.Y., 1885). Important are A. L. Conger, *The Rise of U. S. Grant* (N.Y., 1931), and J. F. C. Fuller, *The Generalship of Ulysses S. Grant* (London, 1929). Alfred H. Burne analyzes the 1864-65 campaigns in his, *Lee, Grant and Sherman* (N.Y., 1939), while Clarence E. Macartney has some criticism of Grant in his *Grant and His Generals* (N.Y., 1953).

An important source for Grant's concern for the freedmen in his command is *Grant, Lincoln and the Freedmen* (N.Y., 1907) by John Eaton, and the newspaperman, Sylvanus Cadwallader, contributed some controversial material in a work, edited by Benjamin P. Thomas, which became available to the public many years after the death of both Grant and Cadwallader. This is *Three Years with Grant: As Recalled by War Correspondent Sylvanus Cadwallader* (N.Y., 1955). A recent commentary is *Grant, Lee, Lincoln and the Radicals*, ed. Grady McWhiney ([Evanston], 1964). An important work on Grant's military record as well as a general appraisal of Civil War leadership on the Union side is the monumental work by Kenneth P. Williams, *Lincoln Finds a General* (5 vols., N.Y., 1949-1959).

Three works dominate the period of Grant's presidency: William B. Hesseltine, *Ulysses S. Grant, Politician* (N.Y., 1935), Allan Nevins, *Hamilton Fish: The Inner History of the Grant Administration* (2 vols., N.Y., 1936), and Adam Badeau, *Grant in Peace: From Appomattox to Mount McGregor* (Hartford, 1887). The first two are definitive, scholarly works, none too flattering to Grant and written before Reconstruction historiography underwent significant change. The last was written by a close associate of Grant and contains much personal material not to be found elsewhere.

The last years are covered in John Russell Young, *Around the World With General Grant* (2 vols., N.Y., 1879), which includes a wealth of information on other phases of Grant's life as well as a detailed account of the journey, and *General Grant's Last Stand: A Biography* (N.Y., 1936), by Horace Green, grandnephew of Dr. John H. Douglas, Grant's physician in his final illness.

Some of Grant's contemporaries have left behind written accounts of their war experiences which furnish significant material on Grant. Mention has already been made of Badeau, Eaton, and Cadwallader. In addition, there is the candid *Personal Memoirs of Gen. W. T. Sherman* (3d ed., 2 vols., N.Y., 1890), and *The Life and Letters of George Gordon Meade*, by George Meade, edited by George G. Meade (2 vols., N.Y., 1913). In the same category are: William F. Smith's unflattering *From Chattanooga to Petersburg Under Generals Grant and Bulter: A Contribution to the History of the War, and a Personal Vindication* (Boston, 1893), George R. Agassiz, ed., *Meade's Headquarters, 1863–1865: Letters of Colonel Theodore Lyman from the Wilderness to Appomattox* (Boston, 1922), and Horace Porter, *Campaigning with Grant* (N.Y., 1897).

So much of high merit has been written on the military aspects of the Civil War it is impossible to mention more than a few of the most significant works. Indispensible is *The War of the Rebellion: The Official Records of the Union and Confederate Armies* (128 vols., Washington, 1880–1891). Allan Nevins, *The War for the Union* (2 vols., N.Y., 1959, 1960), covers the story of the war to the middle of 1863 and is unsurpassed for comprehensiveness and literary quality. Due recognition must be given *Battles and Leaders of the Civil War*, ed. Robert U. Johnson and Clarence C. Buel (4 vols., N.Y., 1884–1888) a collection of articles by many of the active participants in the war, including Grant.

In addition to the works by Bruce Catton already cited, mention must be made of two more of his Civil War volumes, *A Stillness at Appomattox* (Garden City, 1953), and *Never Call Retreat* (Garden City, 1965). An informative critique of the military leadership of the Civil War is T. Harry Williams, *Lincoln and His Generals* (N.Y., 1952), which recognizes Lincoln's contribution to Union victory.

The Scribner Civil War Series has three volumes of particular pertinence for a life of Grant: Francis V. Greene, *The Mississippi* (N.Y., 1882), Andrew A. Humphreys, *The Virginia Campaign of '64 and '65: The Army of the Potomac and the Army of the James* (N.Y., 1883), and George E. Pond, *The Shenandoah Valley in 1864* (N.Y., 1883). An interesting account of the Vicksburg campaign is, Earl S. Miers, *The Web of Victory: Grant at Vicksburg* (N.Y., 1955). Two more recent critiques of considerable merit are, Edward Steere, *The Wilderness Campaign* (Harrisburg, 1960), and Archer Jones, *Confederate Strategy from Shiloh to Vicksburg* (Baton Rouge, 1961).

There are biographies of varying quality of most of Grant's Civil War contemporaries both Union and Confederate. A few of these are: James H. Wilson, *The Life of John A. Rawlins: Lawyer, Assistant Adjutant-General, Chief of Staff, Major General of Volunteers, and Secretary of War* (N.Y., 1916), Douglas S. Freeman, *R.E. Lee* (4 vols., N.Y., 1935), John C. Pemberton, *Pemberton: Defender of Vicksburg* (Chapel Hill, 1942), Richard O'Connor, *Sheridan the Inevitable* (Indianapolis, 1953).

The most authoritative Lincoln biography which covers the period of the Lincoln-Grant relationship is, J.G. Randall and Richard N. Current, *Lincoln the President: Last Full Measure* (N.Y., 1955). Other useful Lincoln biographies are Benjamin P. Thomas, *Abraham Lincoln: A Biography* (N.Y., 1952), and Reinhard H. Luthin, *The Real Abraham Lincoln* (Englewood Cliffs, 1960).

Among the most recent revisionist works on Reconstruction which deserve mention are Kenneth M. Stampp, *The Era of Reconstruction, 1865–1877* (N.Y., 1966), John Hope Franklin, *Reconstruction After the Civil War* (Chicago, 1961), and Rembert W. Patrick, *The Reconstruction of the Nation* (N.Y., 1967). Of the older works the best and the most comprehensive are James Ford Rhodes, *History of the United States from the Compromise of 1850* (7 vols., N.Y., 1893–1906), Ellis P. Oberholtzer, *A History of the United States Since the Civil War* (5 vols., N.Y., 1917–1937), and Robert S. Henry, *The Story of Reconstruction* (N.Y., 1938).

James E. Sefton, *The United States Army and Reconstruction, 1865–1877* (Baton Rouge, 1967) is useful for the period of the Johnson administration, as is Eric McKitrick, *Andrew Johnson and Reconstruction* (Chicago, 1960). Hans L. Trefousse, *Ben Butler: The South Called Him BEAST!* (N.Y., 1957) describes Butler's political role during Grant's presidency. Also useful is Donald B. Chidsey, *The Gentleman from New York: A Life of Roscoe Conkling* (New Haven, 1935).

Henry Adams, *The Great Secession Winter of 1860–61, and Other Essays*, ed. George Hochfield (N.Y., 1958), contains an interesting chapter on the gold conspiracy. For helpful information on the money question during the Reconstruction years see Walter T. K. Nugent, *Money and American Society, 1865–1880* (N.Y., 1968), and Irwin Unger, *The Greenback Era: A Social and Political History of American Finance, 1865–1879* (Princeton, 1964). The civil service reform topic is admirably treated in Ari Hoogenboom, *Outlawing the Spoils: A History of the Civil Service Reform Movement, 1865–1882* (Urbana, 1961), and Leonard D. White, *The Republican Era 1896–1901: A Study in Administrative History* (N.Y., 1958). John G. Sproat, *"The Best Men": Liberal Reformers in the Gilded Age* (N.Y., 1968) offers a good account of the Liberal Republicans.

In addition to the biography of Hamilton Fish by Allan Nevins, already cited, an excellent source of information for the Santo Domingo episode is Charles C. Tansill, *The United States and Santo Domingo, 1798–1873* (Baltimore, 1938). Not as reliable is Jacob D. Cox, "How Judge Hoar ceased to be Attorney-General," *Atlantic Monthly*, LXXVI (1895), 162–173. Grant's Indian peace policy is treated in, R. Pierce Beaver, *Church, State, and the American Indians: Two and a Half Centuries of Partnership in Missions Between Protestant Churches and Government* (St. Louis, 1966), and Elsie M. Rushmore, *The Indian Policy during Grant's Administrations* (Jamaica, N.Y., 1914). Henry V. Boynton's article, "The Whiskey Ring," in the *North American Review*, vol. 123 (1876), 280–327, concentrates on Secretary of the Treasury Benjamin H. Bristow's techniques in uncovering the ring. One of the major figures in the ring, General John A. McDonald, wrote *Secrets of the Great Whiskey Ring* (St. Louis, 1880) as an anti-Grant tract in the election year 1880. It purports to be the inside story but is far from reliable. For the events surrounding the disputed election of 1876 the definitive work is C. Vann Woodward, *Reunion and Reaction: The Compromise of 1877 and the End of Reconstruction* (Boston, 1951).

A number of Grant's contemporaries in the Reconstruction years either kept diaries or wrote memoirs. These contain valuable information for the events of that period. Indispensible for the Johnson years are *Diary of Gideon Welles*, ed. Howard K. Beale (3 vols., N.Y., 1960), and *The Diary of Orville Hickman Browning* (2 vols., Springfield, Ill., 1925, 1933). Also useful are: James G. Blaine, *Twenty Years of Congress: from Lincoln to Garfield* (2 vols., Norwich, Conn., 1886), George F. Hoar, *Autobiography of Seventy Years* (2 vols., N.Y., 1903), and George S. Boutwell, *Reminiscences of Sixty Years in Public Affairs* (2 vols., N.Y., 1902).

A few of the biographies of importance for this period are: Benjamin P. Thomas and Harold M. Hyman, *Stanton: The Life and Times of Lincoln's Secretary of War* (N.Y., 1962), Theodore C. Smith, *The Life and Letters of James Abram Garfield* (2 vols., New Haven, 1925), and Albert B. Paine, *Mark Twain: A Biography, the Personal and Literary Life of Samuel Langhorne Clemens* (2 vols., N.Y., 1912).

A slim volume of personal reminiscences by the youngest Grant child is *In the Days of My Father General Grant*, by Jesse R. Grant (N.Y., 1925), and Ishbel Ross has written a satisfactory biography of Mrs. Grant, *The General's Wife: The Life of Mrs. Ulysses S. Grant* (N.Y., 1959).

Two important commentaries on Grant's *Personal Memoirs* are: Matthew Arnold, *Civilization in the United States* (Boston, 1900), and Edmund Wilson, *Patriotic Gore: Studies in the Literature of the American Civil War* (N.Y., 1966).

Index